Cyndi

Enjoy a great

+ enjoy life a

Paul Fig Feger

aka Fantastic Fig

THE ASCENSION OF JERRY
Murder, Hitmen, and the Making of
L.A. Muckraker Jerry Schneiderman

ALSO BY CHIP JACOBS

Smogtown: The Lung-Burning History of Pollution in Los Angeles

*Wheeling the Deal: The Outrageous Legend of Gordon Zahler,
Hollywood's Flashiest Quadriplegic*

Cyndi~
God bless you. May you never meet a reptile like this.

THE ASCENSION OF JERRY
Murder, Hitmen, and the Making of
L.A. Muckraker Jerry Schneiderman

By Chip Jacobs

A Vireo Book, an imprint of Rare Bird Books
Los Angeles | New York

This is A Vireo Book
An imprint of Rare Bird Books

Copyright © 2012 by Chip Jacobs

Distributed in the U.S. by Cameron + Company, Inc.

Printed in the United States of America.

For information and inquiries, address Rare Bird Books, 453 South Spring
Street, Suite 531, Los Angeles, CA 90013.

Design by Tamra Rolf
Set in Goudy Old Style

Cataloging-in-Publication Data for this book is available from the Library
of Congress.

ISBN-13: 978-0-9839255-4-5
ISBN-13: 978-9839255-7-6 (ebook)

Rare Bird Books are available at special discounts for bulk purchases in the
U.S. by corporations, institutions, and other organizations. For more
information, please contact Cameron + Company, 6 Petaluma Blvd.
North, Suite B6, Petaluma, CA 94952 or email info@cameronbooks.com.

10 9 8 7 6 5 4 3 2 1

To the Jerrys and other accidental underdogs of the planet: sometimes the best way to squash evil is by fooling it into cannibalizing its own flimsy soul. Just don't neglect your own scars afterwards or you may not recognize the victory.

The only thing necessary for the triumph of evil is for good men to do nothing.
—Edmund Burke

ACKNOWLEDGEMENTS

Real life horror stories have a tendency of outliving their initial trauma, and this tale was no different. It was shaped into a book only through the extraordinary willingness of people webbed into a *Kafkaesque* 1979 murder triangle to share their memories of those churning times. I am honored that so many of them opened up to me, knowing that most of these people spent years trying to forget the painful ordeal that I was pressing them to remember in granular detail. Jerry's family—the woman married to him throughout this bedlam, the current spouse who lived it vicariously, and the son who might have been butchered by it—couldn't have been more gracious. The victim's first wife—a woman who still weeps for him and carries his name thirty-three years after losing him—nobly shared her recollections, too. It was her hope in taking me back to that ghastly era that her deceased husband's daughters might better understand him.

Members of the Argentinean family swept up as well by these events were just as welcoming, and their resilient spirit shines. Besides the Buonsanti family, my heartfelt appreciation goes out to Armand Arabian; Mike Consol; Paul Fegen; David Ferris; Alex Young; Lynn Price; David Honda; Kay Lang; Richard Lehman; Brie Levine; Bert Makabali; Rick Nathanson; Carol Rosenthal; Dominick Smacchia; Carlos Villalvazo; Ken Vorzimer; Dean Kuipers; Sharon White; Marc Wax; and a woman named Arlene. Former Los Angeles Police Department detectives Richard Jameson and Howard Landgren provided crisp, helpful recollections. Forthcoming as they were, the lead prosecutor in the case—recently retired Los Angeles County Assistant District Attorney Jeffrey Jonas—was my true shepherd here. Without him, I never could have understood how the grim details surrounding a single bullet could have woven into the bigger picture of trauma and triumph. Tyson Cornell and the staff at Rare Bird Books themselves deserve crackling applause. Not only did they believe in the uniqueness of Jerry's story where others faltered, their unflinching integrity and creativity helped restore my faith in the publishing game. As always, my loving family was there to catch me and prop me up—and believe me—I needed it during this book's eventful journey to print. To all of them, and those I neglected to mention, you have my eternal thanks. May there never be another reptile like this in your life.

NOTE TO READERS

Chronicling a thirty-three year old murder and the human tapestry woven into it requires the donning of a lot of hats. The writer must be a storyteller, historian, truth seeker, and busybody searching for coherence where it doesn't always exist. As such, the tale presented here is not a formal journalistic rendition of what happened, because who can say confidently what the absolute truth of any calamity is? Rather, this is primarily Jerry Schneiderman's narrative—his journey—as told by him to me over the years. But it is not Jerry's story exclusively, because he was not the only one afflicted by the events of March 27, 1979. I've supplemented his memories by interviewing many of the other people involved and scouring thousands of pages of court testimony, police interviews, prosecutorial memos, business documents, personal correspondence, and more.

There are other things you should know about this book. Almost all of the dialogue and the majority of background settings where the action occurs was approximated based on participants' recollections, witness testimony, and other knowable facts. In a few instances, I compressed timelines for brevity. When faced with conflicting accounts of the same event or a disputed timeline, I chose what I believed was the most probable scenario.

I also made promises to people, mostly victims, that I'd give them and their kin a measure of security and privacy. Because of this and other factors, I have altered the names of roughly one quarter of the characters in these pages and modified their physical descriptions. None of the names changed are public figures, government officials, or anyone formally charged with a crime. For clarity, the following names were modified in whole or part: *Tammy, Jude and Daphne Schneiderman; Richard, Paige, Sara, Rebecca, and Rachel Kasparov; Ari Allon; Neddy Hertel; Benjamin Wynn; Nicholas Torrini; Victor Platte;* and the company referenced as *Smythe & Hargill.* Again, these are names that I invented exclusively for this book and any resemblance to real individuals in any way is strictly inadvertent. Dollar values represented here are from their respective periods.

While I am not including a bibliography, I want to acknowledge the publications from which I drew background material and a few select quotes. These include: *The Daily News of Los Angeles; Los Angeles Times; Los Angeles Magazine; Los Angeles CityBeat; L.A. Weekly; The Los Angeles Business Journal;* and *Forbes.* Two books by Kevin Roderick were also helpful: *The San Fernando Valley: America's Suburb* (Los Angeles Times Books, 2001) and *Wilshire Boulevard: Grand Concourse of Los Angeles* (Angel City Press, 2005).

PART I

MURDER

CHAPTER ONE

A CIVIC PAIN IN THE ASS

The grand opening of Hollywood's newest homeless facility promised goodies straight from a sinful dream. "Free food, drink, condoms, syringes, and surprise packages to all homeless guests," announced leaflets distributed in August 1995. Jackie Goldberg, the area's liberal councilwoman, was providing the indulgences. Or so hinted the flyers stenciled with cutesy balloons.

Word of the event shot through the streets, and feet started shuffling. Some of the indigents hoofed it to Gower Street with their shopping carts to haul their swag home. Others caught the bus. When the small mob showed up for the ribald, ribbon cutting ceremony, they were certainly hell bent to party. They shoved so hard on the front of the building that some of the people inside worried about a stampede and barricaded the door. *Where were the freebies*, they bellowed when the doors finally parted? And what about those guaranteed good times?

Goldberg's blindsided crew stuttered that they didn't know what the street people were talking about. There was no christening underway because there was nothing to christen. They were still discussing whether to either erect the facility there at the Assistance League of Southern California or someplace else, and that was going to take months. Besides, a city sponsored condom-syringe goodie bag? Think about it. Goldberg's chief of staff was beet red at the spectacle unfolding around her. An orderly meeting had nearly degenerated into a vagrants' riot. She made the Los Angeles Police Department promise that they would uncover whoever was responsible.

Gerald "Jerry" Schneiderman, the man who devised the bogus invitations and handed them out with aides around downtown Los Angeles, welcomed the outrage directed at him with a steely contentment. He would be glad to tell the cops all about it because the stunt was his way of swinging at a bigger injustice. To the bearded, mid-forties real estate developer the notion of furnishing jobs, counseling, healthcare, and other services there to the needy was egghead liberalism—if not political subterfuge worthy of the ridicule being aimed its way. It would surely drag down local property values, including the five small office buildings he controlled nearby, by beckoning the homeless and derelict across Southern California to the neighborhood. Goldberg had discreetly planned to bus them in from Beverly Hills and other spots and not bus them back. Throw in a few new liquor stores and flophouses and another Hollywood skid row might fester.

Jerry—just then dipping his toes into urban activism—had nothing against helping the downtrodden. Far from it, in fact. He merely believed that somebody needed to stand up for the existing residents who would have to live with the consequences. So, here was his handcrafted preview: a dozen or so restive homeless with nothing to do except loiter. Left unsaid, of course, was that Jerry had skin in the game beyond the value of his properties and the vigor of his moral register. The double divorcé accustomed to the suburbs was living alone in one of his Hollywood buildings, agitated behind the smiling face he presented to friends. No statute of limitations existed for the post-traumatic scars still gnawing him.

The woman who Jerry had humiliated, nonetheless, was no timid politician apt to cower in her office. Jackie Goldberg was one who normally made enemies tremble. A rotund woman with apple cheeks and a strident tone—one of California's first openly lesbian lawmakers—she had built such a legacy confronting entrenched interests for progressive causes that critics nicknamed her "Hurricane Jackie." Her baptism had come during the 1960s Free Speech movement, and later on with the hidebound Los Angeles Unified School District, where she had seen her fair allotment of kooky stunts.

Hurricane Jackie, all the same, had probably never encountered an odd duck as focused as Jerry. The leaflets had just been political theater. He had also written directly to the building owner on behalf of area businesses and residents pledging to sue if he leased it for the homeless. Goldberg, who would later win a California Assembly seat, knew when she had been thumped. Not long after those motley vagrants banged on the door pining for syringes, rubbers, and hooch, she gave up on the Gower Street site and chose a different location. Prolonging her war with Mr. Schneiderman seemed unwise. There was something too callous, too demented about a guy who would resort to such tactics on principle, as if psychic ghosts were fueling them.

Soon enough, that all became clear, because there was no rolling Jerry back into the obscurity of private life after his jousting with her. He was on the cusp of years worth of the most original, ballsy activism that historically unpolitical Southern California had witnessed since the sixties. Jerry, in retrospect, was merely stretching his legs battling the homeless complex. Construction of the city's stubby two billion dollar subway in Hollywood in the mid-1990s became his central target. Through it, he forged an identity as a sort of a property rights Robin Hood crusading for the trampled under-foot (albeit a Robin Hood with a highly evolved sense for mischief).

Jerry's transformation from "nobody" developer to merry muckraker began when giant excavating machines carving subway tunnels beneath western Hollywood Boulevard destabilized the foundations of dozens of office buildings and storefronts. The subterranean shaking had a jackham-mer effect that crinkled floors, bowed load-bearing walls, cracked sidewalks, and left property owners screaming holy hell. Distressingly, the rumbling hit just after another construction screw-up on the eastern part of the bou-levard where a massive sinkhole caved open in full view. A public works project costing three-hundred-million-dollars-a-mile shouldn't be riddled with incompetence and indifference to those it harms, but that was Metro Rail's identity.

So Jerry walked California's legendary street tallying the concrete destruction. He discovered the Snow White Coffee Shop had fissures in its wooden floors and a leather gifts store that sloped cockamamie at its entrance. Along the Hollywood Walk of Fame, he saw brass and terrazzo stars crumbling from the ground up and behind them lopsided buildings that had probably driven their architects to drink. Hearing reports about wobbled architecture, the agency responsible for it—Los Angeles County's Metropolitan Transportation Authority (MTA)—initially harrumphed that most of the damage was exaggerated. The bad news media had sensational-ized it in a smear job to sell papers, officials said. Later, they added Jerry to the naysayers, writing him off as an "operator," a tie-wearing subversive trying to hog attention.

They would pay for that misreading because, over the next several years, Jerry and his associates hemmed together roughly three thousand property owners and merchants in a two billion dollar, multi-plaintiff lawsuit that became national news. The legal filings made it official: Jerry—a loving father of five, a man with virtually no political experience, a guy who had once trusted all—was a civic pain-in-the-ass. He intended to show the MTA he meant business about compromised structures and lost income to shopowners from dusty, barricade-strewn streets. No longer could the agency throw claimants lowball, take-it-or-leave-it settlements anymore and be done with them. Jerry interviewed lawyers to represent Metro Rail victims and went big. He tapped the firm spearheaded by Thomas Girardi, who had recently earned tens of millions of dollars in the California groundwater-poisoning case that made busty paralegal Erin Brockovich an environmental rock star. Not too shabby for a subversive.

Jerry also outdid himself again in September 1996 as subway work choked off more and more small businesses unable to entice customers into the construction turmoil. Many felt the MTA had given them the cold shoulder, only doling out survival money to the well-connected. Reading the situation, Jerry schemed for justice as Mahatma Gandhi might have. He took a blind Hollywood talent agent forced to abandon his drooping building on five minutes' notice and spotlighted his plight where the political pooh-bahs could not ignore it. Tim Shumaker, courtesy of Jerry, sat in front of then-Mayor Richard Riordan's office inside Los Angeles City Hall in a two-day hunger strike that surprised even the jaded.

The papers and television news gobbled the story up because—let's admit it—human suffering sells. The image of a disabled businessman with a guide dog starving himself in that marble-floored landmark to make a point was not something people saw every day in a glamourous town like L.A. Jerry's stagecraft depicting the heartless MTA worked flawlessly, and in shame the agency wrote a check. It released two million dollars to assist merchants and others, including Shumaker, with their mortgage payments. Afterwards, Jerry was hero of the boulevard. Shop owners, many of them foreigners and unshaven old timers, bear-hugged him on the street, plying him with store trinkets as thanks. "You saved us," they said. "You saved us."

The politicians and public officials who Jerry channeled his gadfly barrages at had another response: *Why?* Why was Jerry Schneiderman flogging the MTA? Why was he spreading his activist wings to schools built over toxic land and fishy redevelopment areas? Even fellow developers Jerry had exposed for taking public money that they shouldn't have were wrestling with the question: *Why was he doing this?* Only a masochist or someone's loony patsy, the argument went, would dare such stunts, let alone spread rumors of an avenging creature or reveal a back-scratching deal between a slumlord and a powerful lawmaker. Nobody understood his inner motivations for these shenanigans, and neither would I until I knew his backstory. Shrewd Jerry had a chest filled with rage.

Mystifying as his crusading might have been, it also bore risks that could have buried him. Jerry had provoked an adversary in the MTA with no intention of flag-waving like Jackie Goldberg had done. A latticework of rail projects in a car-besotted city was in the hopper—big money all of it—and officials had no use for downers like him howling about short term casualties. The agency's general counsel warned Jerry that if he went through with his lawsuit he would come of it "bankrupted." A subway contractor was nastier, suggesting that Jerry should "be afraid to walk the streets alone" and that a remote ignition starter would be a smart purchase for his car.

Decades earlier, the killer itching to wrap his fingers around Jerry's neck would have said something similarly diabolical, but this time Jerry was better armed. He had stopped carrying a handgun for protection against unwholesome people able to cloak the barbarity inside them. His weaponry was now rediscovered self-confidence and the hard-earned realization that there are far worse fates than antagonizing a multi-billion dollar bureaucracy protected by lawyers, politicians, and their bullying cronies. Nineteen-seventy-nine still roamed his blood.

CHAPTER TWO

THE SPACE MEN OF MIRACLE MILE

A quarter century earlier, Jerry pulled up a chair inside a tacky Mexican restaurant, Don Ricardo's, gazing into the face of a man excited about a little greed. Richard Kasparov—Jerry's coiffed, older partner—was already in presentation mode by the time Jerry strolled in from Pico Boulevard, with a sales chart poking from his breast pocket and a schedule cleared for the afternoon. Jerry, unable to recall the last time that he arrived to a meeting after his pathologically late associate, had to blurt what he felt.

"Wow, Richard. This must be a big deal."

"Be nice," Richard answered with a Cheshire grin. "You're going to be thanking me later."

During the next ninety minutes, Richard tried showing why with an impassioned appeal about how they could enrich themselves by expanding their business. It was simple, really. Up until now, their space planning shop had operated like his brethren in Los Angeles: it eyeballed blank office space and then sketched where everything went on drawings given to contractors to "build out." Richard's notion was now to keep that suite construction in-house. They would install the executive offices, secretarial pods, hallways, wall-coverings, and light fixtures. They would furrow where the electrical outlets went and handle the dozens of other nitpicky construction details. Job complete, they would bathe in the profit margins.

"Think about it," Richard said mid-pitch. "We've been in real estate forever. We know the trades. We have the back office staff. Stop me whenever I reach a negative. Besides, you've got to say yes. Look where we are."

Both men chuckled with a whimsical tinge. Don Ricardo's was wedged in the basement of the checkerboard-mirrored office building where they had hatched their cleverly named firm, "Space Matters," eighteen months earlier. The pair had scarfed down many a burrito here under the cramped stucco ceiling before they had relocated to a bigger office once their fortunes improved. Something, though, was different, something striking. Jerry had never seen Richard's face so lively, not even in their early days working until sun up until the caffeine gave way.

"Take a look at this," he said, "while I hit the head. It'll get your heart pumping."

Richard slid over a freehanded chart showing projected sales figures curling upwards like an elf's boot. Jerry noticed another thing, too. As Richard walked off, several attractive female lunch patrons beamed him flirtatious glances without his libido even broadcasting interest. "Never changes," Jerry said under his breath, and it never did.

At thirty-eight, Richard could have fallen out of a GQ spread as a beautiful California male. He was 6'1", with a lean frame, and a rakish smile. A fussily-trimmed beard and moustache combination with a mane of lustrous brown hair sold the package well, synergism taking it from there so even his blocky forehead and pouty lips amplified the appeal. Also, clothes loved him. Whether in tailored suits at a meeting or a used Army jacket flipping burgers, Richard evoked a hunky flash that seduced the available.

Jerry, by contrast, had none of Richard's sizzle, and as a bright, self-conscious sort, little of his partner's gregariousness. He was a skinny 5'10", 160 lbs., with medium-brown hair that twirled into a natural frizz and an unlined, youthful face that some confused for a college student or flunky intern. Sleepy, green-brown eyes and faint smile lines gave Jerry a mousy cuteness, and he strove to look older than his twenty-six years with a first-rate wardrobe.

"And I don't want to stop just at office buildings, either," Richard continued, scooting up his ratty Naugahyde chair. "I want us to move into high-end home renovations, too. I already have a bunch of rich people interested in us doing their houses. I just don't see much downside, only blue sky that might not come again."

Jerry lightly quizzed Richard about specifics on his idea that they erect offices and then expand into residential remodels. Richard's answers floated out as half sales job, half seduction, and Jerry was smart enough to appreciate that if he could be bowled over by Richard's vision of a full-service de-sign shop, clients would smack their lips for it, too. Crummy people-reader that he was, Jerry also knew this day was inevitable when he had persuaded Richard that they were too talented to stay at the suffocating design con-glomerate where they had met. Sooner or later, Richard's quest for bigger paydays and his wandering attention span were bound to crave more. After another twenty minutes that day in February 1978, Jerry held up his palm to halt Richard's dog-and-pony show. "You sold me," he smiled. "Let's do it."

"Here's to grabbing wonderful things," Richard gushed. "And pouncing on what others haven't."

A clink of their margarita glasses was the kickoff. They christened their suite building offshoot "CM-2," as in "Construction Management, Too." *You have to start trusting sometime,* Jerry reminded himself. So what if the frijoles went cold while Richard emceed their futures?

From the restaurant, Jerry steered his white Mercedes convertible north onto La Cienega Boulevard and flipped a right onto Wilshire Boulevard, where some of Los Angeles' signature architecture lined the grand dame street with building-mounted clocks and garish concrete. A few miles east of the brackish La Brea Tar Pits, he pulled into the company parking lot and scurried inside. The "office" that swallowed Jerry for blocks of daylight fifty to sixty hours a week was actually a funky, Spanish mansion on the edge of Hancock Park, one of L.A.'s oldest blue blood communities. Jerry and Richard had wanted a headquarters with curb appeal as unique as the layouts they were hawking, and the old mansion with a red tile roof and pimply, white stucco exterior delivered it. High ceilings and French doors accented the interior, with wrought iron railings across the upper floor, and the haunting bust of a woman in front. The dozen draftsmen and designers, as well as Richard, had offices on the second level. Jerry occupied the only bottom-floor space, cherishing the room to think.

On the day his firm took its dive into construction, Jerry's precocious success churned around him. He watched Bert, one of several Filipino em-ployees on staff, checking an architectural rendering, and overheard his French-born decorator, Lillian, speaking frenetically to a supplier. The din was inspiring—the crinkle of unfurling blueprints, the thud of the front door closing as someone dashed out for an appointment. So after he re-turned from Don Ricardo's and caught up on messages, Jerry galloped up the stairs, moving from desk to desk to ensure that his people had their projects well managed. When he was done, he returned to his own paper-teetering office so he could get to drawing again.

The next time Jerry looked up from his sketches and down at his watch, he was shocked to see that the hour hand had been in a full sprint, and at 7:45 P.M. he was the only one left in the place. Before plucking his car keys out, he took another walk upstairs, sniffing a few fabric samples piled on a desk. It was heart-pumping, indeed. They were on pace to finish the year with about $400,000 in net profits, a handsome dividend for an upstart firm. All his hard work had crystallized. Jerry—well before thirty—was earning triple what his father had made, and as the youngest person in his own office. All without a lick of management experience.

He daydreamed about it all on a commute home that whisked him through the posh streets of Hancock Park, across Hollywood's Vine Street, by the stacked-disk Capitol Records building, and onto the roadway brushing up against Universal Studios. When he got to the new 118 freeway, taking him west, the radio he usually kept on for company repeated its lead story: the body of a twenty year old woman had just been discovered in the trunk of an orange Datsun in a canyon off of Angeles Crest Highway, northwest of where Jerry had grown up. Authorities assumed the murder was the handiwork of the "Hillside Strangler," but with so many predators crisscrossing L.A., no one was sure.

Pretty soon Jerry was at his exit climbing the road toward his house under the mustardy foothills on the western scrim of the San Fernando Valley. When he opened the door, his peppy wife, Tammy, was there with her one month old son cooing in her arms. "Congratulate me," he said with wry fatigue. "We're in construction now."

"And was your shirt collar screwed up like this all day?" Tammy giggled, trying to squish it down.

"Of course," he smiled.

Sometimes as he lay in bed trying to quiet his flywheel mind, Jerry bounced his legs on the mattress as a reality check. This splendid life he was cobbling was no hoax. It was at hand.

***

The men of Space Matters realized that it would take more than hustle and sales cards to launch their new spin-off. They needed experience. Neither of the two college educated designers had gotten their own fingernails smudged cutting carpet padding or hanging solid core doors for a living. Richard, in fact, had already been scolded that his lack of expertise could backfire on him by a colleague who had briefly considered merging his shop with Space Matters. "What do you guys know about the technical side?" the executive had asked. "It's a lot more intense than room measurements." And what about managing those rough-hewn construction crews? "Animal training," that's what they called it. Richard had no glossy retort for those doubts then, but he had derived a solution since. They had to hire a field superintendant, a foreman who could juggle multiple jobsites, run crews, troubleshoot on the fly, and read blueprints. Without those skills, CM-2 would be sunk before it began.

They asked colleagues if they knew anybody qualified, and Richard widened the net. He placed an ad in the *Los Angeles Times* and other papers seeking a "superintendant familiar with high-rise interiors." A man who noticed the solicitation phoned Richard expressing his interest. His chief reference was his last boss at the local branch of New York-based Smythe & Hargill, which at the time owned and managed millions of square feet of real estate across the county. Richard called Smythe & Hargill's L.A. chief about Howard Garrett, and the executive, Victor Platte, deemed Howard solid and capable. Platte said that you could erect a small skyline from the cumulative remodels that Howard had supervised during his thirty odd years in the business, from the historic Roosevelt and Jewelry Mart buildings downtown to the Wilshire-Comstock Apartments on the Westside. Name a major property in town and chances are Howard had either worked in it or knew someone who did.

Richard, tickled at what somebody with Howard's credentials could mean, invited him in for a sitdown interview at the mansion in early spring 1978. Howard Landis Garrett, Jr. was polite, reserved, a little coarse, and wholly positive that he could handle CM-2's jobsites. He could practically do it one-armed, he said, compared with some of the hairier projects he had directed for Smythe & Hargill and realtor Alma Smith as an independent foreman-contractor in their bullpens over the years. Ever had to fix a disabled fire alarm system in a subterranean garage, or pour a massive foundation with a skeleton staff? *He* had. Ever frame hundreds of square feet of drywall over a weekend with a trick-back? Yep, *he* had done it.

Forty-seven year old Howard was not going to win any men's beauty pageants, not with his grizzled looks, nor any personality contests with his de-meanor. He was a wiry 6'1," with flat, leathery jowls, penetrating blue-green eyes, and stringy, dirty-blond hair that splayed over his collar. Pouching under his shirt was a small beer belly. Some acquaintances compared him to a fairer-skinned Charles Bronson; Jerry thought he could have passed for a trail-riding cowboy. In reality, Howard was the sort of wind-burned, seen-it-all who called his superiors "chief" and idiots "clowns." Someone who could light a cigarette with one hand while toting a nail gun in the other. He had a subdued toughness suggesting he might have been in the military, and lived in Pasadena in a shaky second marriage.

Old Howard, nevertheless, could smile, and when he laughed it was the bronchial phlegm laugh of a man who tamed his stress with nicotine. Richard was more impressed with the applicant's entrepreneurial spirit. Not only did he stockpile his own carpentry equipment and maintain two small design businesses in Arcadia, northwest of downtown, Howard said that he had once overflowed with so many clients that he had needed to lease a small L.A. office himself. Richard was so positive that he had found an ideal match out of the chute that he ended the job search with one candidate.

They talked salary and Howard said he could accept twenty-two thou-sand dollars for openers. Truth be known, Howard was bringing more than field experience to the mansion. He owned a golden ticket in his long-held California general contractor's license, the one he had agreed to let Rich-ard and Jerry use to jump start their construction jobsites legitimately with city building inspectors. That certification was everything because it would swallow up a year or more for the partners to bone up and pass the state exam themselves. Who knew where fickle California real estate would be by then?

About the only stumbling block for Howard's employment was his spring schedule. Howard told Richard that he hated bringing it up, but a standing obligation left him no choice. In March, he would need a week off—two weeks tops—to be in San Bernardino, the sparsely populated, un-der-developed county east of Los Angeles County. Howard explained that he was a witness in a court case starting then, and the district attorney was depending on his testimony to put a crook away. Prosecutors had been un-sympathetic when Howard had informed them that his mandatory appear-ances inland might disrupt his first weeks at a new job in Los Angeles. They had threatened to subpoena him and that wasn't something law-abiding

Howard said he could ignore. He apologized for the inconvenience that his absence might cause.

Richard, still visualizing a construction money machine within his grasp, told Howard not to fret about the commitment. Nobody's schedule is entirely their own. After Howard finished testifying in San Bernardino, Richard assured him that he would have a position waiting for him at CM-2. If he wanted to, he could start before the trial. As Richard knew firsthand and Jerry did not, even the best employees tote complex histories.

***

Space Matters would never be the same after the two-man team of Richard and Jerry became a three-headed hydra. Responsibilities had to be divvied up. Jerry continued space planning for their money clients while tending to some of the administration. Rainmaking Richard added their new construction services to his sales calls and other duties. Howard, meanwhile, supervised the flannel-and-boots laborers they hired ad hoc for suite remodeling and home renovations. Brains, flash, and grit: it had the makings of a dynamite trio.

There was little doubt about success when CM-2 found takers right away. Under Howard's watch, suite building commenced at the Pacific Stock Exchange downtown, a few neck-wrenching skyscrapers close by, and at the manse of a smarmy Valley tax lawyer that Jerry knew from school. Sweet opportunity popped next. A Westside OBGYN, impressed with the update CM-2 completed at his office, asked Richard and Howard if they wanted to join him in a real estate side venture. Dr. Joseph Marmet yearned to develop a 160-home subdivision from scruffy land that he owned in western San Bernardino County, sensing in Jerry's associates the expertise he sorely lacked.

"What about it boys?" he asked. "Interested?"

"Absolutely," they both said.

Rehabbing so many properties simultaneously made for lots of driving around and sometimes pleasant surprises like the doctor's solicitation. Here was the latest one. Richard and Howard, men with personalities as dissimilar as their appearances, struck up a minor friendship from their time together in the field. After work one day, they had had drinks at Richard's Valley house and gotten acquainted. When they discovered that they would both be in Palm Springs in the desert east of L.A. with their spouses for a Father's Day weekend getaway, they took advantage. They had dinner together at Pal Joey's, a local landmark favored by suntanning celebrities.

Jerry, in the early months, kept his head down. Swept up in the grind of co-running a business, he never heard much about that meal in Palm Springs or a speculative subdivision in San Bernardino. His inbox contained too much to do. Clients in the belt-cinching mode as the U.S. crept towards recession—and, worse, dreaded "stagflation"—contracted with them for one-stop space planning and suite remodeling. Richard's salesmanship reeled in more affluent homeowners that bulked Jerry's load. Thankfully, Howard was just the vet they needed to shepherd these different projects. Whatever the staff impression of him as a taciturn redneck who left ear wax on the office phone and occasionally swore around clients, the man rode his projects to completion. Richard had effused about blue skies ahead if they took a chance with construction. So far, Jerry liked the outlook.

It was still a strange dynamic that he had going here: him, the shy workaholic from grubby North Hollywood who dreamt up the company; and Richard, the West L.A. charmer who outsiders assumed was the lead partner. Also bizarre was Space Matters' prosperity at a time when America's cantankerous mood had infected once immune California. Behind the squeals of Disneyland crowds, and the shimmer of golden beach days—away from Star Wars premieres and hoopla over the new Space Shuttle program—grumpy citizens wanted relief. Angry lines snaked around rationing gas stations. Political appointees were hung in effigy. Abused wives got even with sadistic husbands. Tax reformers were the new gods. Where were the shades of mellow "Hotel California" that the Eagles had crooned about years earlier? Only the part about killing the beast with "steely knives" seemed recognizable, except now the beast was the dispiriting times.

The exhilarating point for Jerry was that none of that collective anger affected him much with the partners he had in alignment. How, in fact, could he not be bullish about their prospects when he peered around the mansion? Space Matters today, a bonanza tomorrow.

CHAPTER THREE

RUSHING SUCCESS

By the time he had thrown off his bedsheets that morning, Jerry was already rushed. Rushed to plant himself behind his desk or a jobsite and get cracking as if he never left the night before. Rushed to create and supervise. After coffee and a goodbye peck to Tammy and his son, Jude, Jerry made himself a haze in his Mercedes, hurtling south on the Santa Monica Freeway. Thirty-seven minutes later, yawning and still rushing, he pulled his car into the world's largest parking garage beneath the recently finished Century Plaza Towers.

At nearly six hundred feet tall, the enormous northern tower and its southerly twin didn't so much dominate the West L.A. skyline as own the sky with their black and gray, triangular shape. The aluminum high rises—designed by the same architect behind Manhattan's World Trade Center buildings—had a formidable height that threw shadowy blades across the Ahmanson Theater and other swanky area landmarks. Jerry got to the nineteenth floor, where workmen were building out a law suite that he had designed to boast hardwood floors and Old World charm, and stood idle. There was an Erector Set rhythm to the work that was engrossing to watch, a magic coupling of power tools and skilled hands. Jerry, however, could only gawk at it for so long because when the racket died down he had to stop watching the show and help to start running it.

Soon, the cabinet guy, carpet man, and other craftsmen, ambled up to him with questions and updates about the multi-million dollar renovation underway. Most of them had a good twenty years on the "skinny kid" in the blue suit, as they dubbed him. Still, seniority wasn't directing the modular, sawing-framing frenzy. Planning—Jerry's planning—was the last word, and if there was a detail that he didn't remember off the top of his head he spread his dog-eared schematic across a sawhorse and traced his finger to the answer. This was not a job that Jerry could fumble. Paul Fegen, the oddball real estate magnate who had hired him, was leaning toward using Jerry's design here as the prototype for other spaces in the towers that he controlled. Hence, Jerry had to be sharp and needed to suppress his mild fear of heights. With his boyish face and deferential manner, it was already challenging enough for him to inspire confidence from the wrinkled men in paint-splattered boots that he could quarterback a first class makeover like this. Appearing as though he needed to sit down lest he barf from acrophobia was no way to galvanize belief in his leadership.

Jerry's nausea tapered some back at the office that underscored his success was no fluke. The mansion halfway between the jagged skyline of downtown L.A. and the boutiques of Beverly Hills rose at the southwesterly corner of Wilshire and Fremont Place. This put it on the southern tip of Hancock Park, the city's ultimate exclusive neighborhood, where palm trees and sweeping driveways that led to dynastic estates that never died. Some of California's most august families—The Chandlers, The Dohenys—had lived there for generations, and so had the city's mayors in the official "Getty House" residence. Space Matters, though no gilded enterprise, echoed the area's privileged ambience. A pair of enormous, white Tudor columns along Fremont protruded in front of the mansion like aristocratic tongs, with superstar neighbors nearby like Mick Jagger, Muhammad Ali, and the Archbishop of Los Angeles.

The company was surrounded by nostalgia as well as fame. To the east of them, toward downtown, was the luxurious, flesh-colored Ambassador Hotel, where Hollywood's biggest stars once socialized and Robert F. Kennedy was assassinated by a Palestinian-born stable boy in June 1968. To the west a few blocks was the "Miracle Mile," an historic corridor of audacious architecture, iridescent green theaters, and wing-shaped apartments dating to the 1920s. When Jerry wasn't slobbering over the design styles there, he often dreamt about cultivating business inside of them.

Those jobs would come in good time. Inside his office that afternoon, roughly two months after they had entered the construction game, Jerry gazed out the window at the company parking lot, feeling the pressure paddle his blood stream. Space Matters employed four draftsmen, and one of them might have been the most skilled in town. Three decorators—including a prancing daisy of a man, and a woman whose husband allegedly worked for the Las Vegas mob—were on the payroll, too, racking up hours, as was Howard. In addition, there were secretaries, a gofer, a messenger service, lawyers on retainer, life-insurance policies, and other piling expenses. *Sketch and build*, Jerry chanted to himself when the strain choked him.

Stress and all, Jerry had to concede the go-getting motor inside him sometimes enjoyed the duress. They were juggling forty space planning clients, among them heavyweights like the Bank of America building in Beverly Hills, the Prudential and Equitable Life Insurance properties mid-city, and the scores of high rises across the country leased by Fegen's empire. Executives there all depended on Space Matters to organize their offices, often on grueling deadlines, and Jerry's dark-ringed eyes showed his determination to please them. Besides, he loved what he was doing here when he hadn't loved much else. Every night when he left for home, part of his heart stayed in his office drawer. Amid Jerry's other ambitions, he was collecting full sets of blueprints for every substantial building in Los Angeles—hundreds of them—to get a leg up on rivals during bidding competitions. Know a structure from its innards out and your proposals to organize a floor were organically enriched.

And make no mistake: Jerry was an assassin with his pen. Most space planners, or interior architects, invested their energies turning office space into aesthetic delights—bright wallpaper, dreamy waiting rooms. Jerry—incorporating client needs, natural light, traffic flow, and other factors—was less about the "pretty" and more about being devastatingly efficient. Hallways in his sketches sometimes lined building perimeters to optimize square footage. Bulky file cabinets that no one had known what to do with before hung from the ceiling in Jerry's layout. The geometry of it came as naturally to him as salesmanship oozed from Richard.

Together, they tried nailing down every deal they could. They attended "roof topping" parties for future skyscrapers, where Richard flirted with daughters of big space owners as the wind rustled through the wall-less floors and Jerry negotiated with his acrophobia. They organized layouts for Synanon, a controversial drug rehabilitation group that practiced primal scream, and a similarly operating family therapy center hot on cathartic nudity and pot smoking. Whether for a conglomerate, chiropractor, or pop psychology franchise, Richard and Jerry had a space plan for all. Jerry expected a corresponding uptick in profits by 1979 would follow.

Considering that optimism, Jerry was a tad stunned a few weeks after his trip to the Century Plaza Towers when the company accountant said he needed a minute of his and Richard's time. The bookkeeper was worried. Richard's construction spin-off, he said, had already spread its available money around too thin and was close to eking into moderate arrears. Velocity was the issue. CM-2 was growing faster than the internal cash flow required to sustain it before the clients paid up. A money transfusion was needed before the debt worsened. Richard a few days later assured Jerry that these types of cash flow gullies had to be toughed out. Every survivor in real estate suffered shortfalls. Richard believed what they needed was bridge financing and a big picture mindset. "Leave it to me," he said. "I have something in the works."

One morning while Jerry was gone, Richard waved Howard into his office and smiled sheepishly. After some pleasantries, Richard admitted that they had dug themselves a little hole and required slurry to patch it. One obvious answer, he suggested, was staring them in the face. What if they kept their construction jobs going by financing materials through Howard's personal credit lines with materials' suppliers? The ones he had maintained for years with his old freelance jobs. They would only have to tap it for a few months. Eventually, client checks would surge in, cash flow would stabilize, and they would continue kicking ass as if there had never been a problem.

Howard sighed. Helpful as he wanted to be, he wasn't sure he could go along with this favor. He had already put up his contractor's license for them that the state could suspend if it discovered any monkey business. Before deciding now, Howard said he needed to understand what was so wrong with the partners' finances that they couldn't repair their own missteps. Golden-tongued Richard had anticipated that question. Approaching a bank for such measly sums, he explained, would transmit the wrong message about their prospects. Transferring money from Space Matters was no better, since "co-mingling" cash flow invited tax headaches. Until they could get their own credit line raised, they needed about three thousand dollars a month to make a CM-2 payroll or two and a place for them to finance wood, paint, drywall, caulking, nails, drop-cloths, and so forth. "What do you say?"

Howard sat there for a moment, thinking. He had been around the industry long enough to decipher the meaning of Richard's linguistic finery, and an interesting meaning it was. Translation: *he* would be keeping CM-2 afloat if he nodded to the request. Richard could sugarcoat their predicament all he wanted with management gibberish. The truth was that this was no interruption of construction cash flow. It was a crisis. Right then and there, Howard knew he had bargaining power, and he tilted it his way because that's what he did in his world. In exchange for opening up his precious credit lines, Howard said he wanted a one-third equity interest in CM-2, just as if he were a partner. He also needed his salary fattened from twenty-two thousand dollars a year to thirty-five thousand dollars. Grayscale did not exist. It was take it or leave it.

Richard said, "Deal!" Why would he ask this of someone he just met? Because Richard regarded it more as a gentleman's agreement sealed with a handshake than a binding contract thick with obligation. Howard was his friendly banker.

***

Every day in this period, Jerry's eyes raced through the business section of the *Los Angeles Times* until he had found his description for Southern California's real estate environment: "schizophrenic." On one hand, the area boasted the planet's glitziest residential market—with soaring home values and Proposition 13, the watershed, property-tax-slashing initiative that voters approved in 1978—a jackpot for remodeling firms limber enough to get homeowners to sign on the dotted line. The land Babylon glittered in retail, as well, with hundreds of millions of dollars being poured into outlets in places like Arcadia, Santa Monica and other marquee suburbs. Indoor malls, consumer Astrodomes where department stores sold underwear next to corn dogs-on-stick kiosks, were in early reign.

Inside the commercial office market that was Space Matters' core business, however, it was a more brutish scene. Space had grown so tight that few were touring empty floors to lease or space plan anymore. Most executives just renewed existing leases. By 1981, there would be work galore for Space Matters and its rivals with fifty new buildings citywide and a one billion dollar redevelopment plan for downtown. Surviving until then would take mettle and improvisation, and that's why Richard told Jerry he had to be out hustling deals more than ever.

A dilapidated, castle-like Victorian near them in Hancock Park was exactly the sort of project that Richard believed they had to suckle through the lean months. The vintage property on June Street required a floor-to-ceiling refurbishing managed by fussy professionals. The owners had already fired a couple of inept, high-billing yentas who thought they could take the update on. Richard was supposed to have met with the woman of the house to review the eighty-thousand dollar job and then flaked out on his first appointment, forcing Jerry and his trustiest draftsmen, Bert, to drop everything and perform the necessary measurements. Richard had been skipping more appointments of late, and Jerry was becoming concerned about his AWOL routines. "How many meetings can one man blow off?" he asked on the ride home with his tape measure. Quite a few, it turned out.

When Richard finally did materialize on June Street, so did his conceptual wizardry. Ideas on where to relocate a bathroom and how to open up the kitchen sprang from his imagination. The Victorian, its owners knew, needed him. Jerry required something else as the calendar moved towards summer. He had to figure out how to keep Richard around more to help him hack through their problems. If that ate into Richard's rainmaking and schmoozing, he would have to adapt.

Jerry certainly would've liked him there when he received a surprise call from an ungainly hospital shoehorned up against the Harbor Freeway downtown. An administrator there had phoned to say that they had admitted a man with a Space Matters business card in his wallet. A "Howard Garrett" had been rushed in unconscious after passing out in the ground-floor bar of the Roosevelt Building. Doctors had brought him out of a coma with medication, and he was drifting in and out of sleeps since then. Little of it made sense until Jerry drove by himself to the hospital and was briefed about the turmoil inside Howard's anatomy.

Unknown to Jerry, his foreman was an insulin-dependent (or Type-1) diabetic. Jerry asked a nurse what that involved and was informed it was a relentless condition that erupts when a person's immune system destroys insulin-producing bodies made in the pancreas. Without the insulin hormone, glucose that cells desperately need for nourishment can't be absorbed and the disease takes root when unprocessed glucose (or blood sugar) lingers at high levels. As Howard must've learned, hard booze teeming with carbohydrates can propel blood-sugar to pass-out levels. Twice a day, he injected himself with insulin that he kept chilled in a thermos and must've forgotten to take extra as he was getting crocked. Jerry was astonished. Hard-boiled

Howard, partly anyway, was made of glass.

He was in a chair next to Howard's bed when he awoke. Noticing his visitor, Howard flipped his body toward Jerry in a night-gown speckled with blood. Then he curled his yellow teeth into a smile.

"Oh, Jerry, thanks for coming, man. You have no idea how much it means."

"Don't mention it. I'm just surprised the hospital called to say you'd been admitted. I had no idea."

"Me, either, brother. One minute I'm drinking and the next I'm here with all these tubes and crap connected to me."

Jerry nodded kindly, trying not to expose his phobia about hospital germs, as he listened to Howard recount his duel with diabetes. Twenty minutes later he gripped the armrest of the hospital chair, hoping to get outside and chimney fresh air in his lungs. More out of politeness than duty, he asked Howard if there was anything he could do. Howard's response gave him momentary tachycardia.

"How about a hug, man?"

There was nothing Jerry could say and he didn't want to seem rude. He lifted himself halfway out of the chair and embraced Howard's torso. It was stronger than it appeared under the loose Hawaiian shirts that Howard favored and gamey with un-showered B.O.

"If this headache will go away and I can get my (blood sugar) levels back, I'll be on the job by tomorrow."

"Take your time," Jerry said. "Don't worry if you miss a couple days. We're okay for now. The jobs aren't going anyplace."

"Not my style," Howard said. "I'll be back tomorrow, assuming they'll God damn release me."

Jerry doubted that was possible, but what did he know about the human metabolism? Howard made it all moot anyway by showing up the next day gaunt and puffing a Kool, his preferred menthol cigarette. Promise made, promise kept.

***

As the weeks passed, Howard's hospitalization proved to be less alarming than Richard's tendency to be absent when needed. Twenty years before cell phones, when pagers constituted wireless communication, you'd have an easier time tracking Sasquatch in the Great Northwest than locating Richard in Greater Los Angeles.

Jerry was near-frantic to get face time with him before any number of internal tribulations spiraled into emergencies. Invoices for construction materials were too high for their projects on the books. A rumor circled the office grapevine about somebody padding bills. The building slowdown concerned Jerry immensely. And then there was creep-management. An executive told Jerry over a boozy dinner that if Space Matters wanted work at what would become the First Interstate skyscraper downtown, somebody from the firm was going to have to "suck a little cock." Jerry didn't know if the creep meant it literally. So again, he asked, "Where the hell is Richard?"

The better question might've been who Richard was, and calling him a walking dichotomy was a good start. Yes, he was a debonair deal-closer and quick-wit appreciated on downer-Mondays. Sure he could score the best after-work ganja and still hold forth like a university professor about the nuances of post-modern architecture or the playful fruitiness of a Merlot. For every attribute, Richard acted as if he had a lifetime pass on responsibility when he felt like it. People torched enough by his flakery and the favors he sought came to question whether he was intentionally sabotaging himself or just believed that part of friendship with him was shoveling up his messes.

Besides his disappearances, there was another issue cresting in Richard that much of the office witnessed: pointed mood swings that struck some as either manic-depressive behavior or anger-syndrome. Richard, no matter that Westside confidence he carried himself with or the lanky charm that made women swoon, had trouble getting through an average day without lashing out. Anyone irritating him when he was in one of his moods had to prepare themselves for Richard to yell, peal rubber in his car, fastball a piece of office-equipment against the wall or stomp around. Anything could set him off. A client had recently mentioned a small flaw in one of Richard's designs and after he hung up Richard sledge-hammered the receiver down so fiercely that it sloshed coffee on the blueprints. Underlings feeling unsteady about their boss's short fuse had to deal with it, and so did Jerry.

Other times, that flash-temper dissolved and the lovable him reappeared. The spontaneous-Richard would order lunch for associates from a steak house and pay a taxi to deliver it. The sensitive-Richard was good for a five-minute, pick-me-up phone call to a blue friend, and a supervisor who genuinely enjoyed extracting creativity from his people. Certainly, nobody else at Space Matters could infuse clients with exuberance during sales meetings like he did, or make associates laugh later at his Johnny Mathis impressions and British humor recitations. These and other shadings of his partner bewildered Jerry, who understood real estate nut-cakes and Popeye-ish landlords better than his cohort. All Jerry could assume was that Richard's heavy workload coupled with a move into a new house with a pregnant wife must've been wearing on him.

Assumptions, though, have scant value when problems rip stem to stern. Kay, the pretty, young designer, was making noises about resigning. She had picked up on Jerry's anxiety about the un-reconciled books, and didn't appreciate his "all-business" vibe or Richard's coy flirtations. Kay had been logging nervous calls from clients asking her when their remodel would begin or pre-paid furniture would arrive, and she had made excuses until her mouth got sick of them. The next time Kay saw Richard he was all smiles and bonhomie, oblivious to any anxieties having been absent so much. Done with it all, Kay piled her design binders up to her neck, clomped up the stairs and before Richard could as much as chime good morning dropped them into his lap. "I quit," she said. "I can't take this anymore."

Jerry, too, was beginning to suspect that something shady was afoot when the bookkeeper still could not explain why some jobsites were over-ordering construction materials. Accounting ledgers aren't usually this perplexing. Jerry nearly tripped on the mansion's stairs dwelling about it. He ran through scenarios in his mind while Tammy described her day over dinner with him. He knew it was a mystery unlikely to solve itself. During a project update meeting one morning, Jerry finally girded himself to ask supremely uncomfortable things. Richard was much happier giving grand sales presentations using his trademark line—*Don't watch what I say, watch what I do*—and teasing clients with what else he had up his sleeve than hearing Jerry's insulting questions about ethics. Rank interrogation smelled like this.

"Wait," he said, "you're suggesting that I'm involved? Oh, come on, man. This is silly."

"I know," Jerry answered, "but what would you think if you were me?"

From Jerry's first query to his last, Richard professed ignorance about any over-billing and allowed resentment to drench his voice. He had been running himself ragged for the business, and now he was getting the fifth degree about screwy work orders the dumb accountant couldn't untangle?

Richard, suave, womanizing, and social-climbing, the one who had spent more time partying with his coke-loving friend in Pip's and the Friars Club than Jerry had spent in bars his entire life, shook his head dismissively. This small money stuff was too petty to belabor when they had companies to grow. Outside of an audit, Jerry felt powerless.

Over the next few nights, he stayed late to pour over the ledgers again comparing expense entries with color-coded job codes. No incriminating, *ah-ha* revelation emerged, just a bad headache that drained his aspirin bottle. He continued tapping a pen to his temple thinking of another tack. If Richard was lining his own pockets by secretly bilking him, Howard might know the specifics. They were always paired up at clanging worksites together.

One day while Richard was out shopping space plans, Jerry gently told Howard that they needed to talk and was delighted that Howard was agreeable. Except for the hospital visit, they had hardly been alone in the months that Howard had been on staff. Few at Space Matters knew the man beyond the superficial, which was just how he wanted it. Howard was a keep-to-yourself sort disinterested in water-cooler gossip. His stern ethic was that you did your job and went home with no disturbances in between.

Jerry tried not stuttering as he asked Howard to promise not to repeat their conversation, which Howard vowed he would. For the next ten minutes, Jerry questioned him about Richard's behavior. Had he seen any skullduggery—a client-kickback, skimming, doctored paperwork, whispering to suppliers? They reviewed each construction site. Howard's refrain was he hadn't witnessed anything overtly underhanded and, like Richard, disliked being hooked into Jerry's suspicions.

"Anything else?" Howard asked. Jerry shoved his files back in his desk to indicate they were done. Howard celebrated with a cigarette, blowing a smoky lungful towards his co-boss.

"You should still watch him," Howard said, picking a fleck of tobacco off his lip.

"What do you mean?"

"You heard me."

"But you said he wasn't doing anything wrong? Am I missing something?"

"No. But let's just say there's more than one Richard in Richard."

"I don't understand. You're making me think I should hire a lawyer."

"What you're missing is the point. I'm just telling you that I've dealt with lots of people like Richard over the years, and they can start believing their own bullshit when they get moving too fast."

"I thought Richard's been burning the candle. CM-2, a new house, a kid on the way..."

"Jerry," Howard interrupted. "Figure it out for yourself. You're smart."

Jerry said fine, thanks for the time, overjoyed by what he did *not* hear: dirtbag details about the man whose flair he idolized scamming him. It must have been Richard's schmoozing style that Howard was badmouthing—the two-dollar words, the Happy Hour elbow-rubbing that Howard's Budweiser-ethic had trouble appreciating. Yes, that had to be it. Howard could implicate himself if he was lying. He might stare like a buzzard and observe more than speak, but he had an industry reputation to maintain and that stern ethic to uphold

Thinking about that, Jerry's stress melted. Maybe it was an accounting blunder, after all.

"Hold it for a sec," Jerry told Howard as Howard wiggled his hips to leave. "I want to show you something I think you'll get a kick out of." Jerry, grinning now, reached his hand into the office plant on the corner of his desk and extracted a small, black dictation recording device with spools still spinning. He had hoped that Howard would interpret his secret recording of their conversation as a sign of his determination to get to the bottom of the bookkeeping stumper and prove he had stones despite his adolescent-looking face. He had hoped wrong. Howard looked down at the gizmo in Jerry's small palm as if it were sludge and walked away brooding. "Thanks for your time," Jerry said weakly.

Jerry refused to let that exit or the nagging feeling that there was more to all of this demoralize him. He needed to recharge his batteries, and took his wife and baby son to Waikiki for lazy time under the tropical breezes. He realized his problems would be festering when he jetted home to California. And they were. Even so, the months sped by anyway, and everybody seemed to be doing their jobs. If he could just crack why some jobsites were over-ordering materials when everybody said they were meticulously following procedures, it would sure make for a calmer gut.

In a conversation with Richard about the situation in November 1978, Richard told Jerry to stop being such a namby-pamby about accounting. He needed him instead to start combing his Rolodex. Jerry cocked his head, confused, so Richard simplified it for him. "Howard just quit," he said. "Suddenly, angrily quit. Made himself quite a little scene, too" Richard added.

Before he had huffed out the door, Howard had typed up a resignation letter, snapping down hard on his IBM Selectric with tobacco-stained fingers. When he finished, he slapped the page into Richard's mid-section. "There!" he had announced in a hushed snarl in the middle of the mansion. "We're official." Richard said he had gingerly requested Howard step into a side room to spare the staff the hubbub. Howard there said with his departure that he expected to be repaid for everything he was owed, and that included the payrolls he had covered, the missing salary he was due, a string of unauthorized charges on his credit line, and another thirty-five thousand dollars for his one-third stake in CM-2. Add it up and it exceeded forty-five thousand dollars.

Richard said he told Howard that he had to be kidding, because nobody had that type of cash liquid. And yet Howard didn't appear to be joshing on his last day at Fremont Place. Ignore these debts, he promised, and his lawyers would make them wish he and Jerry had never gone into business. They would slap liens on every project to suffocate their cash flow. The next sounds were Space Matters' front door slamming shut and the metallic cough of Howard's V-8 Chevy pulling away on Wilshire.

Jerry was distressed, picking at a scab on his forearm and showing his youth by the time Richard was through detailing Howard's departure. They didn't have forty-five thousand dollars lying around. Hell, they couldn't even pay off suppliers billing them for unsought materials. Basically, they needed a millionaire-benefactor and a fallback plan. With Howard gone, Jerry asked who would be their field supervisor and where they would find someone else with a contractor's license in a matter of weeks. "Great," Jerry said, puffing air out of his cheeks. "We haven't been this behind the eight-ball since we were back on Pico."

Richard exhorted Jerry to take a breath, that this was not as disastrous as it seemed. If the recession deepened, there'd be no shortage of qualified foreman ravenous for work. As for Howard, Richard said he was probably shooting off his mouth about hiring lawyers and raising Cain. Howard had only been with the company for what, seven-eight months? He would likely fade into the woodwork or be satisfied having a little of what he claimed he was owed thrown at him. He needed to work again. Troublemakers generally don't get called.

Listening to Richard's ironclad logic, Jerry started feeling less panicked. He had experienced false relief before, but Richard's faith that they had weather Howard's exit had a cottony reassurance. As they talked about the companies' post-Howard era, Richard commented that they were probably better off without him in their fold.

"What do you mean?" Jerry asked. "The guy knew how to manage a site."

"True. But there are things about Howard you don't want to know."

"Like what?"

"Stuff."

"Stuff? What do you mean?"

"Well, he's not just a blue collar guy who keeps his mouth shut. There's a mean side to him that can slip out. He's got secrets from before he was here. Not that he shared them."

"Secrets? Funny you mention that because he told me that you were the one with the secrets."

"I don't care if he tried smearing me, Jerry. That's wasting our time. What we need to do is concentrate on finding a replacement for him and keeping our projects moving. Next year could be gigantic for us."

"Agreed. But don't you think you should've alerted me that our foreman was not the person I thought?"

"Yeah, maybe, but I knew you'd overreact."

CHAPTER FOUR

SPACE INVADERS

In mid-November, 1978, weeks after commemorating their second wedding anniversary, Richard and his goddess-faced wife split up. As a rule, it's typically the husband who moves out while his spouse sobs in his absence. In this instance, Paige fled with their infant, Rebecca, and some suitcases and they called it a mutual separation. Neither of the couple hunted for sympathetic ears to unload the specifics. The reason for the parting would've sounded melodramatic, even paranoid. At its core, Paige could no longer tolerate so many spooky developments with a newborn to protect. Richard, having skewered the second marriage that might've saved him from his lesser self, was in no mood to advertise it.

Up until then, it had been a satisfying union between two people with fun-loving, compatible dispositions. The fifteen-year age gap between them had been narrowed by Paige's spunky maturity and Richard's loose view of responsibilities. Both could be combustible, stubborn individuals, particularly Richard, and they quarreled and made up with a welder's heat. Away from the house, a glamorous sheen spritzed off the two, and diners at a chic restaurant could be excused for mistaking them for James Brolin and Cheryl Ladd lovey-dovey at a side table. Celebrities no, but their union was coated in the Cinderella-ish magic of a wayward bachelor sweeping a country girl off her sandals. It was the happily-ever-after business where the Richard-Paige storybook lost its binding.

They had met at the West Hollywood apartment complex that they unwittingly shared around the time Richard and Jerry founded Space Matters.

Richard had parked his beige two-tone Cougar in Paige's designated space one day and walked off. When she drove up in her yellow Volkswagen Bug with the flower-stickers adorning it, she discovered her taken spot and went searching for the presumptuous jerk to make him leave. Whoever did it wasn't outside, so Paige marched into the building and right into the handsome scofflaw. "What gives you the right to park there?" she asked. "Who do you think *you* are?" Richard responded with caddish passion. He swept the woman whose name he barely caught into his arms and kissed her spontaneously. Before the encounter was over, Paige had agreed to have dinner with him. Three whirlwind months later, on Halloween 1976, they were married at the flamingo-pink Beverly Hills Hotel.

Paige was twenty-four, only a few years younger than Jerry, when she became Mrs. Richard Kasparov. She had come from a tight-knit, middle-class family in Northern California and had breezed down to L.A. after graduating from state college with aspirations of being a teacher or fashion designer. One thing was for sure: Paige was not your average blonde hottie in a town of them. Hers was an explosive beauty—smoky eyes, Farrah Fawcett cheekbones—that one could imagine lovelorn songwriters penning ballads about. For a small-town girl, she adapted quickly to the big city, frolicking until sunrise and watching girlfriends date English rock stars. Meld all the traits and her Christian background and she might as well have been a GPS-beacon for Richard, a non-practicing Jew antsy for thrills, gentile or otherwise.

Then again, Richard hailed from a different California than either Jerry or Paige. His upbringing was enmeshed in affluent West L.A., home of pampered children and big expectations. He had gone to good schools there, been given a car, showed a talent for drawing and attended the prestigious USC School of Architecture, though nobody remembers seeing a diploma. Richard's father was a tough, self-made businessman who wished Richard was more athletic instead of the creative, right-brain type that he was. When he died of a heart attack at a relatively early age, it seared in Richard a fear he would, too. Some later wondered if it was self-fulfilling. After college, he bumped around the space-planning world, underachieving most of the way, and married a sweet, dark-haired secretary from Long Beach in the mid-1960s. The relationship lasted nine, stormy years and produced an adorable daughter who probably wished her dad was more attentive. Paige, for this reason, had been Richard's shot at salvation. She was his do-over to be the gallant breadwinner who finally shed his flightiness for something bigger than himself.

They moved into a house on Wonderland Avenue in chic Laurel Canyon not far from where a quadruple-murder involving ex-porn star John Holmes would taint the street and inspire the movie *Boogie Nights*. Once Space Matters netted dividends, the couple swapped the house for a comfortable, two-story home in Van Nuys set back from its woodsy street. Freeway-strewn as it was, their new town of urbanized suburbia in the center of the San Fernando Valley maintained everything a new couple could need: a private high school (Notre Dame) that a future child might attend, banks, a Chinese food "palace," gas stations, even a psychic. If you didn't require a marble fountain, or define your ego by your zip code, Van Nuys teased bliss.

Paige's first indication that domesticity would be more nettlesome than she imagined roped her when she learned she was pregnant. She was over the moon, joyous tears streaming down hot cheeks, but not Richard. Her announcement left him unexcited and strangely detached. She had expected he would be strutting about Space Matters with a virile grin handing out celebratory stogies, not behaving as if he ensnared himself into a bummer commitment he would rather ignore. Paige tried snapping him out of his lethargy, this commitment-phobia that had dogged him most of his life. He would have none of it. As her tummy rounded, she tried projecting what her situation would be in ten year, foreseeing only lonely terrain. Consequently, when Richard vanished the day she was wheeled into the delivery room to give birth for the first time, Paige prayed to God to grant her a daughter. A little boy with all that testosterone sloshing in him would be tough to bring up alone as a single parent, because that's what Paige reckoned she would be. Maybe the cosmos understood that since the healthy, redheaded bundle she gave birth to was a girl.

Hardly as wondrous, Paige's formerly frisky husband reappeared after Rebecca was born and Paige returned to a svelte 114 pounds. Richard informed her that he was ready to be the baby's father if he hadn't already tanked their marriage. No longer was he in the emotional wilderness, his favorite place to hide when living up to adult responsibilities didn't much feel like his idea of living. "Give me a second try," Richard said. Sanity had resumed. Paige probably could have accepted that rosy outlook and even forgiven Richard for the infidelities that he denied committing had it not been for the arrival of two outsiders. Suddenly, Page had new dilemmas to straddle, and Richard had somebody harder than her to mollify.

The calls first came in the heat of the summer, when Richard, Paige and the baby had only been in the house for a handful of months. As soon as Richard drove off to work, usually in the 9:00 A.M. to 10:00 A.M. range, Howard phoned on the house line. He was calling about Richard, yet not to speak to him directly. It was Paige he was seeking as the lady of the house. Howard wanted her to convince her husband to repay him the money he owed him from their time in business together. Some of the debt was from CM-2, the other part more complicated. It wasn't so much that he badgered for repayment as a collection agency would that caused Paige unease. It was the frequency with which he called. "Richard owes me. Make him pay," Howard told her repeatedly. After Richard refused to comply, Howard's words took on an icier cadence. "He better pay me or there's *going* to be a problem."

Paige rarely said anything to Howard, who she had met on several occasions, and he only mouthed a couple of sentences on each call before hanging up. Judging by the timing, Paige could have sworn that he had a spy outside monitoring their driveway. Some days barely twenty seconds elapsed from Richard's car backing out to Howard phoning in. Paige several times had looked out the house windows and down her block for a beady-eyed accomplice watching them. Annoyingly, all she saw were the typical morning pulses of suburbia – moms in station wagons, gardeners behind lawnmowers.

At first, she strove to ignore the huffy calls as Richard encouraged her. He told her Howard was a blowhard opportunist too cautious to attempt anything more than nuisance-making. When his calls persisted, Richard's words began losing their soothing power. Eventually, Richard understood his wife was frightened on a primitive level where logic did not always reside. In his best reassuring voice, the same one he used with Jerry, he explained to her that he had no intention of paying Howard whatever amount he conjured up that he was owed. The money he claimed he was due was inflated and mostly fabricated. Richard had already lent Howard the Datsun 280-Z that he had originally purchased for Paige in a gesture of good faith that he would meet his minor obligations to him. Howard, among other grievances, now was miffed that the bank wanted to repossess the car because Richard had stopped making payments on it.

The next time the phone rang, Richard happened to be there. He seized the receiver, walked into the kitchen and proceeded to bark at Howard for ten minutes for harassing his poor wife. After Richard hung up, he reported that Howard had gotten the message. Howard, indeed, had gotten it all right. He waited two days the next time to call and berated Paige that her husband was the real vermin here. That was it. The following morning over breakfast Paige yelled at Richard that the calls had to stop. It was pesticide on her motherly chromosomes. "GET HIM OUT OF OUR LIVES! YOU HEAR ME? OUT OF OUR LIVES!"

Paige's teary outburst shook the house without dislodging Richard's hard-headed stance. He believed that Paige was not only over-reacting to the calls, she was underestimating the effect of post-childbirth hormones on her disposition. Who knows? Richard's theory might've warranted legitimacy if an even creepier sort had not shown up.

***

Isabel, the squat Guatemalan woman who watched Richard and Paige's baby and did their housecleaning while they were at work, always had a sharp eye for shadows. One late afternoon in early November 1978 as she dusted near the bar, she noticed dark strands obstructing the sunlight from the ground-floor window. Isabel stood erect for a closer look and with a better view realized that the strands were actually a pair of legs in dark pants outside the glass. Near it were a set of exterior stairs leading to a deck attached to the home's bedrooms. The eyes of the middle-aged nanny knew this for fact. Those legs shouldn't be there.

Something bad was unfolding. A rookie meter-reader or neighbor would never stray this far inside the property, and neither would a disoriented guest that Richard or Paige forgot to mention was dropping by. So, when the legs that caught Isabel's attention disappeared up the stairs, she released the duster from her hand and tried following them. Up the interior staircase she bounded, running into the master bedroom, where she was delirious to find no sign of the uninvited man. Isabel jogged into the baby's bedroom next and exhaled relief seeing the infant asleep in her crib. *Gracias a Dios.* Then she looked south. Standing outside on the deck was a muscular man with light hair and dark clothing and he was not there for bird-watching.

One of his hands was clasped around the handle of the sliding glass door while his other fiddled with the frame. He was trying to jimmy and shimmy the door loose. If Isabel shrieked in fear at all this, she had her motivation. The man had spotted her watching him, and hadn't scampered off the premises like a cat burglar limiting himself to unoccupied homes. Entry was really up to him. Should he be unable to finesse the door over its claw-like metal latch, he could always just shatter the window. To Isabel, glass must never have seemed so porous. Behind that feeble barrier, her eyes scanned the baby's room, where you'd usually find a wind-up mobile, a hamper, talcum powder, jumpers and hardly anything to weaponize. Nothing useful appeared to her as the jiggling glass-door rumbled like private thunder. They were feet apart, the housekeeper and the stranger, separated by that pane and probably wishing early deaths for each other. Isabel's goldfish eyes continued searching the infant's room, dizzyingly so, hoping for inspiration or salvation. The glass was shaking harder. The intruder was resolute.

Just when she might've been tempted to grab the baby and sprint out the front door onto Chandler Boulevard, Isabel noticed what she needed. Upright in a corner, close to the diaper-changing table, was an old broomstick handle. It was about 4" long and a ½-inch in diameter, and had had its whisks removed. Richard and Paige would lay the cylinder in the metal track of the sliding glass door as a poor-man's burglar deterrent when they were away overnight. With that broom-stick inserted there, even somebody who managed to break the lock couldn't slide the window more than a finger's width.

In one fluid motion Isabel grabbed the broom from the corner and dropped it into the slot. The hollow, metallic clang it produced might've angered her adversary. Then again, he could have one-upped her by wrapping his hand in his jacket and punching the glass. He would be inside the baby's room before all the shards settled. All he would have to do was knock Isabel out, or just kill her, and then steal what he had come here in broad daylight to take. And, from the best she could gauge, it was the baby he wanted. The chocolate-skinned woman had no clue why someone would want to snatch a baby-girl any more than what the man would do next. After a few more terrifying seconds, another choice she hadn't considered prevailed: the would-be kidnapper from God-knows-where tired of her resistance. He backed away from the sliding glass door blocked with the broom handle to exit the same way he entered, by way of the stairs.

Hours later, when Paige arrived home from her Ventura Boulevard interior-design shop, Isabel replayed the incident to her with broken-English and air-slashing hands, Paige clutching Rebecca closer with every detail. Afterwards, Paige sobbed a bit, and door locks were double-checked. When Richard walked in the door, a fusillade of questions from his shaken wife enveloped him. Should they contact a security company to install a burglar alarm, she asked? File a police report? Richard, dazed as he appeared, cautioned that they shouldn't panic. He speculated that the man on the deck might have been a drug-jonesing robber who would never press his luck in a return visit. Just to be sure that Rebecca was safe, Paige slept with her in her arms that night.

A threshold had been snapped. In the coming days, the intrusion and Howard's debt-collection calls became too much for Paige to rationalize away as bleak coincidence. Richard had this reinforced to him shortly before Thanksgiving when Paige floored him with her announcement. She said that the next time that Howard phoned, he could answer it, because she and the baby were pushing the ejection button for someplace safer.

CHAPTER FIVE

DWEEB AT THE POLO LOUNGE

When Paige pressed Jerry's doorbell that morning in December 1978, her head might well have slumped into the arch as if it had lost any purpose to stay upright. A year ago at this time, she reasonably could have expected a new home like Jerry and Tammy's would've been her and Richard's next yuppie move-up. Sadly, relocation after the last weeks had taken on a bitterer connotation, as she beseeched friends to let her and the baby stay in anything vacant they had while subsisting on Kraft Macaroni and Cheese. Life estranged from Richard, self-imposed or not, was a hard-scrabble existence. Paige's only blessing was auditory. The ringing phone no longer mortified her, but even that would soon change.

Before they separated, Paige and Richard could barely handle twenty minutes in the same room with dorky-Jerry and what they ridiculed as his "Praying Mantis" hands—Jerry's habit of rubbing his palms together when money was in discussion or when he was jittery. They devised insulting names for him behind his back, the "weasel" giving way to "twerp," and the Praying Mantis supplemented the caricature. Yet here Paige was, because that's what being desperate does to you. It makes you align yourself with someone you only knew from derogatory labels and shallow impressions. So why not use Jerry's smarts to compel Richard to pay the child support he was refusing to pay. There would be elliptical irony if the twerp managed the feat.

He finally answered the door, studying Paige's rawboned face and inviting her in. *Worst I've ever seen her,* Jerry thought. The last time that she

50

had been there was for a birthday party. Paige herself might have noticed if she had been vigilant that day that Jerry's place had an unfinished aura, with no window coverings and few decorative flourishes. For all that, the clapboard tract home was the largest model on Jerry's twisting block. It was a white-painted, green-trimmed house, set against the bright foothills, with wood columns and a picket fence. Inside were five bedrooms, a master suite, a bonus room, a three-car garage, excellent natural light, a pool and an oversized television antenna. It could have swallowed up Paige's current rental several times over.

Jerry told Paige they would speak in the kitchen. She followed him into a regulation egg-white room where Tammy was slicing the crust from a peanut-butter-and jelly sandwich and brewing coffee. Tammy stuck the plate in the fridge and checked the baby monitor. She then directed Jerry and Paige to sit down to talk *this* out for everybody's benefit. Jerry navigated Paige to a chair, having barely touched her before except a glancing cheek-kiss, and Paige went along morosely. About the only occasions where the partners and their wives had socialized was a weekend trip to a Medieval Renaissance Faire, where Jerry had worn passé bell-bottoms, and an "Alamo Party" thrown by the owners of that eyesore Victorian. That had been a seeming lifetime ago.

Paige sat in Jerry's kitchen and tugged out a wad of crumpled tissues from her sweater. She sniffled goose-like and plopped her head into hands, still torn over her presence here. Tammy handed them coffee and they took courtesy sips. After a minute, Paige composed herself and spoke up. It boiled down to this: she could no longer tolerate Richard's unwillingness and obstinacy about paying full child support. The court had ordered him to give her $265 a month, and just like that he had stiffed her for most of it.

Without money from him and other funds out of reach, Paige said she had missed rent and was evicted from the first place she had leased after the breakup. Her ouster had forced her to decamp with the baby to a smallish home not far from here. The owner was married to one of her girlfriends, and had taken pity on her by offering her discounted rent. If that arrangement collapsed, Paige would be out of Plan Bs, except maybe to book it home to Northern California, she was that broke and malnourished. Richard, Paige elaborated, wasn't rebuffing her out of principle or because he was tapped-out. He was digging in his heels because she had had the unbridled temerity to walk out on *him*.

When Paige had phoned Jerry to arrange this meeting, he had been catching up on paperwork stacked taller than his toddler son. All Jerry heard on the other end of the line was Paige's blubbering and the fragments of words, "stealing" being the highlight. Since then, he had been a wreck, sleep-walking through his days and barely wanting to eat. A few remodeling clients had also called him to confide there was something underhanded about how Richard was billing the work. A jolt of regret soon clapped his head. He should've trusted his own suspicions about Richard—or Howard's.

Paige repeated in person what she had sniveled over the phone. Richard was skimming money from Space Matters with deliberately hidden transactions. Whatever trouble Jerry had deciphering people's motives and pasts, he knew Paige was being honest. It was in her froggy voice, in her bloodshot eyes. She even said written proof of Richard's deceptions was squirreled away in a Manila folder in his study. She had tripped across it when she had gone to their Van Nuys house to pick up more of her and the baby's stuff and on her way out couldn't resist the temptation to snoop. She began rooting around Richard's desk, scouting for nothing in particular, when her eyes fell on a bulging folder stuffed in the far end of his file drawer. Paige removed it and opened it in her lap. It was tantamount to finding a cheater's diary.

Inside Richard's secret folder were Xeroxed copies of checks for tens-of-thousands of dollars made out to Richard personally by people that Tammy said she had never heard of before save for a few. On the note-line of the checks clients had scrawled words like "home remodeling" and "redesign." Next to each invoice amount in the ledger, Paige recalled, were a string of numbers and letters. Jerry almost blew coffee out of his nose when he heard them. He asked Paige to repeat the code and after she did Jerry grasped the ploy Richard had chosen to bamboozle him. It was on the CM-2 books all along in that over-ordering. Richard had been intentionally diverting lumber, drywall, vinyl, metal studs, paint and other supplies intended for commercial suite-building and home-renovations to worksites for *his* stealthily founded company. Clients paying bills paid it to Kasparov & Co. or to him personally.

Jerry felt not so much queasy as flush. The beans had been spilled, the despicable scheme revealed. He had been deceived by the man who had gushed about those "wonderful things" they would accomplish as expanding partners at Don Ricardo's. It had all been a mirage. Richard was no different than most of Jerry's old corporate bosses. To them, he was little more than a nebbish squirt from North Hollywood, not a quirky prodigy worth cultivating. What did it matter that people were so impressed with his high spatial I.Q. that they joked he should be working in the ergonomics division at JPL or on the next Rubik's Cube when he had been mauled like this? The company bookkeeper had been right in flagging the over ordering. The issue *was* internal. It just happened to be Richard cleaning them out.

Jerry's problem-solving brain was already spinning about how to respond when it struck him that there was but one pathway. They needed to grab Richard's accounting of his own fraud to use against him. You get defrauded, you go to the source. They couldn't delay, either, because if Richard caught wind he might well destroy the paper-trail. Jerry tried soft-pedaling this to Paige, who was crying again, and flubbed his words. Tammy elbowed him to give it another whirl. As a young mother herself, she empathized with Paige's heartbreak. As Jerry's wife, she needed him to do whatever it took to preserve their future, namely the businesses' equity.

Resetting himself, Jerry looked Paige square in the eye, cleared his throat and repeated that ledger was their ammunition to retrieve the money that was rightfully theirs. Paige responded she still wasn't sure that she had it in her. She did confess that she had weighed taking the folder before, deciding against in fear that Richard might've come home unexpectedly. Being alone inside of there, she said, was scary enough after that unexplained man appeared on their deck. Jerry was baffled by this last bit. Richard had never confided anything about an intruder trying to break in or, for that matter, Howard's debt-collection calls.

For the moment, the bombshell folder that Paige discovered in Richard's back-drawer consumed Jerry. As he chewed over tactics about how to gain access to it, he noticed that he had begun rubbing his hands. Paige was watching it, too, as she dabbed her eyes with a sodden tissue. Jerry, shaky around weepy women, said for both their kids' sake, Paige needed to pull herself together long enough to sneak into the house and collect the evidence so they could copy it. Even if it was scary, even if it was a hairball incursion against the man to whom she had said "I do," Richard had left them no choice. Afterwards, they would replace the folder in the desk just as they found it without Richard realizing it had been disturbed.

Paige listened afterwards to Jerry itemize Richard's fishy deeds that he had witnessed. Toted up it could make any wife slouch in her chair, particularly one who had just agreed to skulk into her old house for damning papers. Tammy, who normally spoke in kinetic sentences, said little about the plan, being a hear-no-evil sort of person. Jerry and Paige could have used some liquid-courage or maybe something stronger to embolden them there in Jerry's kitchen. They had made their decision about Operation-Bust-Richard. They were launching it that afternoon to exploit their new joint enemy. Richard would be tied up in appointments the rest of the day.

Paige used her key to re-enter the house, going straight to Richard's desk. In and out in a whirl, she wedged the Manila folder with the ledger inside under her arm and jumped into her car. A few minutes later she met Jerry and Tammy in the pre-arranged locale, a Ralph's supermarket parking lot near the house. Next door to it was a copy shop. Paige and Tammy chatted about children and children only while Jerry sweated near the droning machines. He jogged out when it was done, his back moist, and handed the folder to Paige. Jerry reminded her that when he was ready to spring the evidence on Richard, he would give her a heads-up so she could take the findings to court to impel Richard to pay the child support the judge had decreed. Paige nodded she understood and drove back to return the papers with a slate face.

***

The young doorman in burgundy polyester at the front of the Beverly Hills Hotel greeted Jerry with a practiced nod, military crisp. You had to watch closely for the once-over that the doorman performed afterwards, as if Jerry was a four-eyed poindexter crashing the bitchin' peoples' prom. Jerry maintained his public smile anyway, having made a compact with himself to stay composed here no matter how awkward he felt because he held the advantage now. You think anyone could manage this? Cornering Richard took a brass neck, and those who believed Jerry lacked one had conflated his bashfulness for meekness.

"Welcome to the Beverly Hills Hotel," the doorman said, reaching for the ornately-cast door handle. "Your first time here, sir?"

"Hardly," Jerry answered, straightening the unobliging collar of his best suit. "I was at the Polo Lounge a few weeks ago."

"Very good, sir. I assume, then, you remember the way to the hostess station."

"Of course." Jerry wanted to tell the smug punk in epaulets to go suck car fumes. He had treated his highest rolling clients to the Polo Lounge inside the hotel, and well-recalled his sister's wedding here. By then, the doorman wouldn't have listened, anyway. He was fawning over a fresh arrival of an actor who better belonged here.

A luscious hostess in a billowy dress escorted Jerry to the table he had requested. No "power lunch" today. He was seated just inside the glass walls from the garden patio, where the flowers bloomed and the sun glistened off eye-blinding silverware. It was 1:08 P.M., and the place was buzzing with actors, agents, producers, insurance-brokers-to-the-stars, coke-dealers-to-the-famous, fashion photographers and wealthy executives with their entourages. Outside, the parking lot was overrun by Germany—BMWs, Mercedes, Audis. Indoors, the menu was Continental, with exquisitely-prepared, arrogantly-priced fare served on monogrammed accoutrements. Then again, everyone knew the grub was a fig leaf for the Polo Lounge's true nutritional value – of just being seen at the Polo Lounge.

Husky laughs and the tittering of female voices did little to dent Jerry's concentration. He ran through the script that was supposed to play out, filling his bladder with a half-gallon of iced tea along the way, and only once stared at the hullabaloo over who messed up some hotshot's pate. Benjamin Wynn, his business lawyer, was at his table standing with his hand extended when Jerry shook out of his reverie. "Finally," Jerry said, "a friendly face. Iced tea?" Benjamin was a rangy, skeletal man with lamb-chop sideburns that gave him the profile of a 1970s Ichabod Crane. Though he was thirty-two, his regal nose, dandruff drifts on his suit shoulder and intellectual's demeanor made him appear as if he had bypassed his youth for a ruffled fifty-five. He and Jerry went through another rehearsal for today's action before Richard arrived. Depending on how Richard reacted, it would be either exultant relief or a trip downtown to the District Attorney's office afterwards to notify them about his embezzlement. Jerry, remembering Paige's sunken face that day she visited him, wasn't sure how Richard tolerated mirrors.

Jerry on his own end had never attempted a subterfuge like this. Just the notion of baiting Richard to a legendary restaurant with a premeditated lie would've once sent him running to the men's room with intestinal cramps. But that was the old Jerry. With Benjamin's craft, he had built an airtight case against Richard over the course of the past seven-eight weeks.

The partnership disillusion that Jerry planned next was his chance to il-
lustrate that he wasn't just another sucker willing to get jobbed and write it
off to experience. In the near future, he was promoting himself to be the
exclusive boss of Space Matters. And the future began tomorrow. He just
had to endure a lunch of false pretenses to get there.

Richard's infectious laugh trumpeted his arrival. It lilted in from a table
close to the entrance, where somebody must've waved him down for a quick
hello. This was understandable, for Richard knew loads of the Westside
cognoscenti. He had grown up around the kids of movie people, real estate
barons and other wealthy sorts, and then partied and negotiated within
their breed as an adult. He spoke their language, shopped at the same high-
end boutiques. It was later, when everybody had parted, he moped that
he wasn't a standard multi-millionaire like them, or that he lived in the
bourgeoisie Valley while they reclined in wainscotted mansions. At thirty-
nine, Richard's underachieving was his personal ghoul. Nevertheless, up
he walked to the immaculate table with more forks and glasses than there
were uses for them as if he had rolled out of hedge-happy Bel Air. He wore
a tan suit and an assured grin that the matronly woman overdrizzled with
Chanel couldn't stop gaping at from the adjoining table. Show-time was
approaching. Richard was thirty-six minutes late.

He shook hands with Jerry's table-mate, who Jerry had represented as
a property owner shopping for space-planning bids. Richard had a canned
whopper ready about why he was behind schedule, and Jerry and Benjamin
played along at his fabrication. "You won't believe this happened. As I was
getting ready to leave ..." A raconteur par excellence, Richard transitioned
from what had waylaid him right into a mini-presentation of what Space
Matters could do *for* Benjamin. They let him wrap up his ten-minute pitch
the way Richard customarily did. He tore a sheaf of graph paper off and
sketched a rendition of the plan they had recently composed for another
client. Richard free-handed the layout upside down so Benjamin could
examine it without having to crane his neck from across the table. *What a
talent*, Jerry thought, *and what a waste*. When the sketching ended, Richard
handed Benjamin his business card and asked him to fire off any questions.

Richard, figuring he just reeled in another sale, reclined in his chair self-
satisfied. It was then Benjamin spoke something other than hello. "Richard,"
he said. "I want to show *you* some papers." Benjamin dipped his fingers
into his briefcase and gave Richard a multi-page document stapled onto a

blue backing. Richard accepted it with a quizzical brow. "You see, Richard," Benjamin said. "I'm Jerry's personal lawyer and you've just been served!"

Richard's mouth withered into a small "o." He contorted his body sideways in his chair, as if to deflect the implications of the document. At that exact moment, naturally, the waitress swung by the table asking if everybody had selected what they wanted for lunch. Richard, dizzy from the trap he had sashayed into, mistakenly placed the lawsuit onto her tray rather than his menu. The waitress glanced at the papers bemused. "What this?" she giggled, giving it back. "Sir, I think it belongs to you. I just need your menu if you know what you'd like." Richard replied that he would be skipping any entrees. Jerry and Benjamin, deciding their appetites deserved rewarding, submitted their orders and the waitress flitted off.

"Richard, you better take this seriously," Benjamin said. "When you read through the entire suit, you'll see we've attached your assets, including your house in Van Nuys. The intelligent move for you would be to resolve this immediately by giving up your share of the companies to Jerry. If you don't, the consequences will be devastating. Have I made myself understood?"

Richard mumbled something to the effect that Benjamin had.

"I'm sorry it came to this, Richard," Jerry added softly. "But I'm mostly sorry you did this to me."

Richard hadn't known that for the past weeks, Jerry's rendezvous with Paige became his gateway to snoop into his partner's off-the-book activities. When Jerry had totaled them up, anywhere between one hundred thirty thousand dollars and one hundred fifty thousand dollars had gone missing. Basically, Richard had been living a double life as the co-boss of Space Matters and CM-2, and as the sole proprietor of Kasparov & Co. Richard had never bothered in acknowledging to Jerry that he had founded a company under his own name, probably because it was specifically and surgically devised to plunder him. It was all in the suit and its painstakingly researched attachments.

There was a quiet at the table surrounded by the Polo Lounge clatter. Jerry resisted the impulse to say something to fill in the heavy silence and Richard swallowed his tongue. He didn't stomp away, tell Jerry that he misunderstood his actions, or try concocting a preposterous explanation for his skimming. He just sat there for a few minutes until he abruptly said he had to leave, as if he had remembered he had left the gas stove on at home. He lumbered from the restaurant on stone legs, not slowing to talk to any acquaintances en route to the parking lot.

Jerry and Benjamin stayed for lunch at the table set for three. They made friendly wagers about whether Richard would fight them or walk away from the businesses having now been exposed as a thief. Benjamin expected Richard to concede; Jerry wasn't sure he was done with Richard's machinations. Once the plates were cleared, Benjamin left to return to his Westwood office at about 2:55 P.M. Jerry told him that he didn't mind sticking around to pay the tab.

An odd sensation flapped through Jerry as he sat alone in his Polo Lounge window seat. Pangs of victory and wistfulness that gyrated inside him gave him a rush that he had never felt before. It made him want to hang around the status-junkies for a while longer. You know, observe the scene. He wasn't about to help a draftsman recalculate the square footage on some CEO's corner office on a day like today. *It's all on me from now on,* he thought.

He removed his suit jacket, and soon found himself strolling along the hotel's botanical pathways fragrant with pink cherry blossoms. As he walked, he reminisced about how, at first, he and Richard used to meet prospective clients during the day and then draw all night at their Pico Boulevard office, an office that topped out with two drafting desks and no chairs. Back then, they had a gimmick to distinguish themselves from the established firms—the ones that didn't have to trade architectural services for free rent with their landlord like they did. They branded themselves the "fastest space planners in town," gunslingers with a T-square if you will. Short of handstands, they would do anything to win your business.

Jerry also remembered the reason he had enlisted Richard to be his associate. Early on, he recognized that a stodgy property-owner was more likely to trust a planner with industry lingo down pat and road-wear on his face than someone whose voice they expected to crack when he spoke. Jerry quickly learned something else once they were in business. Whatever heads Richard turned with his electric appeal, there was a vague distress inside him, a fatalistic root system that their fun, hectic beginnings could not completely mask. Its presence was one of the reasons that Jerry had agreed to Richard's sales-job to start CM-2. He had rarely seen Richard so genuinely happy.

And now he had screwed Jerry when they had tens-of-millions of dollars in real estate deals streaming across the office, and Jerry was lost for the reason. Was it to give Paige a sapphire lifestyle and her eyes away from a younger man or a richer gent? Was there a secret debt haunting him? To Jerry, creative challenges and a rising salary was a cause for loyalty, but Richard apparently felt otherwise. He had believed in the beauty of a little greed. That he had known about the uncharacteristic bravado Jerry had mustered to give Space Matters a running start made it all the more devastating, too.

Before he had resigned at his last corporate job in 1976, Jerry had taken a slew of his building-owning clients to lunch. With puppy dog eyes, he had asked them whether he should stick where he was or stride out on his own when he was already leaning towards leaving. The landlords, many of them aging curmudgeons who had scraped for every square foot they had accumulated, were so impressed that the young buck across the table had sought out their counsel that they willingly transferred their business to Space Matters. Predictably, Jerry's gumption enraged his ex-boss after Jerry hung out the Space Matters' shingle. *Ungrateful bastard.* He phoned Jerry at the Plaza Hotel in New York, where he was staying on his honeymoon, fuming that he wanted to sue him *and* kill him. Jerry's client-persuasion campaign might well have been his industry embalming had his former superior not been protecting a slimy tryst. A married man, he had knocked up his mistress and bribed her into having an abortion with a new BMW that he had financed through an illegal company kickback. Jerry, by chance, had been privy to the entire sexcapade because his then-superior had unwittingly sublet his concubine's apartment from Tammy's cousin, and flapping lips soon enough educated him. So when the philanderer threatened to eradicate Jerry, he calmly mentioned things he had never intended to, and the man's indignation screeched to defeated silence.

The ugliness of what Richard had done years later rabbit-punched Jerry, but that punch subsequently passed just like the threats from his corrupt, horny ex-boss. Without revealing to anyone at the mansion about what he had uncovered or the legal counter attack he had in the pike, he had done his mourning and came out of it convinced he had survived the jagged crucible he knew awaited him sometime in his career. He had graduated into another phase—a heartier Jerry that could handle pressure cookers like the Beverly Hills Hotel. Zoological fact: some snakes sport feathered hair.

He circled round on the path towards the restaurant, when he came upon a tinted window reflecting his image in it. Jerry wasn't sure, but he seemed to look older, as if he had grown into his unblemished face over the course of the afternoon. Maybe, preserving his own scalp had hardened him. Walking out to his car that afternoon anxious and upbeat, Jerry believed the worst was over when in reality it had scarcely begun.

***

As 1979 got underway, Jerry presumed all that was between him and better days were Howard's money-hawk lawyers that he had to tolerate during settlement talks. Ronald Allen, Marc Frenkel and a third attorney kept an office on a fleabag stretch of Beverly Boulevard north of downtown. Allen, a thickset, florid man with a bombastic voice and bomb-proof swagger, did most of the talking there, cutting the cliché pose of a pinstriped jerk. The discussions kick-started just how you'd expect, too: with a demand to cow wet-behind-the-ears Jerry into submission. Howard's attorneys were zealous about converting his claims against Space Matters and CM-2 into a five-figure settlement, and they would bleed the companies' kitty if they had to. They had already filed liens against most of the CM-2's jobs to inflict their first cut. They snorted that Howard was entitled to a one-third ownership share of CM-2 after he agreed to supply his contractor's license to the state, plus unpaid back-salary and remuneration for the construction materials that Richard had dastardly rung up on Howard's credit lines. Here it was. Either, Jerry cough-up fifty-thousand dollars or they would napalm him in a lawsuit.

Jerry couldn't wait to leave the meeting, though he had to admit that it had been informative. Richard, he learned, had not just cheated him. He had also swindled Howard by charging thousands of dollars worth of building materials on Howard's credit line that wildly exceeded what Howard had authorized for CM-2. Black smoke just about billowed from Howard's ears whenever his lawyers spoke of the damage Richard had done to those accounts by ordering supplies that Richard had no damn right to order. One of the few remarks that Howard offered with Jerry sitting at his lawyers' table was that he hadn't logged all these years in construction to be back-stabbed by a charming "liar and thief." Jerry knew the existential truth now.

He listened to the haughty attorneys during the one or two meetings he attended and later kept abreast of their correspondence with his lawyer, Benjamin. He quickly got fed up with the heavy-handed tactics, instructing Benjamin to tell Howard's lawyers that if Howard would agree to cancel the liens then he could take ownership of CM-2. A whole company, in other words, for his hassle. Gruffly, Howard's representatives declined. They had Howard's directions to follow and their client demanded money, not a fraud-riddled company on life support.

Just in case anyone doubted Howard's tenacity to be made whole, he reiterated his grievances in an emotional, blistering letter that he mailed to Jerry at work and Tammy at home in January 1979. He wanted to sensitize the couple to the depth of his misery – him woozy in debt, his wife suffering with "a nervous condition"—sparked by this mistreatment. What better way than with personal correspondence? Howard's jeremiad roared with he-man colloquialisms about how he had spent "more time in the pay line" than Jerry had "in the chow line." How he would rather "be damned and go to hell" than allow himself to be used. He portrayed what happened to him at the mansion working for Jerry and Richard as a "fucking mess" making his life more wretched by the day.

Another of Howard's irritations involved the IBM typewriter, calculators and other personal belongings that he left behind when he had quit. Phone calls and badgering about having them returned had done nothing so far. Richard was supposed to have handled it, but then Jerry uncovered his illicit deals and Richard had more urgent matters to concentrate on than reuniting Howard with his beloved stuff. It only would've required stuffing a couple of boxes and a quick phone call to a delivery company. Howard never gave up trying to recoup them, acting bat-shit-crazy that Richard had snubbed him over things of no consequence to him.

Mercifully, that wasn't Jerry's problem anymore, and soon Howard—the overwound violin string—wouldn't be, either. After weeks of "admit this, stipulate that," Howard's lawyers announced that they would settle the claim for a paltry seven-thousand dollars. No longer were they waving the flimsy contention that Howard had been a partner in CM-2 for putting up his contractor's license. Jerry wasn't sure why Howard had tired of the negotiations and ordered his lawyers to hammer out a compromise. If signing one meant he was ridding himself sooner of him and Richard, that was good enough because Jerry was pining to start space-planning his own future again.

CHAPTER SIX

HOWARD'S BLOOD, INC.

H oward began hatching his own recovery plan for 1979 from the moment that he tramped out of Space Matters on the day that he resigned. He was going into a specialty business, just as his old employer cleverly had, though no state license would be necessary. Tapping his management skills and knack for discreet savagery, Howard had decided to charter a murder-for-profit corporation that he would operate out of his Pasadena apartment on Del Mar Boulevard a stone's throw from the Rose Parade route. His enterprise, like all good ones, had a tightly focused objective. It would rob, strong-arm and kill a handpicked group of local, real estate white-collars who had either fleeced him over the years or presented ridiculously easy targets now. Each project would be inside jobs committed by someone that he hired (and could scapegoat if necessary), with hundreds-of-thousands of dollars there for the plucking. Richard and Jerry would be the opening assignments, because the rage marinating inside Howard towards them no lawyers could settle.

Howard had met his first "employee" approximately six months before he joined CM-2. He and career-robber Robert "Frenchy" Gaines Freeman had shaken hands in October 1977 behind bars in the San Bernardino County lockup when neither man was riding high. Howard then was trying to make bail on a felony charge for an unspeakable find in the San Bernardino desert; Robert was there for a burglary. Fourteen months later, in December 1978, Robert was back in jail there again on another charge. Flat-broke, he recommended that his wife call his old, cell-mate to see if he would bail him out in time for Christmas. Elena Freeman did as requested, telling Howard that Robert's freedom would only cost three-thousand dollars. Howard, mulling his New Year's agenda, answered the woman that she had come to the right place. Out he went to San Bernardino, probably smoking and plotting, and back he came with his future assassin.

Robert, thirty-six, was good-looking and light-skinned, a man with a prison-built physique, a heroin addiction he was struggling to unwind and scant employable skills. This all made Howard his godsend. Not only had he paid his bail, he had given him some walking-around money as well as use of his prized, metallic blue 1975 El Camino, the one with the new white camper shell and chrome-magnesium wheels. He had even agreed to allow Robert to drive it home to San Francisco. "This is yours," Howard told him in a fatherly lilt. "Do with it as you want. But when I tell you I need it, I want it back immediately, okay, like that day." Conditions accepted, Robert said. And thank you!

Robert returned to Southern California a few days after Christmas for an exploratory business meeting with his benefactor. It might've been on this trip south, gliding around those holiday wreaths and oversized candy canes that some Pasadena civic group lovingly arranged on Lake Avenue, that Howard began revealing to Robert the murder-for-profit corporation that he was establishing. They then went to Howard's second-floor apartment, where Howard showed Robert the thousands of dollars of invoices that Howard's ex-boss Richard had deceitfully billed to his credit line. Howard griped that that smudge of bad money had spread, and now he was a full twenty-thousand dollars in debt, an insurmountable hole.

After visiting a liquor store for refreshments, Howard finally revealed his desire. He wanted—*needed*—Robert to execute Richard, among others, for the financial benefit it would produce and the spray of satisfaction it would bring. If Robert sincerely wanted to repay his generosity for bailing him out when he had and providing him with a chance to earn some money that was how. Richard had to die. Robert, acting intrigued, told Howard that he would consider the proposition as he made his way home again to the Bay Area. Howard once more let him leave in the El Camino, and this time he threw in his Mobil gas card. Yet unlike the last trip, Howard intended to supervise Robert's schedule because they had entered an employment relationship. Howard cemented that transition by phoning Robert obsessively with the same question: could he be counted on for the contract-murder of

Richard Kasparov? Robert finally told Howard what he wanted to hear. He would pull the job.

Howard's initial conception was for Robert to shoot Richard dead before New Year's Day while he and his wife, Carol, a Thrifty Drugstore manager, were "on vacation" with an alibi half a state away in his new hit-man's hometown. Believing he had staged everything, Howard motored off to San Francisco with Carol in the Datsun 280-Z that Richard had lent Howard until he could repay him the money that he owed. Somewhere in that irony-savoring head of his, Howard must've been snickering at the paradox of him driving the imported, Japanese sports car of the man whose murder he just ordered up. Carol had no inkling about the plot because that's the way Howard wanted it under his violence sequestration.

Inside-jokes notwithstanding, his criminal franchise got off to the lamest of starts. First, the Datsun's engine blew up in Fresno, forcing Carol and Howard to catch a Greyhound bus to the Bay Area. There Howard learned that his specially selected hit-man had decided to stay put at home rather than drive to the San Fernando Valley to eliminate Richard. Howard buttonholed Robert about it at the first opening. If Robert was too much of a yellow-belly to carry out the job, say it, Howard grunted. He would hire someone with requisite spine to do it. Just don't be wishy-washy. The reprimand, if not Howard's attendant frown, shook Robert up. He vowed to fulfill his obligation in the Valley, and soon.

Two weeks later, Robert was down in L.A learning the finer points of being Howard's assassin. The boss swung his trainee by Richard's house several times to point out the house, explain the neighborhood and calmly take any questions. They used the El Camino on one trip, Richard's now-repaired 280-Z on the next. Howard wanted his carnage handled with lightning efficiency. He said that if Robert spotted Richard's Cougar parked in his driveway, Robert was to knock on the front door and blast away with the .45 that Howard had lent him. Should Richard refuse to open up, Robert was to fire through the door and muscle his way inside. Robert then was to shoot Robert point-blank in the head and murder anybody else in the house. Howard repeated the point. No witnesses tolerated!

Howard believed in options, as well, and his other suggested scenario was a ruse on Richard's vanity. Robert could call him pretending to be a wealthy homeowner who had admired the remodeling work that CM-2 had performed for Joseph Marmet, the doctor with the desert land he hoped to subdivide. Was it possible, Robert would inquire, for Richard to drive out to his place for a bid? Howard and Robert would concoct an address, some lot off Mulholland Drive perhaps, and gun Richard down when he showed up for the presentation.

His boss' instructions ringing in his ears, Robert drove the roughly fifty miles from Ontario to Chandler Boulevard and knocked on Richard's front door. Nobody answered. Robert made a return trek soon afterwards and it was the same as before. Strike one, strike two; Howard was growing antsy, but he knew that with patience Richard's corpse was worth the annoyance. Once more, he escorted Robert on a nighttime recon to Van Nuys. This time, there were lights on in the upper bedroom of Richard's house. Howard reminded Robert as they idled at the curb what to do if these circumstances existed when he returned.

For Robert's third attempt on Richard, Howard leapt on the first plausible excuse for getting out of town. Carol's birthday was January 29, and Howard was taking her to Las Vegas to celebrate and gamble from January 27 to February 2. The trickle of independent construction jobs he had lined up after leaving Space Matters could wait. What's life without a little celebration (and a $5.99 Vegas steak dinner)? As before, Howard was plotting with geography. The police could not possibly implicate him for a murder in Van Nuys if he was 230 miles away in Nevada's hustle-town when the bullets flew.

Howard's preparation list runneth over first. Modifying his .45 caliber pistol to flummox the LAPD forensic technicians that he knew would be summoned to investigate Richard's homicide was a priority. For a former carpenter like him, this was kid stuff. With a saw, hammer and other implements from his old shop, Howard cut and flattened the barrel so any bullets fired out of the pistol would not reveal the telltale marks of the registered weapon that'd discharged them. When he was done, he handed Robert back the gun and cautioned him to baby it. Long ago, a Canadian Royal Mountie had given the .45 as a collector's item to Howard's father, who later bestowed it on a son with no gooey nostalgia to fasten it on a wall as an heirloom. More and more, Howard must've realized guns were his new tools.

Financing was another loose end and Howard decided they would use a remote Ontario gas station as an office to discuss it. Once Robert drove up in the El Camino, Howard set his briefcase on the hood of the 280-Z, unclasped the lock and withdrew from the case eight, one-hundred dollar bills. Robert couldn't recall the last time he had that much scratch. Take it, Howard said. Robert was to lie to anybody inquisitive about the money with a cover story. He was to say his boss had advanced it so Robert could purchase cement for a "construction job" deep in Orange County.

Howard's real intent for the eight-hundred dollars was for a pair of get-away cars to throw the cops off their scent. The plan was for Robert to buy a jalopy down in Long Beach as transportation to Richard's house. After the killing was over, Robert would drive the junker to a Valley motel close by and dump it for a prepositioned car waiting for him there. Robert then could either drive that second car home to San Francisco or to Los Angeles International Airport for a flight up north. Shoot, ditch the car and flee: your basic, three-step execution. Before they parted, Howard also gave Robert a signed blank check for miscellaneous expenses. Howard emphasized that Robert was to call him at the Vegas Hilton to promptly notify him that he had honored his commitment. Howard said he was prepared to stay in Nevada for as long as it required. But, he warned, the effort better not require another road trip across the Mojave Desert.

Observing the gas station meeting from inside the El Camino was Ros Ann Dyer, a twenty-nine-year-old, single mom from nearby Mount Baldy. Richard had recently picked her up at a local nightclub, telling her that he was Howard's "contractor apprentice." Ros Ann, who worked at an advertising agency, was fascinated by Robert's employment, never quite able to pin him down with what his job entailed or the unorthodox hours it required. Now, watching Howard transfer that cash to her boyfriend—at a God-forsaken gas-pump no less—she had fresh material to needle him about the squishiness of his so-called career. "That's a lot of money," she quipped when Robert got back behind the wheel. "What, do you have to kill somebody for that?" A limp, bloodless expression waxed over Robert's face hearing the woman's speculation, and Ros probably understood from his reaction that she might have just yucked her way into peril. Within a few weeks she broke up with him.

If that was painful, spectacular new misery was about to make Robert forget it. Besides his modified .45, Howard also had lent him his shotgun. Since it was registered in his name, Howard wanted Robert to shorten its barrel in a further act of trail covering; it would also make it easier to conceal. So, while Howard and Carol tore east from Pasadena to Vegas, Robert got busy outside with a handsaw, probably at his sister's house in Ontario.

Back and forth he went, the saw's aluminum teeth ripping into the muzzle with a screechy whine, when out of nowhere came an air-bursting crackle that wrecked the rest of Robert's day. Seems the shotgun that was never supposed to harm its user had discharged accidentally. *Bah-wusssh.* Before the rifle's echo died out, Robert grabbed his face unsure if it was all there.

A tiny metallic shaving pried up during the sawing laid cratered in Robert's eye. Within five minutes it was swollen shut and he could barely see out of it by dinner. Robert wasn't sure what to do. Howard expected him to fulfill his obligation, and Robert-the-felon wasn't accustomed to accessing healthcare. As his eye grew puffier and infected, he knew he would become a Cyclops loser unless he found a physician who would treat him without posing nosey questions. After a batch of calls and scrambling around, he located one who removed the filing and prescribed him medication. By then, Robert appreciated he was boxed inside of a bigger dilemma.

The psychological effect of his lacerated cornea was graver than its physical ache. Robert was at another crossroads of bad choices, where Lord knows he had been before. He had spent more time in jail than outside of it. Robbery and burglary for profit that he began at seventeen had left him broke. Hurting others had mostly harmed him. And now Howard had sunk his talons into him. Whether as debt-repayment or criminal employment, Howard expected him to not only kill Richard and any potential witnesses, but after that help him extort and/or murder Jerry. If that didn't work, they would kidnap and maim Jerry's diapered son. Once done there, Howard wanted Robert to lead a home takeover invasion of an immigrant auto body shop owner and real estate investor that Howard and his mother knew intimately. Robert, depending on how things went, might have to slaughter them, too. After that were a series of wealthy executives that Howard aimed to pillage and kill. Pondering his transformation from hapless robber to potential mass-murderer, Robert probably felt as though his gashed eye would throb out of its socket.

Robert had tried reasoning with Howard to re-evaluate his gory agenda even before the eye injury. As diplomatically as possible, he inquired if Howard was certain he wanted to execute Richard when the LAPD would certainly suspect him after examining the pair's entanglements. Disfiguring Jerry's kid, Robert added, would be even riskier, because the FBI got involved in violence against children. Howard listened as long as he could until he shook his head disgustedly, hearing cowardice and not cold logic in

Robert's words. There'd be no pullback, he countered. Or more excuses. Or further delays. Robert just had to fire a bullet into Richard temple and wait for future orders. Understand?

Unluckily, he did. Over the next few days, Robert mulled where this was leading and how he might trench an escape route out. Pixel by pixel, an answer as inspired as it was semi-suicidal came to him. He, in effect, would replace himself. He would dilute his involvement in Howard's aspirations so smoothly, so amicably that Howard wouldn't care that Robert had recruited someone else to kill Richard, Jerry and the others. Dilution, then duck out became Robert's strategy to sever Howard from his life. The first step was painless enough, even promising. Robert contacted Johnny Williams, a longtime pal from his native Ontario and an ardent gun enthusiast. Quietly, Robert acknowledged to Johnny the capers that Howard was organizing. Did he want to split the money that Howard was offering for knocking his former-supervisor off? Johnny answered hell yes he wanted in. To Robert's relief, Howard was equally keen on a two-man job, which Robert had broached with him before he left for Vegas. There it was. Johnny was Robert's first draftee to replace him.

Johnny Harold Williams, thirty-seven, was a diminutive, addict-thin man with bushy brown hair, oversized glasses and a trapezoidal forehead that loomed over a puckered face. He hadn't had much to smile about during his life so he often wore a fixed sneer while expanding his six-page rap sheet. Robbery, car-thefts, fish-and-game violations, forgery, statutory rape, drug possession, etc; Johnny was versatile in his criminality. But he wasn't omniscient. Not even close. If he had been, he would have known that Robert and his bulbous eye had already returned to San Francisco in the El Camino fully determined to breaking from Howard's murder conglomeration.

Howard nearly stroked out when he heard from Nevada that Robert had returned home. Veins popping, he got in the 280-Z, told Carol to jump in and they drove to San Francisco. Robert was going to keep his promise with or without Johnny, even if Howard had to drag him back by the nostrils. For a second time now, Howard tracked Robert down hundreds of miles from the target to interrogate him. "*Why'd you disappear?*" he probably asked. "*Why didn't you deal with Richard? What about the $800 I gave you? Why'd you have to fuck it up again?*"

Robert once more apologized to the incensed boss who rarely raised his voice. He explained how the shotgun had discharged while he had been sawing off the barrel, and how his enflamed eye left him morose about his future. He promised to do better, no more excuses, re-committing to murders he had decided not to commit. Robert then prudently changed the subject, convincing Howard to agree to give a lift to several friends back to L.A. On February 15, 1979, Robert and his buddies—one a cross-dressing thief, the other a knucklehead junkie—crammed into the El Camino for the trip south. Robert's pals, if nothing else, were buffers in case Howard's fury about his hit-man's failures needed a physical outlet.

The next day, Robert was in Howard's Pasadena apartment on a short leash as Howard offered him a refresher on how to eliminate Richard. In broken-record fashion, Howard told his subordinate that he would travel to Santa Barbara, Vacaville or some other place for his latest alibi and Robert said he understood. Howard must have bought it, because Robert still had Howard's approval to drive the El Camino despite the serial goof-ups and disappearances. The day after Howard frog-marched him south, Robert took the car to his sister's place in Ontario just outside Los Angeles County's eastern border. He should've just driven off a cliff.

Out there, equidistant from desert and mountains, the L.A.-dream felt several steps removed. Unlike Van Nuys, Pasadena or Gucci-fied West L.A., the California sun was duller in Ontario, the opportunities less thrilling. Instead of backward swimming pools, people deposited old cars and sofas on dirt lawns. Ontario, as its neighbors, had undergone breakneck growth at the turn of the century. It erected health resorts, dug citrus fields and planted olive groves. "Iowa under Palm Trees" was the civic slogan; it was West Coast weather with Midwestern sensibility. General Electric and defense companies came, and the subdivisions followed. The future, however, was unrewarding. When some of the factories shut, the city of ninety-thousand could only boast a speedway and a second-rate airport owned by L.A. City Hall. Gangs, some sprouting from Latino families who once hoed the local farmland, found fresh blood in the underclass. By the late 1970s, Ontario was in full stagnation, stuck on its haunches without ever enjoying a prime. It was not that different than Robert.

Wouldn't you know, back in these digs, he was snake-bit again. While Robert had slept at his sister's house, his junkie-friend snuck off in the El Camino on an improvised trip to score drugs. Before he got to his dealer, he plowed Howard's pride and joy into another vehicle and ditched the car.

Authorities investigating the hit and run located the El Camino and towed it to an impound lot until the accident was resolved. Howard was unable to control himself this time, howling his dismay when Robert broke the news to him. He couldn't have his automobile attracting needless police attention so close to the pending killings-for-profit. Showstoppers happen this way. Robert begged Howard not to blow his friend's head off in pique. He's not worth it, he said. "*Like you know anything,*" Howard might've answered.

The night of the accident, Howard had a favor to ask of Robert, who comprehended he needed to make amends for his own life-expectancy. Howard wanted to know where *he* could buy some heroin or cocaine for personal enjoyment, and he had no patience for dithering. Robert replied no problem. Johnny Williams had connections, and so did Johnny's brother, who fraternized with the local Hells Angels. Robert, in fact, volunteered to arrange a narcotics party in Howard's name that evening and Howard said that was more like it. Sure enough, Howard turned up on Maitland Street anxious for a good high. Robert knew then that he would breathe another day.

Johnny's pad was a makeshift bedroom that he converted inside his father's garage. For Johnny and his mates, those four walls constituted a secure zone to party, scheme, and condemn their worldly enemies. Howard, Johnny and Robert were there, and so was Robert's short, drag-queen-thief friend, James "Jaime" Jones. Among them all were well over one-hundred felony charges. Needles plunged into skin. Crystallized fluff vacuumed into nostrils. And Howard sat on Johnny's bed contentedly ripped as could be. He now had a fresh drug-source via a man he basically owned.

Stoned and all that evening, Robert wanted out from underneath Howard's thumb as badly as ever. Freeing himself permanently, however, required that he re-assert his dilution plan without tipping his hand. Johnny already was on the team, and Robert hoped to enroll James next. To lend the impression he remained Howard's lieutenant, Robert explained at the drug soiree the underpinnings of Howard's franchise: why they needed Richard dead, what they would do to Jerry and his son, how they would rob Howard's family friend and the follow up robbery-killings. Each one would be inside jobs, Robert told everybody; high payoff, low risk.

Howard was comforted listening to Robert's presentation. Besides, as he surveyed the garage gang that night, he knew he could manipulate the bunch. To a one, he was older, smarter, meaner and, comparatively speaking, a Rockefeller next to them. He owned business licenses and called millionaire-executives by their first name. Robert, Johnny and the others were fortunate the state issued them driver's licenses with the asinine frequency in which they shuttled in and out of prison. Howard, who sported a panther tattoo on his left arm and a skull-figure on his right, knew he need not speak much. He tacitly controlled the room.

Once Howard had driven home to Pasadena, Robert dangled more money for his enlistees. He promised to disperse twenty-five hundred dollars to both Johnny and James in addition to the $3,750 apiece that Howard would pay them for Richard's execution. Grease a human being and earn $6,250: that was the compensation here. Neither realized that Robert was cutting himself out of the money because for all they knew, he had his own salary package with Howard.

February, by most probabilities, should have been Richard's last earthly month with Howard's men on the hunt. The trip from depressing Ontario to pleasant Van Nuys became a commute. Johnny accompanied Robert one night and—ever the attack dog—sauntered up to the front door and knocked. No surprise, the place was empty. Soon, the two friends were back on Chandler Boulevard for another stab. Johnny rapped again, but this time he elicited what he had desired: a response from inside. Richard and an unknown woman peeked out from the upstairs window over the garage to see who was there, exciting Johnny to finger his gun. He might've even been able to take them out with a spray of bullets if they hadn't backed out of his sightline.

***

While Howard fretted about his contract-murder corporation becoming the gang-that-couldn't-shoot-anything, Jerry toiled to separate his company's legitimate deals from Richard's shady ones. Richard, using the attorney that his mother was helping pay for, had agreed in principle weeks after his Polo Lounge bushwhacking to yield his interest in the companies in exchange for his hide. The last thing he needed with all his troubles was a white-collar prosecution and punitive damages liable to bankrupt him.

Until they signed the final dissolution papers, Richard was expected to assist Jerry straighten out the jumble he had made of CM-2's supposedly sensational future. Jerry considered it a teeth-gnashing epilogue. *When we're done, I'll never have to see his face again,* he told himself. As it was, Jerry was feverish with mistrust towards him. Whenever Richard was expected to drop by Fremont Place to sort through the paperwork, Jerry the shy, even-keeled, young businessman disappeared and the headless chicken in him emerged. Having Richard back in the mansion pretzeled him in stress, because who knows what he was capable of? Jerry's office housekeeping order applied to all. No job spreadsheets, account ledgers or any other sensitive documents could be open on anybody's desk when Richard walked through the door. Jerry wouldn't put it past him to twist anything to his advantage.

The crew went along, even the more flamboyant designers once loyal to Richard. Nearly everybody knew that he had cheated Jerry and that meant he had cheated them by proxy. Few of the staff tried soliciting Richard's version of events if he was around. Quite the opposite: they cast him suspicious glances and tracked his movements. For someone with Richard's sense of prestige– someone quick to say that he resided in "Los Angeles," not gauche Van Nuys– it must've been 500 PSI of embarrassment.

Richard, nonetheless, refused to slip into another bout of moldy depression as he had after his first divorce in the early-1970s. There'd be no beautiful loser in him. Hell, he was not even forty yet in a city that applauded second chances. Maybe it wasn't even too late to re-approach some of his ex-believers if he would acknowledge the disaster he had been inside. He had at least bottomed out enough to begin seeing a Pico Boulevard psychiatrist. After years of dabbling with est and other self-help movements offering more wackiness than enlightenment, he was giving convention a try.

So no, Richard wasn't giving up and in fact hoped to re-unite with his estranged wife, Paige. To demonstrate that she still had title on his heart, he bought her a four-hundred dollar ladies-Cartier watch and clothes for baby Rebecca. Instead of being touched by the gesture, though, Paige was gape-mouthed by it. The blue outfits that Richard had purchased for their little girl were designed for a boy. And what was she to do with a Cartier, official timepiece of the affluent, when Richard was denying her court-ordered financial support to the point that she could barely afford an In-And-Out Burger for dinner? Richard's head seemed to be orbiting Mars, whatever his efforts to depict himself as grounded.

He did have one woman steadfast to him as he bit down on his dignity and assisted Jerry with the disarray he had instigated. Brie Levine, a free-spirit who believed in karma and crystals while resembling an Italian model in tight pants and loose tops, had dated Richard for several years after his first marriage flamed out. They had remained friends despite Richard's cruel romantic treatment of her, and a few months before things collapsed with Jerry in late-1978 Richard hired her. He anointed her as Space Matters' unofficial office manager, tasking her to bring order to the company's pell-mell files and fuzzy procedures. Now that he had to periodically return to an office that he had fleeced, Richard was relieved that Brie had stuck it out.

Everybody else who had encountered Richard during his pinnacle saw something else: his accelerating dishevelment over the last months. The same mesmeric personality who on his best day made space-planning sexy looked to be unraveling molecularly, with cow-lick hair, badly wrinkled clothes and a patent aimlessness. Dark stories about his behavior trailed him. A client fond of him in spite of his flightiness reported that he had stashed a drawer full of Quaaludes and tried to sell him a batch. Another client had gone to fetch his newspaper early one morning only to notice Richard parked on his driveway asleep in his car. Was it because he was too wasted to drive and needed to crash or a more chilling explanation: he sensed monsters were after him.

One afternoon in early-1979, after Howard's hitmen had commenced their numerous quests to kill him, Richard could fake it no more. He dropped the charade that he was taking his downfall in stride, screeching up to Space Matters with a face corkscrewed with distress. Brie saw it and rushed down the stairs to comfort him. By then, Richard was done with her pep talks, yipping at his loyal ex-girlfriend to leave him alone. He wanted to get to where he was going. Which, at that time, was pretty much nowhere.

By February, there wasn't much clamoring for Richard's company besides his mother and sister. How could there be? His fundamentals sounded like a whistle for anti-depressants: unemployed, in litigation, on the outs with wife No. 2 and self-medicating like crazy. Desperation wafted from him. Even the car he was normally so meticulous about that he would park it blocks from dust-sources was filthy tin. There was no other way to say it. Richard was lost. Knuckle-dragging, don't-shave-for-days, let-the-phone-ring lost.

PART II

HITMEN

CHAPTER SEVEN

A REAL JOHNNY ON THE SPOT

As CEO of his newly minted, real estate murder corporation, Howard made a gutsy personnel decision around this period. He promoted Johnny to lead assassin because he was naturally ferocious and, unlike Robert, an employee who followed orders without reservation. Howard could have held tryouts at simulated crime scenes and still not have pinpointed as good a substitute hitman.

Not that Johnny had been destined to cradle a gun. Early in his life, he had scored high on intelligence tests and exhibited glimpses of a photographic memory. Uncanny, his father once noted, how Johnny could recite paragraphs verbatim from a book years after reading it. Johnny might well have parlayed that brainpower into a fruitful life if not for the accident that redirected his trajectory. It had happened when Johnny was a boy being driven by his mother to see his dad, then a long-distance trucker returning from the road. On the way there, the car door had creaked open and Johnny spilled out, striking his head on the blacktop from a vehicle speeding 45 MPH. The neurological damage was obvious as time passed. The doctors diagnosed Johnny with epilepsy and prescribed him medication for life.

Whether from illness or nature, the criminal inside Johnny percolated up by adolescence. Rather than Boy Scouts and proms, it was Juvenile Hall and parole agents for him. Multiple murders were not in his bulging case file, but they should have been. Johnny, as Howard no doubt discovered, had taken the lives of three people as a late-teen in the little-noticed gang wars along Southern California's eastern wasteland near the Los Angeles-

San Bernardino county border. People shot at him and Johnny returned fire, accurately at that. Not once had local police questioned him about these killings and never was he formally charged for any of them. Johnny must've deduced that society's gnashing for justice excluded dead kids from blistered, bloody streets.

Howard, for his part, saw what he needed in Johnny's fondness for bedlam. They began meeting alone, usually over drugs, in Johnny's garage-bedroom as Howard educated him on a deeper level about his enterprise. James Jones and Johnny's friend Hector "Chaser" Villa were a rung below as lower-tier employees collecting one-hundred to two-hundred dollar weekly stipends from Howard. Unlike in January, the boss was in buoyant spirits now. The killings were about to begin, and his trouble-loving El Camino was back with him without drawing police attention after the hit-and-run.

As chipper as Howard was about the money he would wring from his crimes, his original hit-man, Robert Freeman, was stomping the dirt in frustration. No matter how much he kept returning to the Bay Area to isolate himself from Howard during the early months of 1979, Southern California had a tractor beam on him that landed right back into his master's clutches. Howard, it turns out, held old-fashioned views about people doing what they promised. When Robert failed to meet his obligations on Chandler Avenue after so many efforts, Howard made it personal. He preyed on Robert's family in Ontario with compulsive servings of terror and guilt.

A February 1979 night of cat-and-mouse at the home of Robert's mother was how he began. Howard and Johnny had shown up there hoping to slickly goad "the old lady" into lending them the family's shotgun for what they termed was a "serious situation" in the San Fernando Valley. But the woman, already admonished by her son not to give Howard a weapon unless she wanted it turned on them, lied sweetly that the rifle *was* registered with authorities, whatever Howard's perceptions about it. Sorry to disappoint you, she said; you'll have to try elsewhere. Feeling snubbed, Howard channeled his energy elsewhere. He pressured Robert to arrange transportation so Johnny and James could return to Van Nuys with their own guns. Robert knew he had to placate him or they all might be dead and, as such, committed a deplorable act. He convinced his sister's boyfriend, Mark, to make the drive without explaining the homicidal motivation behind it.

A chilly midnight rain greeted the three when they reached Chandler Boulevard. Being pros, Johnny and James had anticipated the weather and dressed warmly. Catching them flat-footed was the unfamiliar car parked in Richard's driveway. "It looks like he has company tonight," Johnny quipped. "I don't know if we ought to stop by or not." Soon enough, he decided they would and directed Mark to leave. Johnny, as he had done before, strode up to Richard's front door and knocked with the poise of an Amway sales-man. Déjà vu: nobody answered. Johnny trudged back to the street to hatch another ploy.

His associate wanted to help, but James, the cross-dresser, was exas-perated that he was there in pants. He would much have preferred to be outfitted in his favorite skirt, blouse and accessories that just happened to be stuck in the locked camper shell of Howard's El Camino out in Pasadena. Their inaccessibility was a shame, James reasoned, because having him dolled-up might have been their surprise catalyst to get this killing checked off. No one, and certainly not Richard, would expect a killer in lipstick and rouge standing coquettishly on his driveway. Aside from the novelty, James enjoyed invoking his feminine side. Since he was in men's garb for the night, the .32 revolver he was packing would have to be enough.

Johnny, too, was interested in switching things up to secure the blood-shed that had juked them until now. Walking up and knocking cold on Richard's door had been useless. They needed a believable pretext to entice him into opening up his house before he gave it much thought. Something he might've opened up to before. That was it, Johnny realized. They would fabricate an emergency. This time, he would knock on the front door and screech that he had been involved in a motorcycle wreck and needed a phone to alert help. Richard would likely suspend any wariness of strangers for someone who had been in an accident. He would have turn the door knob into his own assassination.

Johnny and James re-approached the driveway with the fake story that they hoped would be the last thing Richard Kasparov heard before the bar-rel exploding. The charade might've been successful, too, except for the negative kismet about to pop. Down the block from them, a woman in a domestic sedan and a lady in a Mustang collided in a metal-crunching col-lision that awoke part of the neighborhood. Howard's men must've stopped on their insoles to gasp at each other; another snag? No, Johnny vowed, not this time. While he realized there'd soon be a convoy of cops, paramed-ics and tow trucks on site, Johnny planned to capitalize on the smash-up. Richard, he knew, had probably heard the accident himself, making Johnny's sham of being a pleading accident victim at his door that much more plausible. Quickly, he rang the doorbell instead of knocking and got what he desired. Two faces–likely Richard and that woman from before–peeked down at them from an upstairs window.

"Hey mister, there's been an accident. Can we use your phone to call the cops?" Johnny shouted through the mist. The faces in the window said nothing. Johnny kept his eyes on them. The faces receded just like before.

Johnny and James were up against it now, stranded a seeming continent from Ontario, in what felt like a snooty L.A. neighborhood. As always, Johnny sustained his composure. He walked over to the accident scene like any other lookey-loos and sidled up next to a man with a Pontiac Firebird. Could he drop him and a buddy off at Corky's, a fifties-style coffee shop not far away, Johnny asked? The stranger agreed. Inside the restaurant, Johnny phoned his elderly dad to pick them up in the faraway town.

Howard could barely restrain his own poise from becoming molten rage after Johnny acknowledged the closest, near-miss yet. Another whiff, another misadventure: they were up to a half-dozen botched or squandered chances now. If Howard didn't know better, he would swear Richard had a guardian angel on *his* payroll.

The man who was already supposed to have mowed him down had nothing divine helping him. After a court hearing on an old charge was delayed the next day, Robert drove downtown to take a physical required for a cross-country, truck-driving job with a company called J&B Produce. Robert had decided that he wanted to wipe his slate clean, if not put time zones between him and you-know-who. Nice thought if it wasn't so farfetched; Howard could track you down in a river. Robert had been in the exam waiting room with a clipboard in his hands when his boss flicked the door open and sauntered over. "I have wasted enough fucking time with you today," Howard said with purplish cheeks in front of the other job applicants. "I have places to go and people to see, and I am not spending any more time here. Come on. Let's go."

Robert left with the gait of a P.O.W. and ducked into the El Camino. Howard drove east out of downtown and then told Robert that he had something explosive to lay on him. Something that Robert might not believe but better remember. Ready? In an acid voice, Howard said Johnny had volunteered to kill him because he had chickened out of murdering Richard and knew too much about their blueprints. Johnny, indeed, was so enthusiastic to do it that he hadn't even asked for any money. "How could you run around with people who called themselves your friend when they would offer to kill you for free?" Howard asked. "Does that sit well with you?"

Back in Ontario a few days later, Robert shuddered with worry. Crocodile, predator, psychotic, ghost: choose your metaphor. If Howard wanted something that you denied him, he would burrow under your house to feast on its contents. Heaven help you if he knew your weaknesses—drugs, embezzlement, gay sex, fear of incarceration. And God save you if he targeted your loved ones. The metaphor went blank then. Robert understood that he had to bolt. Not just for a week. Not for the spring. He had to ditch Southern California and act as though it had sloughed into the ocean after the Big One. The dilution plan had failed. Believing otherwise had been self-serving dreamland.

Everything was upside down. Johnny had tried explaining away his offer to kill him for free as nothing more than smoke-blowing blarney to impress Howard, but Robert knew Johnny was lying. Robert had been clued in about how Johnny had recently pulled aside Robert's step-brother, Nathaniel, asking him if he wanted to make a little money. Johnny said that all he would have to do was to help them kill Robert, his sister, Janice, and their mother in a neatly-packaged triple murder. Thus, Robert escaped in the only conveyance at his disposal: on the knobby wheels of Howard's weathered Chevy. Rolling up Interstate-5 yet another time, Robert must have wondered what would skulk out of L.A. looking for him. Say this, the man had instincts. The question is whether he had a future. Someone had fired a potshot at him as he drove off from his Ontario neighborhood.

The next bullet aimed at him would likely be more accurate, because a few days after arriving in San Francisco Robert stood pale on his block. A car thief had swiped Howard's El Camino from where Robert had parked it. What was it about that ride that imperiled so many people? Robert's wife, Elena, asked about their next step and Robert said that they needed to gauge Howard's temperature with a phone call to his Pasadena apartment. Brace yourself, Robert warned her. An explosion was building.

Howard stayed quiet while Elena explained that someone had pinched the El Camino. He said nothing as she described how Robert was so traumatized about the development that he had subsequently skipped town when he was really secretly listening in on the receiver. He heard her recommend that he report his Chevy stolen to the police or his insurance company to recover his loss. There was a pause on the line after she finished speaking and a flicker of hope that Howard would evoke a spirit of forgiveness.

A flicker? With him? Howard erupted, barking threats like a rabid creature rousted from its cave. It was as if the true Howard was reaching his hand through the transmission lines and around their Adam's apples. "Your husband is a sonofabitch, and you know now he is a dead sonofabitch," Howard shouted. Elena, weeping, tried interrupting the barrage to talk sense. He continued. "A dead man, you hear me. He stole my car." *Click.* Howard hung up to let Elena eat the dial tone.

In the ensuing days, Howard began calling Robert's sister, Janice, to dislodge Robert's whereabouts. "Robert owes me money. He has a job to do. Have him call me" It was important, real important. Robert never responded, spurring Howard to switch to guilt. "I was good enough to get him out of jail, Janice, and now he won't do the work that I've already paid for. I'll ask you again: where is Bob? San Francisco?" Janice said she had no idea.

When Howard saw he wasn't getting anywhere, he and Carol again drove from Southern California to San Francisco. They went to the psychedelic Haight-Ashbury district that they knew Robert frequented and by sheer luck spotted him entering a building. As much as Howard must've wanted to splatter him with a drive-by shooting, he wanted his vehicle back more. They continued searching for it on streets and in alleys, beyond green trolleys and red brick buildings. Minutes later, there it was, shiny-blue on a curb not far from Robert's apartment where the unknown car thief must have returned it. Howard fished out his spare key and plopped in feeling a beat of satisfaction. He knew his welching, lying former assassin would be dead soon.

***

After weeks of gray skies and rain, California's tangerine sun reappeared on March 9. The light shone down just in time for Johnny's return visit to Van Nuys on a day of criminal alchemy unlike than the others. Johnny, with Howard's assent, planned to convert a simple burglary into a demented answer for the hardware for which they had been scavenging.

Johnny and his buddy Chaser, a short, bony Hispanic, moved confidently along Richard's narrow side yard. They snuck into the backyard and up the landing to the upstairs deck, where Johnny used a screwdriver to bash a bathroom window to gain entry. Neither man was packing. They weren't here for carnage, and didn't want the extra prison time if they were nabbed with a firearm. Johnny's implement today was nefarious imagination. They would rob Richard's house and trade in the loot for a murder weapon to use against him.

He and Chaser scooted around the well-decorated home that Paige and the baby had deserted after Howard's menacing calls. They pilfered goodies on sight without perspiring about any alarm system or guard dog that Howard had already briefed them weren't present. They lifted Richard's typewriter and a couple of stereo systems. They pocketed jewelry and trinkets. Filching Richard's yellow Cartier watch was a prize haul itself. Nobody on his Ontario block had probably even held one before.

Richard discovered his ransacked place after a two-day trip, to where nobody knows. Whoever had invaded his house had exited cheekily through the front door. Richard filed a police report about the break-in and apparently took no other precautions. In his inventory of what had been stolen, he had even neglected to notice his men's Cartier was gone. Richard's brain really *was* somewhere else. Had he been worried enough to take the fish-eyed view, he would've seen this was beyond daytime thievery. This was Howard closing in.

Around March 12, Johnny made sure of that. He asked his father, Carl, to take him to Euclid Loan and Jewelry, a pawn shop in downtown Ontario a short hop from the railroad tracks. They were rifle-shopping. Paperwork-wise, it would be Carl purchasing the firearm as a straw-buyer because as a felon his son wasn't allowed to own one. Johnny had stayed quiet about why he needed it, and his father probably didn't want to inquire. At the pawn shop, Carl Williams selected the .30-caliber M-1 rifle that Johnny said he just had to have, plus a five-round clip. Carl paid the $180 bill by hocking the yellow Cartier that Johnny had stolen from Richard's house and tossing in the $50 cash that Howard had given Johnny earlier. Before they exited the store, Johnny was able to complete one transaction himself. He exchanged Richard's IBM Selectric II typewriter for $75, having as much use for a typewriter as a tuxedo.

The sleek weapon now in Johnny's possession had been created for American paratroopers jumping into hotspots in Europe and Asia during World War II. The M-1's semi-automatic mechanism and other features had given the Marines and Army infantrymen firing it a distinct advantage over enemies saddled with bolt-action has-beens. General George Patton had effused the mighty rifle was "the greatest battle implement ever devised." Johnny agreed, ecstatic that he owned a piece of history. He was so jazzed about his antique paratrooper weapon that the same day he acquired it he took it outside and sawed off the barrel. The next night, Johnny test-fired it by pumping rounds into a junker-car owned by a neighbor. He judged the action as fine and calibrated it for a short blast.

Johnny's timing was as impeccable as his marksmanship, because Howard, the following day, announced to him—Chaser and James—that he was tweaking his executive master plan. They were going to interrupt their maddening bids to murder Richard and then go after Jerry for another job that Howard expected to be a confidence-building cinch. Howard would use his old family friend to mark their first success.

Howard's franchise was set to do brisk business after completion of this first round of robbery-murders. They would pillage a Beverly Hills contractor foolish enough to keep one-hundred eighty thousand in company payroll at home. After him was another Beverly Hills businessman who tucked five-hundred thousand dollars away at his residence. If every job worked out, Howard would be pocketing almost eight-hundred thousand dollars, making more in a few months of debauchery than he had earned in twenty years in supposedly rewarding California real estate.

Hearing this news, Johnny was about to bust his buttons. Somewhere inside the Johnny-that'd-never-be was an Army sniper or Olympic skeet-shooter. He enjoyed fingering cold steel, fiddling with the trigger mechanism, cleaning the barrel, just the whole management of firearms. Howard's passion for them was half of Johnny's. It was logistics that occupied him. For now, he reminded his men to be extra cautious. They had already exhausted their quota of mulligans.

CHAPTER EIGHT

STICKING IT TO FRIENDS

On an otherwise forgettable day in mid-March, as Los Angeles talk-radio feasted on 1979's hot names—Ayatollah Khomeini, Patty Hearst, Ronald Reagan, Sid Vicious—Jerry pulled his car into the parking lot of the steel-and-glass Glendale Federal Building in Beverly Hills. Celebrities aside, Paul Fegen ruled the air space here.

Jerry and Fegen had a regular meeting scheduled, as if there was anything "regular" about a leasing mogul who had practically turned exhibitionism into a second vocation. Over to the side of the garage, Jerry noticed Fegen's twin Excaliburs, high-priced specialty cars modeled after a 1920's-era Mercedes Benz SS. One of the automobiles was purple, the other candy-apple green. Jerry knew Fegen often drove them in matching coats and boots.

He took the elevator to Fegen's floor and entered an office that, at roughly fifty-feet by sixty-feet, was larger than a small mansion. The walls inside were spare except for the greeting cards and articles about the man who inhabited the suite. *Yawn.* Jerry had seen it all before. Fegen sat behind his desk wearing boots, tights and a Renaissance-style shirt. The sixties-buccaneer clothes set off Fegen's bright-eyed face, which was curtained by his hallmark hippie-long brown hair and a receding pate. In Jerry's mind, Fegen resembled a bald Jesus. Near him in the office was the German shepherd he taught tricks to and the unicycle he rode in his office when he had the itch.

Jerry ignored the frivolity, and spread out a half-dozen preliminary sketches for Fegen to peruse. Fegen's whirling mind sometimes swept him off to distant galaxies, but he would return to orbit when his leasing required extra attention. Jerry gripped the first blueprint—it was for a skyscraper in Houston—and narrated his vision for it. "Impressive," Fegen said. "I like where you put the doors. Now tell me about the hallways."

Fegen had known Jerry since 1975, pegging him as a "genius" out of the thousands of intelligent Angelenos he had encountered during his fanciful life. Fegen was the archetypal West Coast original, demonstrating not only how profitable it could be reinventing oneself but also how abundantly entertaining. The son of a milkman, he helped put himself through college working as a juggling clown. After time as a personal-injury attorney, he began developing his specialty renting and renovating office space, leading off with his own building in Beverly Hills. Before long he was pre-leasing unheard-of amounts of space, primarily for law firms. His technique became so popular and so copycatted that it was given its own term: "The Fegen Suite."

Fegen on the side was an accomplished, amateur magician and yet there was no sleight of hand in his business philosophy. He had gotten it down to a science of salesmanship and economy. Fegen and his aides would approach building owners—some of them strapped with unoccupied, money-draining properties—and offer to pre-lease entire floors. With their consent, they would build out the expanses into nicely-done, efficiently contoured professional suites. Wasted space was forbidden. In Fegen's model, individual attorneys and law firms were typically arrayed on the perimeter of a floor centered by a reception area. Rimmed this way, tenants could do more with less space since they shared secretaries, law libraries, telephone operators, kitchens and other common services.

Low-cost luxury was the teaser and Fegen's pitches, though speculative, found a chomping audience. His operation became the biggest office-subleasing operation on the planet with U.S. holdings stretching from L.A. to Houston and some six hundred employees. He swiftly realized that he needed a go-to space planner to oil his multi-million dollar outfit, specifically to purchase indor carpeting. Seeing a place for himself inside Fegen's kingdom, Jerry rustled the product up for him at an affordable price, and after that Jerry had Fegen's allegiance. Over the years, he easily space planned more square footage for Fegen's holdings—seven million square feet—than all the commercial square footage in Century City total.

On his end, Jerry had never associated with somebody as uniquely confident, if as unabashedly narcissistic as Fegen. Even in granola California, middle-aged tycoons generally don't drive exotic cars outfitted with microphones so they could flirt with young women or plaster sequins on their faces for hilarity. They don't employ a small army of secretaries drilled in the precise art of pencil sharpening or commission stained-glassed windows of *themselves*. Fegen was a mind-boggling personality, an icon of his own making determined to go to his grave after reaching one-hundred certain there'd never be another like him. He was well on his way. Celebrity and crowds seemed to excite him as much as prodigious leasing. In 1971, Jimi Hendrix and David Bowie performed at his house. After the rock stars left, Fegen threw soirees at four-diamond hotels, where his sea of often purple-clad guests watched a famous Hollywood stylist cut Fegen's nearly equally famous shaggy hair. Never one to shrink from his own legend, he claimed partial inspiration for the 1968-comedy *I Love You, Alice B. Toklas!* about a free-spirited lawyer (played by Peter Sellers) and his "groovy" brownies. Nobody contested it.

Counter-culture leftover that he was, Fegen was still relevant in the late-1970s. He had shown that anyone with a vision, regardless of background or fetish, could enrich themselves in real estate with flinty self-belief. Bald Jesus had plenty to teach his space planner.

***

To the east that same afternoon, skyscraper suites were the furthest thing from Howard's attentions. Once upon a time, he would've done almost anything to champion the man his thugs were about to terrorize. Luis Buonsanti and his family had intersected with Howard just after Luis' family emigrated from Argentina to the same Arcadia neighborhood where Howard and his mother resided earlier in the 1970s. Luis was smallish and fleshy-faced with a jack-of-all-trades skillset, especially in the mechanical field. He would need it. His family was all crowded into the same apartment, and Luis took any dangled jobs to bust them out of there.

Howard, saner back then, valued the South American's work ethic and stuffed money into his pockets every opportunity he could. When he required weekend yard-cleanup at his Coronado Drive home, he paid Luis to do it. When Howard's construction jobs required after-hours demolition, Luis got the call. Sometimes to Luis there seemed to be two Howards: the organized jobsite professional and the after-hours good-timer who guzzled champagne while gunning his old Corvette to 120 MPH on the hairpin Pasadena Freeway. Nevertheless, Luis asserted, when it came to business, Howard knew how to manage construction and remember a friend.

Mabel, Howard's mother, adored the Buonsantis herself. The plump woman with the horn-rimmed glasses and trouble moving around was always digging into her purse for them. One Christmas, she bought the kids a sleigh's worth of toys and gave them donated clothes. The Buonsantis rewarded her benevolence by naming her godmother to their youngest son, Maurice. Manuel, Mabel's husband and Howard's step-father, befriended Luis, as well. Manuel was a tall, gray-haired Latino who smoked a pipe, knocked back hot chilies and probably drank too much. Knowing what he did about Howard, he had his reasons.

Years passed and Luis's industriousness paid dividends with his acquisition of an auto body repair shop in Arcadia, Pasadena's once lily-white neighbor to the southeast. By 1978, he had quietly over-achieved to the point of branching out. In his spare time, he bought two older homes as investments that he repaired and sold for quick profit, also known as "flipping." Luis hoped to load up on more flippers, a lot more, and reasoned that experienced, connected Howard would be the perfect associate. Howard had even done a little construction work on one of Luis' speculative houses.

On March 12, Luis revisited the theme of them flipping houses together full time when Howard pulled his El Camino into Luis' shop for repairs. Luis volunteered that he had located the next property he wanted to acquire, and asked for Howard's assistance in locating a bank willing to offer him a low-interest loan. Luis said that if he couldn't secure a lender, he would pull fifty-five thousand dollars out of his own residence to finance the transaction. Howard, already aware that Luis "had money in his house," said he would ask around about a loan. Luis smiled.

Suddenly, Howard jerked the conversation to the El Camino, which had front-end damage and a crumpled back fender that he wanted restored. Howard acted prickly about his car, grousing about how some people had mistreated it. Just recently, he said, a now ex-friend had torn off to San Francisco in it without his permission. When he had repossessed it, Howard said there were items in the camper shell that he did not recognize. "Strange" items, unsettling items; he refused to even touch them. Luis was too decent to peer through the double subterfuge being applied by his purported close friend. Howard was laying the groundwork to frame Robert Freeman if any of his plots went awry while also keeping his recognizable El Camino absent from the hell that his goons were about to unleash on the man standing next to him. Because Luis could not perceive any of it, he lent Howard a green Fiat four-door, one chum to another, while the El Camino was on the rack. It was Luis' last day of innocence like that.

Twenty-four hours or so later, Howard sat in a car down the street from Luis' green-speckled house in Monrovia, a Mayberryish, foothill suburb where the clapboard houses were well-tended and flag ownership high. Howard wasn't sweating being noticed, having ensconced himself in a car that nobody had seen before. That's because hours earlier, Howard, with Johnny's assistance, had stolen a white and blue 1976 Buick Riviera from the underground parking lot of the Roosevelt building downtown. Howard had worked construction at the property for years, learning its secrets as well as its tenants. The car he took off in belonged to Bruce Freeman, one of Howard's many lawyers, who rented an office there. Gotlieb's vanity license plate was unmistakably smug. It read: J-U-R-Y.

At 8:30 P.M. inside the house of Buonsanti, Luis' family and his shop foreman and wife nibbled appetizers waiting for their late supper. It was just another dull, mid-week night in Jimmy Carter's America. Everybody was in the front of the house except for Luis's eldest boy, Sergio. The high school freshman was in his bedroom in the back, where he preferred watching primetime sitcoms than engaging in the pre-dinner social hour. Unlike him, his eight-year-old kid brother, Maurice, was out with the grownups. So was his big sister, Sandra, a pretty, vivacious brunette looking forward to graduation as an eighteen-year-old high school senior.

The doorbell rang, and Sandra answered it hoping it was her boyfriend. A pair of short men in long, dark coats, instead, stood there framed against the night. One (Johnny) had bushy hair, a goatee and wore brown-suede shoes. The other (Crazy Eddy) was a mite smaller. He brushed his brownish-red hair into a comb-over style that accentuated his bruised, discolored face from a recent fight. "We're here to pick up the car. Can we speak with Luis?" Johnny asked. The car, Sandra inquired? She had hung around her dad's shop and had never heard of a customer traveling to their house. The unannounced men could see that Sandra was puzzled. "You better go get your dad," Johnny suggested.

Luis was as mystified as his daughter when she passed the message along. The only person he could imagine that would show up at this hour was a Cuban customer so finicky about his car that he had requested Luis drive it home to minimize any chance it could be damaged or stolen overnight. Luis realized his Cuban-customer hypothesis was incorrect as soon he stepped onto the entryway. "We're here to get an estimate," Johnny said. Luis was even more confused now, but his clarity was coming. Johnny and Crazy Eddy turned their backs and when they whipped around their orange-gloved hands clutched rifles that'd been shielded under their coats. On instinct, Luis rushed back into the house while Sandra tried slamming the door. Howard's men were too fast. They jammed their rifle butts into the arch and shouldered their way in, knocking father and daughter backwards.

Pandemonium exploded where there'd just been appetizers. Luis sprinted towards the kitchen, reverting to his Spanish to shout, "It's a robbery. Call the police! Police!" He snagged the kitchen phone and tried dialing the operator while continuing to shout "Police" as if he expected they were crouched outside in his hedges. Before Luis reached anybody, Crazy Eddy caught up with him, waving his gun and ordering him to set the phone down. He and Johnny swiftly went about oppressing their six captives. They steered them into the living room and forced them to their knees. Shut up, they said. Keep still. Nobody try being a hero. The intruders next counted heads and Johnny peeled off for a room-by-room search. "Where's the other (child)?" Johnny asked when he returned after a minute. "There's one missing." Luis' near-hysterical wife, Norma, had an answer. "He's at Boy Scouts—a Boy Scout's meeting," she said. "He won't be back until later."

Johnny accepted it, knowing that by the time the boy returned they would be long gone. The issue was what he would find. Johnny and Crazy Eddy weren't positive themselves. In their planning meetings with Howard, he had stressed the robbery and condoned gore if necessary. What should they do if they met resistance, Johnny had asked? Howard's glib retort was, "Just pull the trigger," because Howard loathed recalcitrant hostages as much as disloyalty. As the lead gun-man here, Johnny had the latitude to do what he needed to secure the fifty-five thousand dollars that Howard was certain Luis hid in the house. If after everything Luis was still clamming up about it, Howard told Johnny that he could always shoot Norma or the children one by one to squeeze him for answers.

Crazy Eddy began placing strips of duct tape over the mouths and eyes of everyone except Luis, whom they needed to be able to speak. Johnny followed behind, taping hands behind backs and ankles together.

"What do you want?" Luis asked the men. "You can take anything, ok? Just don't kill nobody."

Johnny walked to go over to the kneeling, groveling patriarch. "You know what we want," he said. "You know why we're here."

"No, no, no," Luis insisted. He did not. They were being too vague. "This is a mistake."

Norma piped up, saying the men were there in error. She begged Crazy Eddy to hurry up with the restraints so they could "go ahead and get this over with." They didn't appreciate hearing her petition and ordered her to pipe down, Johnny in English, Crazy Eddy in Spanish. When she complied, Luis resumed his beseeching.

Johnny went back to binding hands and feet. He understood they didn't have forever, and that Howard expected him to emerge with a satchel of money. Before the takeover, Howard had explained to Johnny that Luis was not the heart-of-gold breadwinner that everybody thought. He believed that Luis paid his workers under the table to avoid taxes and that some of his mechanics might've been illegal aliens from Mexico. Because of that, Luis would not want the U.S. Immigration Service or IRS looking into his affairs, even a stolen fifty-five thousand dollars that would probably decide not to report. What Howard never bothered to tell Johnny was that he was slandering Luis's integrity minus hard facts.

"Don't you have kids?" Norma asked Crazy Eddy teary-eyed as the binding continued. He replied that he did. Little-Maurice himself, meantime, imitated his father's call for calm, unaware of how unlikely that was. "Guys," he muttered under the tape, "stay cool. Take it easy." Luis supposed they were all about to be gunned-down execution-style in the comfy confines of the living room. The men who had hijacked his house hadn't bothered to cover their faces with masks. His daughter, Sandra, had her own trepidation: the intruders would rape her and her mother before this ended. Johnny and Crazy Eddy kept leering at them.

In retrospect, the henchmen should've kept their focus elsewhere. For all of Johnny's enthrallment with guns and Howard's fastidious planning, the intruders had underestimated a mother and child. They never could have guessed that Luis' wife would've been able to deceive them so convincingly about her oldest son being at a Boy Scouts meeting when he wasn't anywhere near this troop. Nor could they have estimated how much Luis' yelp to "Call the police" and the clatter of pounding heels would ricochet down the hallway and into Sergio's bedroom.

The boy had been watching *Laverne & Shirley* in a pair of boxer shorts and T-shirt when the intruders plowed in. *Oh, fuck* he thought. Sergio understood he had to do something macho at fourteen, but what? Brandish his bee-bee gun at the bad guys? Hide someplace until they left? He reconsidered those ideas amid the whimpering from the front of the house, deciding to throw on some pants and unlatch his window.

Sergio dove out head-first, crashing down about eight feet on account of his home's hilly grade. He sprinted to a neighbor's house, knocked on the back door and rocked back and forth waiting for someone to answer. Dennis Cline and his wife, both fiftyish, hadn't heard the boy at their door, let alone the turmoil inside his house. Visualizing what might be happening there, Sergio let himself in and said sorry for the interruption but there was an emergency, got a phone? Dennis dialed the police's number because Sergio was shaking too badly. He handed him the receiver and the boy told the police that strangers were holding his family hostage. "HURRY!"

Monrovia police's response time would've done the Marines proud. Robbery-takeovers were unheard of out in the 'burbs; there were more calls about teenagers partying in the canyons or bears wandering into hot tubs. Within a few minutes, a city patrol car sped by with two officers inside and the siren silent. On their way on Hillcrest, one of the officers noticed a grizzled, middle-aged white man inside a parked Riviera. When they went by him, he suspiciously got out of the car, rubber-necked them and disappeared phantom-like up somebody's side-yard. Sergio was the next person the officers passed. He was on the patio of the Cline's house pacing and crying. Seeing the police car ripping by, he pointed toward his house, shouting, "THEY GOT 'EM IN THERE!"

Inside, it had been taking Johnny and Crazy Eddy longer than expected to get all six people bound and gagged. Johnny was the first of anybody to see they had uninvited visitors outside. Two Monrovia police officers were pulling up to the curb. They would be reaching for their holsters next. "Here come the pigs," Johnny told Crazy Eddy. They conferred in a hasty dialogue in front of the captives. Johnny's instinct was not to skedaddle for the hills but to cut down the first officer dumb enough to come after them. Johnny aimed his M-1 at Luis' front door, reminding himself that when the handle jiggled, he would have his cue. Crazy Eddy, however, acted like he wanted to hightail it. Howard's men were split between valor and retreat.

The Buonsanti's poodles deduced the officers' arrival, too, and began barking and yipping, adding to the anxiety pouring off the walls. Their carrying-on changed the room in one definitive way, because Johnny got his wits back. He stopped pointing his M-1 rifle and tried strategizing his way out. In that moment, he decided that even Howard would accept prudence over a gunfight with the Monrovia police department. NATO would be after them if they killed a small-town cop.

"How do we get out of here?" Johnny asked his captives. "Is there a back door?" Sandra, able to speak beneath the slapdash tape-job over her lips, said as loudly as she could, "Toward the dogs!" One of the two intruders may have asked whether they bite. Neither of them lingered for an answer. They lit out of the rear door, trampling a grave-stake fence rimming the property and leaving a gaggle of bound, red-eyed people behind. Sandra straggled to her feet and waddled towards the entryway. The duct tape around her ankles broke loose, and she managed to unlock the front door to meet the police on the lawn. "They're going out the back door!" she said pointing.

The officers dashed into the house, ordering the Buonsantis and the guests to run next door while they conducted a room-by-room search. The officers looked stunned after their sweep. The restraints and the descriptions of the men's firepower was big-city criminality, not life in quaint Monrovia. One close-range bullet from the M-1 would've blown someone's chest apart. Soon, backup arrived, and the general agreement was that the robbers had vacated the neighborhood by foot and that the Buonsantis were safe. The captives said thank God, and hugged and wept that the boy had rescued them. If Sergio hadn't been in the rear watching "Laverne and Shirley," a mindless comedy about a pair of spunky, working girls from the 1950s—a show whose gibberish theme song began *Schlemiel, schlimazel, hasenpfeffer incorporated*—they might well have been massacred.

Later that evening, after they had deemed the property secure, Monrovia police bore down on a possible person of interest. They searched for slipups in his story. They poked into his background. Not all victims, they knew, are guiltless. Luis was being grilled. "What did you do to have this happen," they asked him. "What's the real story? You in the drug business?" Luis was numb; first, Johnny interrogating him and now the police.

Near midnight, officers drove him to his Arcadia body shop on Las Tunas Drive close by the Santa Anita racetrack. They wanted to ascertain if Luis had any customers who might've organized the takeover. Concentrate, they told him. Who could have done this? The only hazy linkage that drifted into Luis' head was Howard's unsolicited comment about the peculiar stuff left in the cargo hold of the El Camino. He still doubted someone outwardly as decent as Howard could orchestrate such a thing, and he felt awful about implicating him to the men with the badges. But he had to.

Detectives had Luis unlock the El Camino with the Garrett & Associates decal on the side doors. They took a gander inside and what they found was unremarkable: a set of carpentry tools and blueprints. The Howard-connection was soft. The abandoned Riviera with the J-U-R-Y license plate was the evidence gusher. Scattered around the floor mats and seats in plain view were a rifle box containing a carbine-clip and instructions for it, as well as a parking claim-check, cigarettes, and various papers. For Monrovia detectives, the easiest history about the Buick was that it had been reported stolen from a downtown building that afternoon. The hardest element was tying it back to the El Camino and what transpired in Luis' living room. As the police reminded him, Howard was only a suspect and nothing more. Whoever had pulled this off was cagey.

At officers' urging, Luis' family slept somewhere else that night. Sandra's boyfriends' family invited Luis' staggered bunch to their place. They were home the next morning hoping they could erase those men from their thoughts. None of them realized they should've stayed away, because Johnny remained yards from them still holding that gun in his hands.

His cohort, Crazy Eddy, had no hiding place in mind when he had fled the previous night, letting his harried legs transport him through strangers' yards. Johnny kept it basic. He threw himself over a neighbor's wall that shouldered up to the Buonsanti's yard and crawled into a small pool house. Monrovia police soon canvassed most of the area around him with flashlights beaming and revolvers drawn as Johnny sat ready with his World War II rifle cocked. Somehow, officers never bothered to check the shed, an audacious place to hide, and Johnny got so bored waiting for a firefight that never came that he fell asleep.

The next morning he casually walked down the block to Bob's Coffee Shop, where he, Crazy Eddy and Howard had reviewed the operation the previous night. Howard picked him up and Johnny learned something insightful about his boss. Howard was philosophical about his sadism. He joked openly to Johnny about the invasion that they had uncorked on his friend, as if he fully believed they would triumph on a second try for the fifty-five thousand dollars. For Howard, this was blue ribbon mirth. That he had once dressed up as Santa Claus as a Christmas surprise for Luis' children or chugged bubbly with him after a day schlepping drywall brought him no sentimental regret. It brought another demented chortle. Howard's face turned a grayer hue when Richard and Jerry's names were broached.

Luis, meantime, was now patriarch of a family spooked that those short, evil men might reappear. The day after the assault, Luis did something about that. He drove to J.C. Penney and purchased a .30-.30-rifle. He also had a motion detector alarm system installed. Good thing, too, because that night about 3 A.M. the alarm activated.

Luis snatched his new rifle and tiptoed towards the sound. He crept into the living room and when he did, there was a glimmer of light and maybe a signal the men had returned. Reflexively, Luis fired. Nobody else in the house of shattered nerves, thankfully, heard it. The next morning, Maurice, Luis' youngest boy, went through his normal routine in an abnormal time. He filled a bowl up with cereal and squatted down in the living room to watch cartoons. Bugs Bunny or Wiley E. Coyote would've appeared, just as he wanted, had there not been a spiky hole in the set's glass screen. "What happened to the television?" Maurice asked in wonderment. "Dad shot it last night," Sergio answered deadpan

Howard stopped by the shop later that same day grumbling and complaining. He found Luis, who looked five years older overnight, and said the loaner Fiat was worthless. It wasn't in drivable condition; all four tires were bad. Luis apologized, saying his mind was someplace else after those fifteen minutes of duct tape and ultimatums. Luis kept tight-lipped about the police's search of the El Camino, already feeling guilty he had implicated it. Howard listened sympathetically, preserving his own secrets, too. "I'm so sorry, man. Really, Luis. That's just awful." Luis said in response to the incident, he bought a gun, installed an alarm system and was contemplating doing more. "I got to protect myself and my family, you know." Howard opined that Luis was making good choices with all the hoods preying on the area. After consoling him for a few minutes for the crime his subordinates had carried out, Howard muffled his smirk and drove off in his freshly repaired El Camino.

One family's luck would be others' doom. And Jerry believed Howard's lawyers were his weapon of choice.

***

Johnny remained in a killing mood a week after the foiled Buonsanti takeover-robbery. Once he felt he was licensed to shoot somebody, Johnny regarded it as a lifelong assignment. He longed for another opportunity to murder Luis, even if he never saw the man's face before the assault. He would stalk him all the way to Buenos Aires if he must. Johnny broiled with the same homicidal twinge for the other strangers from the operation (the Monrovia cops who responded to the break-in), eager for another chance at them. Mostly, as he waited for Howard's nod to execute Richard once and for all, Johnny dwelled on Robert. He had to kill him, because Howard had sanctified it and the turncoat from his neighborhood deserved it. Johnny had his mission.

With Howard unwilling to ever lend the El Camino out again, Johnny needed to locate another vehicle for their trip. No problem there. He and Chaser traveled to a local Chevy dealer and feigned interest in a black GMC "four-wheel drive" truck; it would be another decade before they were called SUVs. How did it handle in traffic? What about the shocks? Johnny asked the car salesman if they could take the GMC for a test-ride to find out for themselves. By all means, the salesman said. He only needed Johnny's driver license, and do you think Johnny presented him with an authentic one? Before you could say phony ID, Johnny had steered the black truck toward the freeway and throttled it to San Francisco.

When they arrived in their stolen vehicle, Johnny and Chaser drove to Haight-Ashbury. For once in ages, luck picked their team. Robert was there on the street and in the open chatting with five men that Johnny guessed were homosexuals. Robert, the onetime hit-man who dared to flee Howard, was bisexual, according to what Johnny had discerned. Though he was married to Elena now, he had supposedly had male relationships in prison.

Johnny parked the GMC around a corner. He slid out of the driver's seat and told Chaser to keep the motor running and the passenger-side door open. There was going to be street-panic and a police perimeter established if the shooting went the way he envisioned. He was going to mosey up behind Robert to blow his head off wise-guy style with Howard's .357 Smith & Wesson and nonchalantly stride back toward the GMC. Johnny assumed that Robert's gay friends would be too horrified to give chase or memorize the killer's physical description. All they would be able to recount was that he was a short man with a "Dirty Hairy"-type gun.

Johnny and his anxious hands prepared themselves. As he moved closer down the block, Robert was still gabbing with that cluster of men, oblivious to his old neighborhood pal approaching from the rear. Johnny's eyes surveyed the street for any last-minute deal-stoppers one direction at a time. At long last, he was finally going to be able to squeeze off a round. Act like a real assassin. Take control. Five seconds later, he was cursing under his breath at the perpetuation of misaligned stars for Howard's franchise. It couldn't be, he thought. Not again. Yet it was. A San Francisco Police patrol car cruising the block was within yards of Robert. Johnny knew in his depths it would hang around, because that's the way events were panning out.

He had another stressful decision to make: stick with the back-of-the-head-shooting of his Ontario friend and assume he could elude any roadblocks, or scrub the execution so he would be available to get their work done in the Valley? Johnny stopped on his heels with Robert achingly feet away. There was no dilemma, none at all. Murdering Robert would've eliminated him as a potential troublemaker and satisfied Johnny's gushing endorphines. Emphasizing Howard's primary targets, in contrast, would usher in months of enjoyable turmoil and years' worth of money. Johnny, classified by authorities as brain-damaged and bloodthirsty, could think on his toes.

Grudgingly, he pushed the .357 into his jacket and trudged back to the stolen truck. Seeing Johnny's face, Chaser knew Johnny had stumbled and that it was going to be a long, sullen trip to L.A. Once there, they discarded the GMC. All they had to do now was wait for Howard's assassination order for Richard and the torture rack they planned for Jerry. Their luck would have to turn sometime. It just would. The laws of probability apply to all.

CHAPTER NINE

L.A.'s LORD OF DISAPPOINTMENT

Richard, by one yardstick, had accomplished the extraordinary by March 1979: he had managed to keep his head above the water line until then, whatever the psychological currents trying to drag him under. His pallor had a healthier sheen now that spring roses readied to bud after a torrential winter. Nibbles for Kasparov & Co. design work portended activity for antsy hands. After Easter, his soul would have its chance. Richard in April intended to reclaim his wife and daughter by committing himself to be the dependable provider that he had seldom been over a lifetime of fractured relationships. Hopefully, he and Paige would consider a new start in San Francisco, away from the smiling bastards of L.A. and their own turbulent history there. Richard knew that if he could survive last winter, he could acclimate to any latitude.

Hence, as he knocked on the door to Paige's rental home on Saturday, March 24, he had reason to believe he was knocking on his future. It's just that the door that swung wide did not reveal the same woman who had been openly discussing a marital reunion with him. It spotlighted a fragile, young mother quivering on her doorstep.

"What's wrong," he asked? "Is the baby okay? Somebody hurt?"

"Rebecca's fine," Paige said, her jaw barely hinging.

"Where is she?"

"I'm not telling you."

"Let's rewind here. What's going on? Something's up."

"You really want to know?"

"Uh, yeah."

"I just got an anonymous phone call from a woman who said there was a contract out on you, Richard! A fucking murder contract. Somebody wants you dead."

Richard was motionless. "I don't believe it," he said after a second. "A murder contract? It doesn't make sense."

"Now you know why I'm upset."

"When did this all happen?"

"About eleven this morning. I was feeding Rebecca in her high chair, staring at the oven clock. That's when the phone rang."

"But how did this person even find your number? You've already moved twice."

"The phone book or something – you tell me. This woman asked to speak with you and I told her we weren't living together. She wanted to know if I was married to an architect and I said you were a (space) designer."

"What does that matter?"

"Because she wanted to make sure that you were the right person to warn. Haven't you been listening to what I said?"

"Yes, and so far it's no big deal. Have you considered that maybe it was a prank call. A teenager or something?"

"You're just not getting it if that's what you think. This lady dared me to try to list your enemies. She said, 'Why don't you tell your husband to go around making nice to people,' and that you should be careful. She said for me to tell you that. She actually wanted your number but I wouldn't give it to her."

Richard glared at Paige as though she were a mental patient. "What the hell does that mean, 'go around making nice'?"

"I don't know. But you better quit asking questions and start getting to the bottom of this."

"I can't get to the bottom of something when you're telling me that some-body wants me dead? It's ludicrous on its face. Who would want to murder me? Tell me? I can't wait to hear."

"That call didn't come for nothing. This woman asked about *you* – Rich-ard Kasparov. She sounded nervous herself."

"So you say."

"What?"

"There was no call, was there Paige? Admit it. You made it up." Richard made a shoving gesture to imply he was being sandbagged. "You're playing to the court for money. Very sneaky of you."

"I'm confused. How could you think I'd go from discussing getting back together to accusing me of such a thing? I'm scared, okay. Remember the man on the deck with Isabel. Remember (Howard's) calls?"

"Scared, acting, whatever."

"I'm pleading with you, Richard. Don't be stubborn. Go to the police. Figure out who's after you. This could be your life were talking about."

"Quit saying that. Where's my daughter? That's what I'm trying to figure out."

"You're certifiable if you think I'm letting Rebecca go with you when I just receive a call saying somebody wants you dead? No mother on earth would allow that."

"I'll ask again," Richard said crimson-faced. "Where is she?"

"All right. I'll answer again. She's not here."

"Is she with Erica across the street? I'm her father in case you forgot. I'm not a schmuck. I have rights."

"And I have a duty to keep my daughter safe."

"If that's the way you want to play it, the next phone call you'll be getting is from my lawyer. I'll see you in court. I don't have to take this shit."

Richard pivoted, storming towards Erica's home with a body language that'd clear out a crowded post office. Paige's friend, however, was ready to intercept him from her doorway.

"Turn around, Richard. You can stop right there," Erica shouted. "The baby ain't coming with you."

"The hell's she not. I hope you know the law ..."

"I hope YOU know," Erica interrupted, "that I hate your guts and you're going to fucking die if you don't watch it. NOW, GET OFF MY PROPERTY!"

Had anybody noticed Richard's pallor as he returned to his Cougar, they would have seen it was no longer maroon as it had been during his argument with Paige. Forehead to chin, he was chalk.

Richard's hopeful day had been disemboweled by his blow-up on Paige's doorstep. By the time he arrived home to call his attorney, Paige had already beaten him to a lawyer. She had phoned her attorney at home about the mysterious caller and he ordered her to immediately hang up and contact the Los Angeles Police Department. The eight-month-old baby that Erica had brought back to Paige's house lay in her crib as she did. Sometime that day, Paige also phoned Tammy to ask her advice about what to do. Tammy was incredulous about the anonymous threat, preaching common sense. "Paige – this is 1979," she said. "These things don't happen."

The LAPD, then so understaffed that there were a quarter-million un-answered emergency calls the year before, seemed to agree. The officer with whom Paige had spoken to said he understood her anguish about the warn-ing call, but there wasn't anything that the department could do for her husband. There was too little evidence of "a specific threat." Besides, the cop on the line was reluctant to fill a report out. It was the weekend shift.

Paige re-contacted her lawyer to describe the runaround the officer had given her. Afterwards, her attorney phoned Richard's on the Sunday of recriminations. The two bickering lawyers agreed that a judge would referee who was right.

***

Come Monday, March 26, Richard could list few reasons why he should be alone, eating leftovers or deluding himself that he would ever rebound after this latest kick to the stomach. Early that morning, the woman he had been dating phoned him, and Richard was overjoyed with her timing. He was a man in need of gentle handling and a lusty romp, and she thought he was dashing. Outwardly, Susan Sullivan contacted him for a different purpose, inquiring if he could pay her for the clerical work she had previously done for him. Richard mainly cared that she called.

He had met her in February, when a temp agency referred Susan to Space Matters to fill in as the office receptionist. Right away, Richard and his indefatigable libido noticed that the leggy newcomer had the sex-appeal of a *Penthouse* magazine model, not the mothball-scent of a dowager who typed fifty words a minute. Susan, all the same, was confined in an office where Richard was viewed as a crook. Because of that, her ongoing fealty to him made her his personal fan-club, his estrogen analgesic. He had even carped as they had gotten closer that he had received a bad deal in the disso-lution, saying Jerry was the only person with whom he squabbled. Whether he believed his own tripe or not, he promised to phone Susan later that day about getting together. He told her that if they did connect, it would have to be after he attended a "client" meeting. This was not exactly the truth. The meeting that Richard referred to was his official appointment to sign over to Jerry the companies that he had defrauded.

About 3:00 P.M. that afternoon at the Westside office of Jerry's lawyer, Richard relinquished them all: Space Matters, CM-2, the subsidiaries in the works, everything. That night around suppertime an inner voice usurped him. Before his ego protested, he was on the line with his ex-partner pouring out what he hadn't said hours earlier that day: that he was sorry, immensely sorry, for skimming from him, for going seditious on him, for destroying everything they had cobbled from those all-nighters forward. Richard's voice was weepy and he wanted Jerry to know his own chicanery was skinning him inside. Jerry conceded he was hurting, too, and hoped the wound bound.

"I want you to be okay, Richard," Jerry said as they closed out their conversation. "After everything, I still do."

"I appreciate that," Richard said. "You've got to know I never thought it would get to this point. Things snowballed. Thought I could dig my way out. God, do you remember how we started off? The Fegen parties?"

"How could I forget?"

"Probably should've savored them more, huh? Just do me a favor, all right? It's something that has nothing to do with the business or whatever I've done to you."

"Okay."

"If anything happens to me, and I'm not saying it will, make sure Paige and the baby have what they need? You know, check in on them once in a while. I know it sounds melodramatic."

"Are you planning on going someplace, Richard?" Jerry asked, unsure if Richard was suicidal.

"Not directly. I can't explain it. Maybe in the future. Just promise me?"

"Sure. I'll look out for them. I just wish I knew what was going on. You don't want to tell me."

"No. Not today."

***

After that conversation, Richard was a condemned building tumbling inwards in a dust storm of dismemberment after the explosives ignite. Only random frontage remained, and how long can that last? He rang Susan at home just after 4:00 P.M. to further discuss a rendezvous. On top of the money she hoped he would pay her, Susan was anxious to find out whether Richard had had the opportunity to read the script she had given him with the part she was auditioning for. Susan didn't intend on being a temp-secretary forever. She aimed on being a Hollywood actress. Richard answered that he was planning to read the script tonight, so head on over.

She arrived at his house on Chandler Boulevard at 8:45 P.M. in the midst of another rainstorm. Richard met her at the door presenting a together-persona. Behind him, fireplace logs crackled. Upstairs in the master bedroom, the college-basketball title game pitting Magic Johnson against Larry Bird in a clash of future sports mega-stars aired on television. With little chitchat, the two walked up the stairs, entered the bedroom, sat on the bed and kissed. Richard switched off the game and made an announcement. He told Susan that she deserved a nice dinner on him and that he would hear no objections. Susan said it sounded lovely, but what about the creased dress that she was wearing? Richard had a notion how to straighten it out: she could remove it and hang it on the doorknob. Off it went.

And here came what remained. Susan wrapped herself in a vine around Richard as they melted onto the floor. With body heat rising, Richard's mouth made the first move, just not sexually. There on the ground he began inquiring about her financial situation – bills, expenses, rent. The math of L.A. life. He told her that if she needed to economize, she could shave her expenses by moving in with him. Just look at all this space! He had been raising co-habitation with her in recent weeks even as he kindled hopes for a second chance with Paige. Susan, just as before, told him she would have to demur being his roommate. She treasured her independence too much. Still, she was sure glad that she was here.

They shifted onto the bed naked and forgot about cost-of-living calculations. Richard entered her and then pulled out to dab some Vaseline. They went to boinking again, but neither of them climaxed. Richard said that since she didn't seem to be in the mood just yet, why not go eat? Good idea, Susan replied. She put her still-wrinkled skirt back on and stroked her eye makeup while Richard watched a beauty pageant on television.

They were in Richard's Cougar on the hunt for a late dinner by 9:30 P.M. with it damp and romantic outside. The first place they tried, Albian's on Ventura Boulevard, was closed. When they passed it, Richard pointed out the building next door and, forgetting who he was with, proudly said Paige had supplied some of the interior decorating. They drove next to La Serre, also on Ventura Boulevard, and found an open kitchen. Richard ordered impulsively—artichoke hearts, beef, and strawberries. They were back in the toasty house by 11:15 P.M.

Susan sat downstairs near the waning fire and sketched with the pen and pad that she had asked Richard to borrow. She left her bag and sweater by the front door apparently uncertain if she was spending the night. Ten minutes later, the drifting scent of incense disrupted her artwork. She followed the aroma upstairs to the bedroom. Richard, that skunk, was up to something.

***

Johnny knew the call lay spring loaded on Howard's tongue. He just had no way of predicting that his employer would sound the claxon during a pounding storm when he and Chaser had already shot up and were preparing to drift deliriously into the dawn. Not that either man were bellyachers. One of the first lessons that they learned about Howard was that unsolicited, dissenting opinions consigned you to his dog-house, and good luck getting out the same as you went in.

Howard had been drinking at a bar near Johnny's house in Ontario when he hit the payphone around 9:30 P.M. "Let's go take him," he said in a low rasp. Weaponry was gathered. Howard reached for the .357 Magnum that his wife gave him as a thoughtful birthday gift to complement his other firearms. Johnny grabbed his M-1 paratrooper rifle and the carbine clip that he had stashed for it under his bed. Chaser had his own pistol.

They climbed into the front seat of the El Camino that police two weeks earlier had absolved in the Buonsanti house takeover and veered on the freeway westward. From Ontario, it was about an hour's drive to Van Nuys with no corona of red brake-lights in their windshield.

Howard wasn't one for idle chitchat, either to fill the time in until they arrived or just in general. What was even there to say? Chaser, Johnny and Robert had flubbed the job or encountered such stupendously bad luck on so many consecutive efforts—nine, ten times, maybe more—that the only apt summation for it was confounding clusterfuck. Howard, as such, had accepted that he had no recourse except to forget about the alibis he had devised before to remove himself from the future crime scene and handhold his minions through the job. It could be a training mission for future killings. So there the three were on the freeway, knifing through the damp, black night, nobody talking. Next to them on the roads were big-rigs hauling consumer products and dour men traveling to boiler-room jobs.

Had Howard switched on the all-news AM radio, KNX or KFWB, the ones with the Ted-Baxter-voiced newscasters and typewriter soundtracks, he would've heard about an eventful day in his world. Gasoline prices were forecast to blow stratospherically in the wake of an Arab-OPEC decision to raise crude oil costs nine percent, this after two embargoes in the decade. Talking heads predicted that there'd be a free-for-all on the world markets and more pain for commuting Californians at the gas pump. Commuters like Howard.

Competing news burbled out of Salt Lake City, Utah, where the Michigan State Spartans had defeated the Indiana State Sycamores for the NCAA men's basketball championship. Normally, the title game and the tournament that led up to it were only holy days for Vegas bookies and sports nuts. Not anymore. The 1979 matchup attracted a record audience that'd popularize the college basketball playoffs into the big money, bracket-filling gambling juggernaut that it is today. "March Madness" was being born. In the game, the college player of the year, a rangy white-bread forward from French Lick, Indiana named Larry Bird, was hogtied by the Spartan's double-teaming defense. The hero of the championship was from Michigan State, a 6'9" man-child with a solar-flare smile and marquee ball-handling ability. The player's first name was Earvin, though everyone called him "Magic." The NBA's L.A. Lakers would soon draft him as their franchise player. A city in a snit was desperate for his effervescence.

Weather, however, dominated the news cycle, from the sagebrush high desert to L.A.'s curvy coastline. The years' rain totals were already threatening records etched in 1969, when a giant swarm of warm Pacific Ocean water propelled such destructive storms—landsides and mudslides everywhere, four-hundred million dollars in property damage, ninety-one deaths—they still felt like urban myth. A decade later, Angelenos continued overreacting to rainy-days, where most locals drove with the herky-jerky reflexes of someone ice-skating for the first time. Hydroplane spinouts and fender-benders littered the roadways as Howard made his way to Van Nuys. "What pansies," he might have clucked flying past an accident.

From the sounds of the radio updates, the storm was an L.A.-monsoon.

Central boulevards had become asphalt swamps, fallen boulders one-hour bottlenecks. Come nightfall that Monday, no one remembered seeing the sun during its regularly scheduled hours. Not far from where Howard was driving, stretches of Laurel and Coldwater Canyons, rustic enclaves filled with actors, rock stars and other creative sorts, was waterlogged Bohemia. Almost anywhere you went that day, palm trees bent backwards and power lines drooped. Call it a deluge, another storm of the century, or for Howard's murder corporation, a sweet window for score-settling.

Two-thirds of the way there, Howard steered onto the Ventura Freeway and into the corridor slashed through the emerald Verdugo Mountains. They motored through the cities of Glendale and Burbank, home of Walt Disney Company and Warner Brothers, past hilly Forest Lawn Cemetery, and then Universal Studios. Plunging further west, they reached the heartland of manicured single-family houses and cartoonishly repeating strip malls known as the Valley.

Just before Howard hit the San Diego Freeway, he turned north on Woodman Avenue and entered a section of Van Nuys called Sherman Oaks today. Up ahead were glass-framed car dealerships, a General Motors plant, and the Busch beer gardens that nary rated a blink by L.A.'s gaudy standards. Then, too, Howard and his men weren't from here. Nearing Richard's street, they wheeled by spacious homes with basketball hoops in the driveways and Spanish imitations crowned with red-tile roofs. To them, this was the high-rent district. To them, breaks never sprinkled on their families were required for admission here.

Nevertheless, they had made the drive in short time thanks to the late hour, rain and televised basketball-championship that made Magic legend. It was past 11:00 P.M., almost Johnny Carson hour, when they parked around the corner from the home that'd defeated them so many times before. Outside they acted as if they belonged, taking the sidewalk until they got closer to Richard's house. From there, the shadows were easy for them to dissolve in. Richard's street was nearly as wide as an airport runway, divided by a grassy median planted crookedly with pine, magnolias and eucalyptus. The trees and residential landscaping projected green suburban forest, and, in a sense, dangerous privacy. Besides that, Richard's southerly bedroom pointed away from the boulevard, and it was that room that Howard had decided where they would get their business done. Knocking on his front door to bait Richard had gotten his men bumpkis.

Before they went around back, they cupped their hands around their faces to look in through the bottom level of the wood-and-stucco, ranch-style house. The half-burnt logs flickering in the fireplace was just what they hoped to see, tantalizing proof that their target was near, except for the juxtaposition nearby. No cars were in the driveway, Richard's Cougar most notably. "Jesus F Christ," Howard might have muttered. "Not again. This guy is the luckiest sonabitch alive."

They snuck off the property and returned to Howard's car. He wasn't about to call it a night. He flipped the El Camino around and drove through the slippery, slick streets. He turned onto Van Nuys Boulevard and pulled into a local hangout. Corky's, the Art Deco coffee shop with a roof shaped like a weak smile, the same place that Johnny had retreated to after an earlier whiff on Richard, would be their waiting room. The three blew a slow, forty-five minutes inside avoiding any loud discussion of why they were there. They each had coffee, and Howard ordered a bagel. Time-killing by the fry-chefs, that's all this was.

Johnny drove back from Corky's and maybe that rebooted their luck. When they passed the home this time, they each noticed that Richard's Cougar was parked in the crescent driveway. Pulse rates galloped at its presence. Howard ordered Johnny to park the El Camino a few blocks away on a drag facing south toward the Ventura Freeway for their getaway. The trio then set out on foot again in the rain and double-backed toward Chandler Boulevard. Their clothes were still soggy from before.

Reaching the house, they strode past the bushes fronting the property and hurried across the concrete apron. *Swuh, swuh, swuh* – Johnny's wet boots squeaked with every step. They ducked by the garage underneath one of the second-floor rooms and entered a narrow side yard partitioned with two sets of gates that closed automatically. (Johnny and Chaser were familiar with it, having just been here for the burglary.) At the base of the steps leading to the deck, the men paused to scan the grounds and re-secure their hardware. Johnny, the designated shooter, carried his rifle in his pants like a phallic enhancement. Finally, they tiptoed up the stairs. None groaned.

The three were on the back side of Richard's tree-dotted property with no neighbors in sight. So far, advantage them. Hunched in the blackness of the night, they tried gathering their wits and still found their jumpiness hard to contain. The moment that had taunted them might never arrive, as if a hex had interceded to keep Richard Kasparov alive during the two months he should've been dead, was finally ticking down to a flashpoint crescendo. Carefully, they arranged themselves into their pre-attack crouch outside Richard's master bedroom and what a silhouette it must've been: three lurking figures, two of them baring scowls, the other a devious smile, communicating with hand gestures in the rain. Howard had smartly insisted on silence here, knowing the execution they had traveled half a county to carry out demanded precision. They weren't in some outland ghetto crackling with hourly gunfire and lethargic policing. They were in the epitome of protected L.A. suburbia panting steam and thinking mayhem.

They focused their eyes on Richard through a sliding glass window designed to spill California's amber light into the space. Howard was tucked in behind Johnny on one side of the window the way a baseball umpire hunches over the catcher's shoulder. Chaser positioned himself on the other edge of the window. They observed what was happening inside the house, adoring what they saw. Richard, miraculously, was lying there bare-chested ten feet away and within easy striking distance. They were close, deliciously close, with Richard's head at a sideways angle from them. Just one tug of the trigger and they could get on with the plan and out of the frigid night.

The single object between them and their mark was a thin piece of glass, little more than a sheet of fortified silica that a nameless factory disgorged and shipped out. Something the would-be kidnapper who stood here five months earlier could have crumpled with a violent elbow. In the years to come, the fragility of Richard's barrier would unleash haunting questions and ten-thousand tears: how could he have possibly believed that something so eternally delicate, so transparent would protect him when he knew Howard was on the prowl? Why wasn't he under armed guard, or better yet, on a jet to the remotest village in Mexico or Lichtenstein he could locate? Richard had to know he had a bullseye stapled on his back.

Yet he appeared comfortable at home, at least with the California rain crashing down outside. The entire world seemed to be indoors, out of the storm—apart from Howard, Chaser, and Johnny—chilling at fifty-two degrees and dropping. Every now and then, a breeze ruffled their wet trousers, as raindrops plinked rooftops with a drowsy patter and Richard's pool sloshed chlorine whitecaps. Electric blankets were made for these nights.

Just not to Howard. To him, the rainy conditions couldn't have descended at a better time. A tactical benefit attached to it that he dared not squander. Between the gray-cape the storm threw over the starry sky and their obscured position on the flip side of Richard's property, nobody would notice them up on the deck and decide the strangers warranted a phone call to authorities. With apologies to insomniacs and street cleaners, hardly anyone was outside at all. There was just no disputing their meteorological advantage. For Howard, it had sliced potential witnesses down to nothing.

The ample-sized balcony was less beneficial. While there was enough room to accommodate three grown men of varying dimensions, they couldn't be sure in the darkness if there were wrought-iron patio chairs or anything else they might trip over. They had already sidestepped the bougainvillea bush near the top of the landing. Certainly, Johnny and Chaser were all for a wham-bam execution. Back in the comfort of the El Camino, they could warm their fingers over the vents of the cranked-up heater and calculate how long it would be until they could re-blast heroin into their arms. They also needed to keep that to themselves. Howard was enjoying himself too much to ponder a car ride. Blue fingers, potential pneumonia: he didn't care. He had his quarry in sight.

Being pressed up against that plate glass also had complexities. Every time the three exhaled, their breath fogged the pane up with steamy, amoeba-shaped clouds that hazed their view. Johnny probably had to keep wiping the glass with his sleeve to maintain his sightline, and do it with nary a squeak. If one of them so as much as sneezed or lost their balance, the noise would ruin their element of surprise. They would have to retreat down the steps and lope to the car knowing they had blown their gazzilionth chance at Richard, maybe even their last one. Only so many assassination attempts can pass before the intended victim catches on, even Ostrich heads. Neither Chaser nor Johnny wanted to be on the end of Howard's reaction if that came to be. Ask Robert Freeman how failure felt.

The late hour optics was one consideration that they needn't fret over. On this night, practically the only illumination in the 13,000 block of Chandler Boulevard emanated from the lamps and floor-lights beaming through the upstairs sliding glass door. They bathed the upper bedroom in a glow of dull yellow set against the blackest of nights. Viewed from the outside, the effect was that of a well-lit fishbowl, an ocular phenomenon splendid for close onlookers eager to go unnoticed. Richard and Susan, had they peered out the window for any duration, would've seen nothing but back-glare and their own reflections. The deranged faces gazing in at them from the sides might as well have been invisible.

Fishbowl notwithstanding, even the visually impaired have intuition. Evolution embedded man's self-preservation instinct near the top of his genes. An inexplicable creak or a fifth sense could have been Richard's personal air raid warning to save himself. *Dive now and say a prayer. Run out the back door and pound on a neighbor's door for help.* How could Richard have been so unmindful of the monsters close by after the blunt warning call from last weekend? There was only one conceivable answer. His fight-or-flight reflex was on shutoff.

If Johnny or Chaser knew about Howard's reputation in situations like these, they might've used that warm, yellow light from Richard's bedroom to distract them from their employer's countenance. Rumor was that Howard's eyes bugged out with no blinking or peripheral reflex when he was gripped by violent thoughts, as if he were spellbound by a trance. Word also was that the veins running up his neck had their own Dr. Jekyll identity, pulsing to the width of coaxial cables when Howard's stupor locked in. His men probably didn't want to dwell on how that mutation might someday haunt them, so they re-focused on shooting Richard to please the boss. They would, too, when he stopped fidgeting. A quick check of the watch would've shown they had been crouching on the deck for two-and-a-half minutes rather than the hour it must've seemed.

***

Richard was leaned up against the headboard reading the script when Susan strolled into the bedroom, drawn by the incense. He tossed her his pajama top and asked her to join him in bed, perhaps conjuring up a grin about the next few, carnal hours. She disrobed, slipped on his top and jiggled next to him. Richard's king-sized mattress was a dark invitation fitted with blue sheets and a brown-and-white comforter. Susan took the pages from his hands and asked him if she could rehearse her lines for her upcoming audition. Richard said to go for it. He would be her audience of one.

Susan descended into character and Richard listened as raptly as his perforated essence would permit. Feet away outside the bedroom, rain pattered down on the men indifferent to their target's depression. Astoundingly, Richard had briefly stared out the south-facing window sometime *after* Howard and company had assembled on his landing, causing them a scare until it was clear the optics were blinding him to what lingered so near.

Soon enough he was listening to Susan again read from her script, which the deck-bound killers had mistaken for a book.

He had been lying down for about five minutes when his restlessness awoke. A relaxant was needed to draw into the mood, and Richard bounced off the bed for the numbing agent he kept within reach. He walked to his dresser, opened a drawer and removed a brown paper bag. Next, he went to his closet and took a shoebox down from a shelf. With those items in hand, Richard laid back on the mattress next to Susan. In no time, the slender fingers endowed with all that starry ability, the fingers that should have helped him and Jerry get their names emblazoned on the top of a high-rise, had pinched, tamped and rolled a textbook doobie. He returned the brown bag and shoebox to their hiding spots and re-positioned himself halfway down the bed. There was a tasty anticipation to getting stoned on a rainy night.

While Susan read, Richard lit the joint and inhaled a beefy first hit. Smoke coils drifted, and the pleasure ride was instant. He passed the doobie to Susan, who pulled a toke and returned it back to him. The joint's red tip dimmed, but Richard didn't try to relight it, figuring he always could later. Susan went back to reciting her lines for another minute while Richard got cozy again. This time, he situated himself diagonally across the mattress on his stomach with his head near Susan's hips and his hands propping up his chin. It was if he were floating on a cloud with time suspended.

Suddenly from the bedroom's placidity it happened, the termination of a ruined man. The explosion hit like quicksilver with a sharp, muffled bang that vibrated Richard's walls, jostled the bed and petered off as quickly as it struck. *The-waaap.* That was the sound. Susan had been reading her lines when she heard and felt that *The-waaap* and she had questions. Could it have been a small earthquake? What about a sonic boom? A big-rig chugging by wouldn't sway the room like that. She set the script down to address her curiosity. The sound did not repeat. She tapped Richard to solicit his opinion, and he was an un-budging lump. She touched him again with no response, unaware it was connected to the bang. It wasn't until she glanced down the bed, near her pelvis, that Richard's quietness made sense. He wasn't sleeping. If only he were.

No longer up on his elbows, Richard's face was flat on the sheets as scarlet fluid pooled around his head from a gash near his throat. Johnny's bullet had whistled through the sliding glass window like cellophane, flown over Susan's outstretched legs, nailing Richard from an upwards trajectory at a couple thousand miles per hour. As the blood seeped, his breathing grew labored, and his body started behaving like a twitching, dying animal. Ever so slowly, it tried crawling away from where it had been savaged, towards the headboard, with the life gurgling out of it. Richard didn't move far, only a few inches toward Susan, who was on the right side of the bed. The fishbowl had gotten him.

Blood and brain matter splattered Richard's lair red. They stained the mattress, caked the sheets and sprayed around them in a ghastly fantail. The M-1's bullet had clipped him just under the right side of his chin, near his jugular, with a marksman's touch. On impact, it had ripped open a star-shaped wound measuring about half-inch in diameter that turned the area near his Adam's apple to mangled hamburger. The bullet's jacket, destabilized when it pierced the glass, had shredded tissue and flown off when it slammed him; police would later find the cladding in the bedcover. The projectile inside that jacket was responsible for the head shot. After penetrating his throat, it had wended upwards at a sharp angle and come to rest in the back, left side of Richard's brain.

Susan could not help but focus on the slaughterhouse encircling her, as blood spilled from Richard's throat and his body convulsed. She had no comprehension of the mechanics or back story of how he had gotten this way, only the timing. One moment she had been reading in a snug bedroom on a drizzly night and next there was that wall-shaking thump that sprayed red everyplace. Once the atrociousness of the chronology firmed in her, Susan reacted. She cut loose a spine-tingling scream that legend has could be heard for blocks.

After her scream faded, there was a second, white-knuckle moment for Susan to confront—the washed out breathing and scuffling of feet she heard from the upstairs patio a few yards away. She sprinted into Richard's bathroom to get some mass between her and those noises and locked the door. There was a phone in the master bathroom, but there was also a window, and outside of it was the landing where the shot originated. Susan was now even closer to the strangers' than before as she dialed the phone, stifling her sobs, because those killers might hear her. Her call awoke her friend Nicholas Torrini at 12:30 A.M.

"This is Susan," she said in a hushed voice. "I'm in terrible trouble."

"What?" Nicholas said, shaking off his REMs.

"I'm in the house of this man and he's been shot. I think he's dying. I'm hiding in his bathroom right now."

"Oh, Christ."

"Maybe whoever shot him wants to shoot me, too. I don't know what to do." Susan paused for a moment to listen outside. "I think they're still here."

"The bathroom door is locked, right?"

"Yes."

"Why didn't you call the police?"

"I don't know. I don't know. I just called you. You were the first person I thought of. Help me, Nicholas."

"I will. But where are you? I mean, what's the address?"

"I don't know that, either. His house is on Chandler, between Fulton and Woodman (avenues). You're not going to hang up on me, are you?"

"No. Just stay on the line, okay? Don't go away. I'll use my other line to call the cops."

"Hurry!"

Nicholas phoned the LAPD directly; the 911 emergency system hadn't yet been invented. Initially, he got a robotic-sounding recording. When a live officer finally picked up, he informed Nicholas that he had dialed the wrong LAPD dispatch number. Red tape does not bow, even to murder. The officer patched him through to the right colleague, who like the first also questioned why Susan hadn't contacted the department herself. Nicholas said to forget that, send someone out, there'd been a shooting. This officer doubted there'd been gunplay in Van Nuys. Nicholas repeated it was the truth.

He asked Nicholas for the number that Susan was calling from, which Nicholas supplied by jumping back on his other line with her. The officer immediately phoned her, and all it got him was one hair-pulling ring after another because Susan was too paranoid to click over to Richard's second line. What if she got disconnected? It would maroon her with the men on the sundeck and look at what they had done. Luckily for her, Nicholas never panicked. He used his two-line phone to relay instructions from the LAPD to Susan.

The police wanted her to scamper outside to get the street address and call them back with it. Susan agreed, reluctantly, knowing it was either go along or take her chances with the goons a few feet away. She ran from the bathroom, to the curb, then back into the bathroom praying they had gone. After she finally connected with the LAPD on Richard's phone, officers said they had sent out black-and-white patrol units and an ambulance. Susan phoned Nicholas back while she waited, reporting that the man with the hole in his neck was still moaning. Sirens were the next sounds she heard, followed by officers pounding on Richard's front door. "WE'RE HERE," they yelled. "OPEN UP."

Homicide detectives out of the Van Nuys division drove up a half-hour later and by then it was 2:00 A.M. Much later, Nicholas would recall something insightful Susan had told him after the police had been hailed. "You know, it's strange what goes on in your mind," she had said. "Someone must be a very good shot."

Immediately after he fired it, Johnny knew he had a dilemma. In the dark and cold, he couldn't locate the shell casing that might connect him to the killing, and he was disinclined to paw anything that might leave his fingerprints behind. Delicately, he felt around his feet, near Howard's and the shattered window. Nothing. Howard was less bothered by Johnny's anxiety over the wayward casing than the Southern California Rapid Transit District bus unloading passengers nearby on Chandler Boulevard. For an interminable minute, when they weren't sure how quickly the LAPD would respond, Howard made them wait before they descended the stairs and found the El Camino. From start to finish on the sundeck, the mission to execute Richard had lasted sixteen minutes.

Richard's obliterated sliding-glass door continued to crumble well after Howard, Johnny and Chaser dispersed. At flashpoint, the bullet had opened up a spidery hole about a half-inch in diameter. As the weight of the shattered glass sagged through the night, the gap doubled in size. By mid-morning you could stick a fist through the hole and connect it to the foot-long cracks pleating the glass like varicose veins. Only the larger, jagged outer edges of the window remained in the frame by the next day as pre-murder mementos. Much of the rest of the glass around the bullet hole had continued cracking and plopping into the bedroom, just inside the deck. The crystal shards sprayed around the floor, waiting to filet skin at the faintest touch.

CHAPTER TEN

THE REAL MARCH MADNESS

Jerry sat at his desk on Tuesday afternoon, absorbed in a drawing as the sun broke through the coal gray clouds, when Tammy phoned him with the news from Chandler Boulevard. She had herself just heard about it from a frantic Paige, who had been notified about it from the Los Angeles Police Department. The emergency-room doctors at the Valley hospital who had attempted resuscitating Richard had given up their triage at 1:30 A.M. The slug that Johnny had delivered into Richard's brain roughly an hour earlier had destroyed exactly what it was intended, and that was any chance of Richard's future.

From his time-of-death forward, Jerry's former life expired, too, and he entered his second existence panicky and connecting dots. A rifle-shot murder! Of a space planner! Right in his own bed! Off that storybook street! How could it possibly be true? Van Nuys was hardly some banana republic, and Richard could not be mistaken for a tin-pot dictator in his palatial bed. He was a tortured, talented guy unable to square himself. That's it. *Richard can't be dead*, Jerry lectured himself. *He can't be.* The clammy hands era had dawned.

He tugged his lip once the shockwave settled some, lobbing himself questions that someplace inside of him he had already answered. If Richard had been brazenly murdered, who was to say he wasn't next, with no telling what was in store for Jude, Tammy and the second child she was carrying? Reject those theories and there always was the possibility that somebody was trying to frame him for shooting his partner over their disputed finances. *Eliminate Richard, incriminate me,* he thought. Pretty simple from the fifty-thousand-foot view and also pretty unlikely. Jerry had to pick one of the scenarios, so he assumed the scariest was the most probable. After he had, he realized that whoever was behind that bullet was about to have a commanding role in their lives.

The mystery, the fear—Jerry's stomach was clenched, but he knew he had to react only a few minutes after Tammy gob-smacked him with her call. He hopped on the phone with Benjamin, his attorney, to help him buffer what might come next. Good move. Benjamin contacted the LAPD about his client and by that afternoon homicide detectives had interviewed Jerry in Benjamin's office about Richard's enemies list past and present. Jerry was heartened having the police involved. They were something concrete in a haze of disbelief. It was what happened afterwards that made Jerry feel as vulnerable as he ever had. Once the interview ended he was back on the Ventura Freeway, through that metal gnash of traffic, pointed towards Northridge. The spacious house he had been so proud to own there now felt about as sturdy as a papier-mâché hut. *Breathe,* he reminded himself.

At home, he thumbed through his home Yellow Pages searching for security guards able to begin immediately. A credible-enough sounding firm caught his attention, and Jerry explained to the manager about his situation. At Jerry's insistence, the company within a few hours dispatched a pair of lanky, long-haired watch-men in their early thirties. They strode into Jerry's house in leather jackets frayed at the elbows with pistols off their hips. Jerry scanned them, thinking they could be mistaken for rock-band roadies, and crossed his arms. He still had not done enough to safeguard his family. Back on the horn again, he had a Space Matters staffer drive out to tack shades on the windows still missing them, and most were. They undeniably blocked interior views from the street, which was an improvement. Despite it, Jerry and his wife realized that the protection they lined up that afternoon provided their house with only marginal fortification in light of how Richard died. That disquieting sense they were just as exposed as he had been while lying on his blue comforter on his peaceful block was a gremlin in their every room. The front of the Schneiderman house was overrun with windows.

Distance, they needed distance. They stuffed a few suitcases, collected their son and his favorite toys and along with the guards packed into Tammy's red Cadillac Seville. They planned to stay with one of her girlfriends, figuring they would lay low in an anonymous house for a few days and hope for an arrest. But that assumed they had days. When Jerry keyed the ignition in his driveway, a surprising mist of black smoke poured from the front grill, billowing over the windshield and up into the Valley's mocha-colored smog. The guards suspected booby trap. "EVERYONE OUT OF THE CAR," they shouted. "GO!" Hearts stuck in throats as the longhairs waited off to the side, presumably out of the blast zone, before deciding it was safe to pop the hood and investigate. The guards studied the engine block, pointing here and there and failed to see any dynamite or bristling wires hooked to a battery. A film of greasy oil was all they noticed in an indication that the Seville might have needed new head gaskets. If so, it was a rotten time to learn about car care.

They put the smoking engine behind them and schlepped to the home of Tammy's friend. She was hosting a dinner party the night the nomads trundled by her guests in a hot beam of stares. Forty-eight hours later, Jerry and company were back in their own house, as frightened as before about its profusion of glass. Just for precaution, Jerry, Tammy and Jude slept hud-dled together on the floor of the bonus room, away from those sashes and their monotonous routine. Tammy's psyche already reflected the disruption. "I hate California!" she began repeating. "This doesn't happen to normal people."

Up ahead they had Richard's funeral to attend, and there was no pos-sibility it would be normal, either. Jerry, in retrospect, had no explanation for how he or a few others survived the dreadfulness of the sendoff. Hillside Memorial Park, a grassy cemetery accented with waterfalls and marble off the emission-choked San Diego Freeway, was the site. Under Jewish tradi-tion, the dead are to be laid to rest as soon as possible. For this reason, Richard was interred only a few days after the incident that mutilated him above the clavicle. Jewish custom also forbids mourners from viewing the body. Paige-the-Christian herself had tried for a final glimpse, until Rich-ard's mom blocked her from walking around a screen where the casket was parked.

Everybody could see that Richard's young widow was beyond grief, crossed over into the catatonic stage, and barely "there." Paige sat in the front pew of the chapel next to her pal Erica and not with her in-laws, who wanted little to do with her. The setting and gravity of it all was too much for her. It would've clobbered anyone who had received that warning call and watched it ignored. During the middle of the ceremony she had steadily sobbed and spaced out through, her body rebelled. Paige leapt out of the pew and hurried toward a side door, where she puked within earshot of the black-clad mourners. The only victory she managed that day was slipping her wedding band into Richard's coffin when his kin weren't watching.

From his own seat, Jerry regularly peeked over his shoulder to remind himself that he had never heard of anyone being gunned down at a funeral. He wasn't so sure about aggravated assault after some of Richard's family members lobbed him the stink eye. Without them enunciating a word, he knew they were blaming him and Paige for their loss. Their insinuation was reprehensible: that they somehow got "Dick" mixed up with sub-humans who would resort to murder. At other times that day, Richard's clan behaved as if it were a car wreck or cancer that had taken him too early instead of a rifle flash in the night. Denial enameled that part of their grief. If there was a cemetery discussion about whether Richard's actions contributed to his undoing, Jerry was excluded from the conversation. The contents of Richard's wallet that detectives searched spoke more about his unraveling than his relatives dared. Inside was twenty-four dollars, two checks and five credit cards, one of which belonged to Jerry.

For Richard's now fatherless children, none of that mattered. They had enough tears around them to discern accusatory glances among the adults. At the service's conclusion, eight year old Rachel, Richard's daughter from his first marriage, released the balloons she had been gripping. They spiraled upwards, sent to a father in a place where weird killers don't roam, and the handkerchiefs whipped out again. Jerry watched the globes drift and dart into the atmosphere. *What I'd give*, he thought, *to be up there with them*. Few at the funeral were focused on the neon blinking in Jerry's head. A wily murderer was afoot.

After the funeral at Hillside Memorial, Richard's sister hosted the Shiva at her West L.A. home, where things fared no better for Paige or Jerry. Richard's high-strung family returned to their old themes, vilifying Paige as the fast-lane wife who led "Dick" astray while lionizing his first wife as the virtuous ex-woman in the room. There were lots of sore feelings to go round. Months earlier, Paige and Richard's mom had engaged in a screaming match. Paige had sniped about not receiving any child support from her son while Richard's mom pilloried Paige's "expensive" nails and her gumption in reciting Richard's emotional sins to her. If Richard interceded to cool the hostilities, it must've been delicately. He had chafed for years at his family, his Jewish background and, most of all, what he complained was his mother's heavy-handed love.

On Jerry's side of the wake, the accusatory laser-beam that Richard's family aimed at him at the funeral harshly resumed. It was if a tribunal had indicted him. Milling around the cold-cut platters and mourners, he realized what he was up against. The Kasparov's poisonous feelings towards him and Paige were too raw for him to counter with a windy explanation or an extra dollop of condolences. None of it would register today or maybe ever. Plus, as before, he had thornier problems hounding him. What was he going to do to defend his own family if Richard's murder was business related? And what sort of office would he walk into if it was?

Paige, by then, was barely standing. Nobody, not even Jerry, could comprehend the dimensions of her hell, beginning with how she learned of the event that transformed her from estranged wife to unprepared widow and single mother. It was day for new vocabulary. Two murder detectives had shown up at her design shop on Ventura Boulevard, the shop Richard had helped her launch, and rapped on the locked front door with sobering business to attend. It was mid-morning on March 27, about ten hours after the shooting that no one in Richard's circle knew a scintilla about except for Susan. Paige, jumpy after the last months and alone in the storefront, was unnerved by the official men outside. She mouthed that they would have to wait there while she phoned LAPD headquarters to confirm their identities. This annoyed one of the detectives, who pressed his badge up to the glass. Paige unlocked the door.

They asked her name and where she had been the previous night. Paige said with a client and inquired what this was about? "A homicide," a homicide involving your husband, I'm sorry to report, one of the detectives responded. Paige at first was unfamiliar with term. With the officers' continued repetition of it, that changed. She picked up on its macabre inference and began hyperventilating. "Is Richard okay?" she asked, wheezing. "What hospital is he at? What's his condition?" The detectives had her exhale into a bag. There was no calming her breathing, though, after Paige understood that she was being informed of a gruesome act involving her spouse. It devoured her feet from her fabrics and papers.

The detectives wanted to know if there was somebody who could stay with her as the trauma compacted. Just then, Erica returned from an appointment and contacted a doctor. He traveled right over to the shop and gave Paige a Valium shot in the back seat of a friend's car to sedate her. There was no relaxation. In her distraught shape, the Valium was about as tranquilizing as chamomile tea. Paige was driven from the shop to her rental house and by then she was tumbling into full-fledged shock. Her only respite from it came when Isabel brought baby Rebecca to her. It was the sight of her daughter, unharmed and alive, that freed Paige to capitulate to the Valium. She passed out on her bed, temporarily forgetting the decimation of the new word in her lexicon: homicide.

The aftermath was waiting for her when she awoke, and in those early days it would be cruel and absurd. The bloodied master bedroom on Chandler had to be de-soiled and cleansed now that the detectives were done collecting evidence. A crime scene clean-up company commissioned to do the job had backed out of it when employees saw the repulsiveness of the work order. Paige had her own hesitations, too, asking the police if Richard had been shot in the heart. Officers told her no, it was his brain that was what was matting the walls and everything scarlet. Alone, Paige wound up scrubbing and tidying the room, as if Ajax and bleach could erase the effects of what Howard had engineered. Still, she tried, a widow down on hands and knees sopping up the remains of the love or her life. She cleaned it all numbly, coldly, resisting the urge to weep because she feared that once she began she might never cease.

***

They were a hangdog bunch that day, eyes gravitated downward, but they still had to eat. Jerry, Howard and Bert, Jerry's second in command at Space Matters, met for lunch a few days after the funeral to assess their loss. If the mood at Richard's service careened between tense and delusional, it was downright bleak here. The trio was at Langer's Deli, a gastronomic guilty pleasure renowned for pastrami sandwiches the density of gold bricks and a vinyl booth atmosphere ripped from Manhattan. It was Howard's idea to connect at the popular restaurant across from a paddle-boat lake northwest of downtown to honor their fallen colleague. He had even recommended that Bert invite Jerry, and Jerry was all for it, expecting that Howard might offer to drop his legal claims in exchange for freelance work on Richard's unfinished remodels. Perhaps, Jerry speculated, the killing that had knocked him loopy had done the same to Howard. After squeezing into the booth, his ex-foreman disabused him that was his purpose. Remembrance was today's theme, not reconciliation.

Awkwardness hung over the wood-laminate table detectable in the tender talk about how everyone found out and who could have perpetrated such a deed. There had been a brief article about the shooting in the local paper, *The Valley News and Green Sheet* (later renamed *The Daily News of Los Angeles*), and nothing in the *L.A. Times*. Howard muttered into his sandwich about how lacking in details the story buried in the metro-section was, but what did he expect? There was so much carnage and so many serial killers strewing L.A. at the moment that not even the spectacular details of a suburban execution could win the front page. Howard peppered Jerry if he knew anything that wasn't in the article, and Jerry shrugged he didn't. Bert added he didn't either, and that was that.

From outward appearances, Richard had died as inexplicably as he had lived. Whoever had killed him in that private setting—a scorned woman, a jealous husband, an insane acquaintance—had taken precautions not to leave evidence behind. (Jerry stayed quiet about his conversation with the LAPD, as detectives had requested.) The men offered up memories of Richard and his antics, and wondered about the future for Paige and Rebecca. The gathering had a choppy tempo to it obvious in the somber chewing of normally mouthwatering cured-meat. Afterwards, everybody shook hands near Alvarado Boulevard and scattered their own directions.

Back in Northridge, Jerry and Tammy had decisions to finalize about further shielding themselves. After pondering their options, they allowed their schedule to be their solution. They had been booked to fly from L.A. to Detroit to visit Tammy's family during Easter, which landed on April 15. Tammy had earlier called her parents to tell them about what'd happened to Jerry's partner and inquire if they could travel out a few days earlier. Her folks, at first anyway, had difficulty registering the trepidation she and her husband felt in California, urging them to stay on schedule. No need splurging on changed plane-fare, they said.

So, Jerry, Tammy and toddler-Jude stayed on course. They boarded their regularly scheduled flight and made the trek to the Midwest at thirty thousand feet. Tagging along with them was a fantasy: that before their return to the West Coast, a murderer would be in custody and some semblance of normalcy restored. When no suspect was apprehended, there was a crucial alteration in plans. Tammy and Jude remained in Michigan with her family in Ann Arbor outside of Detroit while Jerry boarded the L.A.-bound plane by himself.

It was a teary scene at the airport, as Tammy begged her husband before he clumped down the ramp to stay longer in the peaceful Midwest. Just postpone California for a few more days, she said. Jerry knew he couldn't, just as he knew he had to protect his family from whoever executed his partner with such black-hearted proficiency on that stormy night.

***

He had been home from Michigan for eight days when a gnarled hand tapped on the door of the bookkeeper's office where he was sitting. Jerry had been in the room in the back of the Space Matters mansion, chatting with one of his draftsmen, when the knuckles lined by years of sweat and sawdust hovered in the transom. It was late morning on April 18, 1979, with the media just getting word out that England had elected its first female prime minister. Margaret Thatcher's elevation was historic news, as was the ongoing radiation scare at Pennsylvania's Three Mile Island nuclear-power plant. Important sure, but to the man in the doorway they were trivial blips.

He settled into the chair opposite the desk, and before Jerry's eyes spread a celebration of monochrome, a statement. Howard Garrett wore a blue shirt, blue jeans, blue shoes and blue-tinted sunglasses over his pale, bluish-green eyes. Jerry couldn't decide what surprised him most: Howard's decision to step foot inside Space Matters after pledging he never would again or his hypnotic, one-color couture.

"I'd like to speak with you privately," Howard said softly.

"Geez, Howard, I wish you would've called first. I have to be downtown by noon. Can we talk now?"

Howard shook his head. "I'd really rather go someplace else. I was thinking that we'd grab coffee."

"Nobody will bother us here. The room's not bugged. That was just a one-time thing to find out about Richard. If you need to talk confidentially, shut the door."

Howard considered Jerry's words for a moment before the change swept over him. Skin tightened, and his tranquil face recast itself into something reptilian—burning eyes, recoiling jaw. Something carnivorous he had planned to unveil over coffee. Howard jerked his chair up and bent forward, so close that his chin loomed over the edge of the desk.

"You fucking Jews—you're all alike," Howard said in a smoky half-whisper. "Hitler should have just killed all of you."

Jerry couldn't respond. His tongue was paralyzed.

"I used to think that Richard was the bad one, but now I know you're just as much of a shit as he was. I also know you have one-hundred and fifty thousand dollars in life insurance coming due and I want half of it."

"I don't understand," Jerry said timidly. "Why do you deserve any of it?"

"Because I had Richard killed and did you a favor. Somebody had to get rid of that bastard."

"A favor?"

"You heard me."

Jerry pressed back into his chair, in shock at the topic. "I don't have seventy-five thousand dollars. The money's frozen. Richard's mom filed a claim."

"I don't care."

"But it's up to the insurance company. You know how slow they can be."

"Jerry—you can stop right there, okay. The days of you feeding me horse-shit excuses are over. If the money is frozen, then talk to Tammy's family. They're loaded. You can ask her dad for it."

"I can't do that."

"You better unless Tammy's dad is willing to see her or his grandson get hurt. I'll call him myself about the money if you're too much of a pussy. And you can forget about going to the cops. You want to know why?"

"I guess."

"Because I already have a contract out on you if you do anything I don't like. You're bought and paid for, Jerry, and I'm the only one who can call it off. Got that? The only one! They can send me to prison and throw me in a hole. It won't stop the hit on you. That, I promise."

"Why are you being like this, Howard? I don't get it. I never stole anything from you. I tried treating you right."

"I already told you. I've had enough fucking around with all this money I'm owed. The whole business has caused me more hell than you could ever dream. I have creditors badgering me all day because of what you two did. Not a good way to live, Jerry. Not at all."

"But your lawyers have filed liens against us. This doesn't make sense."

"Oh, screw the lawyers. And screw more talking about talking. You have a week to get me the seventy-five-thousand. I want it in two parts. Maybe you should write this down on one of your fancy pads. I want a twenty-five thousand dollar cashier's check and a fifty-thousand dollar check written out to me. Two parts. Understand?"

"I think. But how do I know what you're saying is true, that this isn't all some trick? You realize what you're saying. You must."

"Oh doubting Jerry. I want you to play a little game with me. You call Paige and ask her about the caliber of the bullet they found at Richard's house and write down what she says on a piece of paper. I'll write my answer down and we'll compare. Then you'll know I arranged it. Go ahead and call her. I've got time. I'll wait."

"I don't want to do that."

"You're in dangerous water, my friend. I've killed before Richard and gotten away with it, and I'll do it again with you."

"Before Richard? What are you talking about? This is insanity."

"Don't you remember that trial in San Bernardino? What do you think it was about, huh? A code violation? It was about murder."

"Murder? Nobody ever told me anything about murder," Jerry said up an octave. "You're only trying to scare me. You were a witness in some minor case that delayed when you could start work here. That's what Richard said."

"Let me clear things up then once and for all. *I* was the one on trial. Me. And like I just told you, I got away with it once without being convicted and will do it again."

"I don't know what to believe anymore."

"I'll go over it a final time. I got even with Richard and now I'm getting even with you, douche bag. Get me my money within a week or you're dead. That's as simple as I can make it. Call me when you have it collected."

With that, Howard, the blue ghost, moseyed out of Space Matters as if he had already pocketed a check.

CHAPTER ELEVEN

UPSIDE DOWN IN LOTUSLAND

Jerry, as he had throughout his role-reversing childhood, was back to questioning what was real and what was illusion after Howard came calling with his bluster about Hitler's "mistake" in not killing all the world's Jews and the demented merits he had awarded himself by having Richard shot. You're not supposed to have one *I-can't-believe-that-just-happened* moment piggybacking on another. First Richard's execution, then Howard's extortion; in Jerry's bones, the world had shifted from bewildering to vicious.

His index finger was punching his lawyer's phone number minutes later. Benjamin had always come through with bankable advice for him, most recently in exposing Richard's deceptions, and never had Jerry needed counsel like this. "Come over right now," Barry said. "We need to take a walk." Jerry heeded the call, ignoring the usual tenets of defensive driving and speeding from Hancock Park to West L.A. with the heavy foot of Mario Andretti. Funny thing about perspective; he would do anything now if an unscrupulous partner who fleeced him for two hundred thousand dollars constituted the worst of his problems.

He listened to the AM news updates about Margaret Thatcher on his way to Benjamin's, hoping for a diversion. Futile try with the geometry imposing itself. He, Richard and Howard were fixed points in a triangle cut by greed, blood lust, and other motivations that Jerry had yet to decipher. Apparently, whatever had shaken out between Howard and Richard was now something razor vectored at him. That's all Jerry knew for sure as he tore through yellow lights, and almost all he could take. When he had met with

125

Benjamin after learning of Richard's murder, he had been dumbfounded but lucid. After Howard's visit, he felt weak-legged, twitchy at unexpected noises, less than sum of his parts.

Up in his office, Benjamin crooked his arm around his client's shoulder the way a consoling uncle might. Uncooked shrimp had a better pallor than Jerry, who appeared on the verge of throwing up. Benjamin patted him that he would be all right, and that they needed to take their stroll. Benjamin knew the incendiary advice he had to dispense was not grist for his secretary or eavesdroppers. Not if he wanted to continue being a lawyer, anyway. At the elevators, Jerry asked him where they were going. Benjamin answered the graveyard.

Benjamin's small law office was cloistered inside an understated highrise bookended by office towers with heliports and luxury apartments fanning western Wilshire Boulevard. The structure, crammed to the particle boards with attorneys and other professionals, probably could have benefited from a healthy space plan to add breathing room. South of the building was Westwood, where UCLA splayed out like a mini city of backpacking youth. To the west a few blocks was the Veterans Administration's 114-acre cemetery. Spacious as those were, Jerry's lawyer opted for a different site for his confidential with Jerry. The Westwood Village Memorial Park, one of the tiniest boneyards in Southern California, lapped close to his office.

The graveyard was really just parkland, too, with none of the chapels or marble adornments to death of Richard's interment. Indeed, the location was so unheralded that most Angelenos whizzed by it on their daily commutes without appreciating the strata of Hollywood luminaries and entertainers reposing there. Today, it's L.A.'s red carpet necropolis, in receipt of Marilyn Monroe, Dean Martin, Roy Orbison, Natalie Wood, Jack Lemmon, Walter Matthau, Burt Lancaster, Bob Crane and Truman Capote, *inter alia*. Jerry fretted he might join them.

He and Benjamin walked for about five minutes when Benjamin halted. This was as good a place as any, he believed, for Jerry to hear his repulsive options.

"Before we get started, you need to know something," Benjamin said.

"What's that?"

"If you ever tell a single soul about this conversation, I'll deny it. Categorically. Agreed?"

"This is going to be heavy, isn't it?" Jerry swiveled his head to check that they were alone. He was confused by Benjamin's stipulation.

"But do you agree? I won't say a word unless you do."

"Yeah, sure. I agree. Let's get on with it."

"Okay, good. We'll keep it linear. As far as I can tell you have three choices, Jerry. Be forewarned: none of them are pleasant. You can pay Howard. You can go to the police. Or, you can kill him. Of these choices, I recommend you kill him."

"You recommend I do *what?*"

"Kill him."

"Tell me you're kidding?"

"No actually I'm not. You asked me for advice so I'm laying out your alternating. You have to decide whether to act on them or not."

"Oh, great."

"Ask yourself who Howard is—what he's capable of doing? From what you've described, it sounds to me as if he were an animal. Like them, he'll always come back for more if you're feeding him. Once he decides you're a threat, or you get tired of paying him, he'll dispose of you and think he'll walk away clean."

"I don't know, Benjamin."

"Well, you better start. Howard has already confessed to killing two people. That's incredibly dangerous information for you to have. You realize that, right?"

"But this is what you're saying? I come to you for legal advice and the best you can do is tell me to commit a felony. What kind of attorney does that?"

"A realistic one. Say you call the police and tell them that Howard has threatened to kill you or your family unless you give him seventy-five thousand dollars. He goes to prison and then what?"

"Like I told you, he said he would have me killed from behind bars?"

"Maybe he could, maybe he couldn't. But what happens if he's released from prison without forgetting about who put him in there? You want to live the rest of your life looking in the rear view mirror? You'll be on tranquilizers by next year."

"Of course I don't want to live that way. If he got out of jail, maybe I'll have to do what you're suggesting. But I have a family to think about right now. A son. A pregnant wife. What about them?"

"You don't believe Howard has other skeletons in his closet?"

"I don't know what I believe. All I know is how scary he was when he dropped by. It was like he came through the walls."

"I'm gathering that. Look, we both know from the settlement meetings that he's a scary individual. Just feel better knowing the police are investigating. It could wind up you won't have to take anything into your own hands; that'd be the best outcome. I'm no criminal lawyer, but I'll bet they're already on to him. It's nothing for them to check rap sheets."

"Too bad we hadn't before we hired him."

"That's something I reminded myself to ask you. How did you come to employ somebody like him?"

"Richard hired him after he answered our ad in *LA. Times*. Richard got a good recommendation for him from his last boss."

"A good recommendation, for that guy?"

"I don't know the specifics. Hard to believe, isn't it?"

"I guess some people know how to blend in until they see an opportunity or get angry. Then they show what's really inside of them."

"I already know what's inside of me. I can't kill anyone. Not even a murderer. With my luck, I'll be the one going to prison. Sorry. I can't do it."

"You sure you don't want to think it over for twenty-four hours? This is a major life decision."

"Yeah, I'm sure."

"Then let's go back to my office and get those homicide detectives out here again. You have a story to tell them."

"I wish that's all it was, too—a story, and not my life."

"Don't get ahead of yourself."

***

Long live the LAPD! God Bless Chief Daryl Gates. Jerry could have sung those lines falsetto, a la Queen's "Bohemian Rhapsody," when homicide detectives sat down with him in Benjamin's conference room a few hours after his graveyard walk. Their mastery of the situation made you glad you paid taxes. Up front, the detectives said that Howard had been their primary suspect from day one. That's why they had shown up with two binders stuffed with information about him. Howard's extortion demand on Jerry, coupled with his knowledge of the Chandler Boulevard crime scene, substantiated their hunches. Howard was a killer or the ringleader of something bigger.

Therein lay Jerry's dilemma. A hunch was not evidence. You could stuff a law library full of briefing books and still not have enough to charge him and win a conviction, not unless there was direct proof linking him to Richard's patio that evening. Motive would be simpler to establish. Howard, as his liens showed, believed he had been swindled. Then there was his past. Detective Richard Jameson, a lanky, amiable man, and Howard Landgren, a shorter, no-nonsense type, bombarded Jerry with questions about Howard. What type of person was he? Did you ever see him cross? What were his dealings with Richard? What did Jerry know about Howard's employment history and home life? Had he and Howard had any personal beefs? Had Richard done something to push Howard's buttons? Why specifically had he quit?

Jerry's responses, though limited, helped detectives exhaust a fresh notepad. Relax, they said. As long as Howard believed he had a fair chance of getting his seventy-five thousand dollars, he would be safe. He could call them anytime. They would send a patrol car periodically by his home and work for peace of mind. After detectives packed up their briefing books and hit the elevators, Jerry reflected on his inverted day. He was relieved about how much history the LAPD had amassed on Howard and simultaneously disappointed that there was no timetable for arresting him. Everybody, it seemed, was taking action except him—mild, threatened him. *I better start adapting, too,* he thought. Benjamin, his preemptive murder recommendation notwithstanding, had performed well but had gone as far as he could. What the situation required from here on was expertise from professionals who had had clients squeezed for money or blood. Clients who had faced their own blue ghost.

For advice, Jerry dialed his sister, Carol, who was attending Loyola University law school, a small, Jesuit-run college in downtown L.A. Carol knew just what to do, calling her dean, Father Richard Matthew Vashon, to say her big brother was in the crosshairs of a killer. Vashon was glad to help, and suggested that Jerry's sister connect him with a Loyola criminal law professor named Michael Lightfoot. The man knew his criminology. Lightfoot said that since no one could predict how long it would take the police to erect a comprehensive case against a practiced adversary like Howard, Jerry should consider retaining his own private eyes to keep tabs on the LAPD investigation. It was the knowledge-power correlation. Better yet, the professor who would never charge Jerry for his advice had a recommendation.

The men that Jerry signed that day made his longhair security guards seem like mall cops. They had both enjoyed long careers—one high up in internal affairs at the LAPD, the other at the L.A. County Sheriff's Department—before retiring early. The older of the two was a friendly Irish American with a moon-shaped face and short-cropped red hair gone gray at the temples. He gave off a fatherly, seen-it-all vibration. The other private eye was the testosterone one, a swarthier, gruffer man with Italian in his bloodline and fearlessness about him. Their *just the facts, ma'am* professional stoicism reminded Jerry of the fictional detectives from one of the few television shows that he watched in his youth. So that's how he painted them in his mind: his "*Dragnet* duo." Professor Lightfoot had served them up for him.

Once Jerry had nailed his private eyes down, Barry told him that he wouldn't allow him to go back to Northridge, not after Howard's visit. He would spend the night with Barry and his family at their place on the Westside. Jerry went where the offer took him, because everything had changed with Howard's ultimatum. Even serving as Fegen's space planning swami was no longer as straightforward as it had been twenty-four hours ago. Jerry's new security team was unhappy with the notion of him traveling to meetings from Hancock Park to Beverly Hills during daylight, when Howard could tail him. Jerry had to explain to them that Fegen was the company's superstar client and the job it could least afford to mishandle. They responded that keeping him safe was *their* job. In the weeks ahead, Jerry and his *Dragnet* duo forged a compromise. Jerry would meet with Fegen only late at night inside Fegen's well-secured office building. And his private eyes would do the driving.

Another person experienced with defeating brutes—albeit one without a city pension or ex-cop haircut—volunteered his services just about this time. Should Jerry require a bodyguard when he traveled to see Tammy and Jude or for other assignments, he wasn't to entertain thoughts of calling anyone else. Some threats demanded specialists. Ari Allon was raring to be Jerry's supplemental security as someone fiercely loyal to friends and comfortable with confrontation. Lump in all the Israeli businessmen residing in Southern California in 1979 and you'd be hard pressed to find anyone close to inimitable Ari. He was a powerfully built man, hairy as an ape, with a pocked complexion and black hair trimmed pageboy style. Like a German shepherd, he cast snapping jaws if he mistrusted you and a warm, protective glow if you were his chum. Ari saw in Howard something different than Jerry did. He saw a redneck ruffian masterful at tormenting average people, which definitely excluded him.

Morocco's French Quarter, where Ari raced camels as a youngster, was his birthplace. Later, he left it for the Middle East, spending years as an Israeli commando and mercenary fighting Arabs all over. During his military stints, Ari had seen things and carried out orders, beneath hill-rattling artillery and around soldiers separated from their limbs that stuck with him, making him at once world weary and fearsome. After his fighting days were done, he immigrated to the West Coast and reinvented himself as a businessman with his commando skills intact.

Jerry had met Ari years before he ran into Howard. Back then, Ari was just starting an L.A. demolition company that put him in the driver's seat of bulldozers, earthmovers and other yellow-painted machinery leveling space for contractors. Jerry, out of all of Ari's local acquaintances, might've been the most impressed with Ari's versatility, especially after his creativity dealing with one of Jerry's problem clients. Ari had been hanging around Space Matters when Jerry mentioned that a Pico Boulevard property owner was refusing to compensate him for some twenty-thousand dollars in planning work. Jerry for weeks had been wavering about whether to retain a collection agency or sic his lawyer on the deadbeat. For some reason that day, Jerry glanced at Ari and felt a swell of possible resolution. When he asked him if he would mind assisting him with the debt, a devilish grin broke across Ari's pitted face.

At about 4:00 P.M., Ari turned up in the lobby of the skinflint property owner. Jerry had suggested Ari make himself a benign nuisance that the other building tenants wouldn't appreciate by loitering around. Ari traded up for a more personal approach. He called Jerry's client from the ground floor and asked him to meet him downstairs for a private conversation. Once the executive approached, he noticed that Ari had a *don't-fuck-with-me* sneer and a pungent stink from bulldozing in the L.A. heat. "You don't pay my friend Jerry, I make parking lot out of building," Ari said in his conjugation-free English. "I bring my bulldozer." Half an hour later the man phoned Jerry with a bargain. If he ordered the intimidating demolition man in grimy jeans to vacate the premises, Jerry would have his money tomorrow by 11:00 A.M. Which Jerry would, no bulldozer required.

After Ari's heroics on Pico, the two cultivated an unlikely friendship, one man expert at flattening buildings with diesel-fueled force, the other gifted at configuring office space with a mechanical pencil. Fervent as he was now to protect Jerry during the spring of 1979, Ari, nonetheless, could hardly have counted how many people spent their days in mortal fear about Howard and his thugs rounding their block. How high can you count? In Haight Ashbury, twitchy eyes peered through blinds for a blue El Camino stalking the city. In Ontario, house locks were replaced and guns hidden. Throughout West L.A., families knowledgeable about how Richard was shot no longer stood in front of large, uncurtained windows. The elderly physician who had tried teaming with Richard and Howard on the San Bernardino subdivision was a wreck. Notified of Richard's murder, Dr. Marmet vomited on the spot.

CHAPTER TWELVE

LIVING LIKE BAIT

From the LAPD's vantage point, Howard might as well enjoy his murder corporation while it lasted because it was about to be summarily liquidated. The department had experience dealing with extortionists like him, and had every intention of arresting him before he duplicated what he did to Richard. Blunt deception was the quickest means to that end. For it, they needed to bend Howard's own bravado against him and Jerry's "assistance" would be essential in the severest sense of the word. It was up to him to trick Howard to drop his guard and admit in court admissible fashion his involvement with Richard's death, and it was up to him to do it in a nose-to-nose meeting at Space Matters that detectives would be secretly monitoring. A phone call was too flaccid for the task. The bigger Howard's mouth, the faster he would be handcuffed. Jerry could never forget that.

On Thursday, April 25, one week after Howard had threatened to exterminate him and perhaps his family unless he forked out seventy-five thousand dollars, Jerry met detectives at 7:00 A.M. at the department's Venice Boulevard station. They had asked him a day or so before if his constitution could absorb such a nail-biting job and Jerry had answered yes without spinning through how many things might go wrong. His response was sheer reflex, because he would say anything if it meant stopping Howard and retrieving his family. He was a space planner by trade, a young comer in what many considered a sissified profession, and his old world was the only one with oxygen for him.

From sunrise on, it certainly was all novel. Jerry had never touched a gun before, let alone spent a morning in a sparse police building. This one was in mid-city, north of the Santa Monica Freeway and a few miles southwest of the Space Matters mansion. Surrounding the station was a row of fast food joints and ramshackle storefronts. Why, Jerry fantasized on the drive over, couldn't he just spend the day at Venice Beach, the city's funky, seaside community rather than on dreary Venice Boulevard. It could be a while before he visited the beach again.

Detective Jameson and his colleagues steered Jerry into a chilly briefing room fitted with a table and chairs. Others would enter to help, and the LAPD would be deploying more personnel that day. Jerry, designated bait, wore gray slacks and a checked sportcoat over a burgundy sweater and white shirt. He was in the room drinking sludgy police coffee for about twenty minutes when the first problem cropped up. Officers were frustrated with Jerry's skinny chest, because it gave away the bulletproof vest they had intended him to wear beneath his clothes in his meeting with Howard. The lead-lined garment pushed his clothing so far away from his meager frame that a glaucoma patient would have seen that Jerry was up to something sneaky. There was no junior size, either.

By 8:00 A.M. it was quandary time. It would be irresponsible for the LAPD to allow to Jerry meet Howard wearing a klutzy, oversized vest. Someone as observant as him would instantly recognize that Jerry was co-operating with authorities and nobody could predict how it would skew the conversation. The prospect of inserting Jerry within arm's length of a killer with no insurance could be even more disastrous, a potentially fatal judgment that'd live in LAPD infamy. So, officers noodled around with the lead garment and Jerry's clothes, smoothing them out and fluffing the layers. They tried it different ways and got the same bloated appearance. Agreement coalesced among the detectives and others and Jerry acquiesced to it. He would meet Howard vest free.

Jerry would face Howard with one artificial object under his clothes. Before the vest fitting trouble, the police had him remove his shirt so technicians could tape a small microphone to his breastbone. A wire connected the microphone to a black, square transmitter about the size of the future Sony Walkman, which was harnessed to the small of Jerry's back. Detectives were banking on the electronic recording gizmo to transmit the tête-à-tête with a crisp signal broadcast into their mobile recording bay, an unmarked LAPD van. The arrangement had brought other murderers down.

Going into his meeting, Jerry wore something much heavier than that black device. It was a muzzle that affected a building full of people, his people. There'd been little consideration of it at the station, what with all time exhausted diddling with the vest and instructing Jerry on how to lure Howard into damaging statements. At the LAPD's insistence, Jerry still hadn't acknowledged to his staff that their former construction chief, the one who used to have a desk on the upstairs floor of the mansion, was responsible for Richard's slaying. Or, that Howard had just ordered him, the surviving partner, to either pay him half the life insurance proceeds or expect to die. Jerry assumed his workers had already surmised that something ominous was afoot based on gut feelings or his own shaky explanation of why Tammy and Jude were staying so long in Michigan. Yet, that hardly qualified as a responsible disclosure about an elevated risk.

Brie, Richard's former girlfriend and Space Matters' current office manager, had intuited Jerry's stressful secret. A man in a jogging suit had knocked on Space Matters' door a few days earlier requesting to speak with Jerry. Protective Brie told the stranger to shove off, and then attempted flinging the door closed on him while he tried walking his way in. The jogging suit man refused to move, and Brie would not back down. Once he noticed the impasse at the door jam, Jerry hurried over, assuring Brie that the man was a friend and safe to enter the premises, which he did. Brie was unaware that the stranger was a plainclothes officer working Richard's homicide case. She just sensed that he was not an old buddy of Jerry's randomly stopping by.

Jerry drove down Wilshire zoning out about all this for as long as he could. He needed to concentrate on practicing the lines the police had given him while he acclimated to the transmitter gouging into his lumbar. Before he had departed the Venice station, Jerry had phoned Howard at his Pasadena apartment and convinced him to meet him at Space Matters at 11:00 A.M. It would have been a week since Howard's threat, and Jerry said they "had to talk." If Howard tried anything violent, detectives assured Jerry that hidden officers would rush in and slam him to the floor. Nearing his office, Jerry felt a lump of hesitations settle into him about the LAPD's controlled choreography. The department, he started comprehending, wouldn't devote this much manpower in a time of record setting murders unless him sticking his head into the lion's mouth to extract prosecutable language risked his decapitation. Jerry shivered his first cold sweat of the day.

At 11:00 A.M. sharp, the Space Matters door swung wide, revealing somebody who definitely was not Howard Garrett. He instead was in his mid-twenties, about half Howard's age, appearing as though he had just thrown on a pair of tan corduroy pants and shirt following a Malibu surfing competition. Michael Bailey was a thin, blonde construction hand who had done a little demolition work and errand running for CM-2 under Howard and then for Howard directly after he quit. In the last weeks, Howard had tried brainwashing his helper about how Jerry and Richard had ruined him to lubricate their own greed. Howard's toady would later say he was undecided whether his boss was justifiably mad or criminally paranoid. He was only here for a day's pay.

Jerry was nowhere around when Michael poked his head into the mansion looking for him. He decided to wait outside, because manufacturing small talk with former workmates about what he was doing at his old office was chancy. After a few minutes Jerry drove up in Tammy's Seville, having gotten a late start from the police station. (Ari was using Jerry's Cadillac in barter for future services.) Jerry immediately saw Howard's gofer waiting for him, and his synapses told him why. Howard had revised the day's schedule for his own advantage. *Oh terrific,* he thought. *I'm already on my heels.* As Michael walked over to explain his unexpected presence, he observed one of the results. The hands Jerry used to clutch his briefcase were shaking.

Michael made himself ignore it, repeating Howard's instructions for how the true meeting would proceed. Michael said Howard wanted him to drive Jerry in the El Camino to Tiny Naylor's coffee shop nearby. Inside, Jerry was to use the restaurant's public phone to call Howard, who would be waiting by the phone bank at another area restaurant, the Beverly Hills Café. That was how they would conduct their conversation. Jerry stuck by his car, feeling better protected with a chassis behind him. Why, he asked Michael, had Howard switched venues after agreeing to meet here? Michael referred to his boss' chestnut: he did not feel comfortable inside Space Matters anymore. *Not comfortable after Richard's brains were scrambled!* Jerry wanted to holler? Go tell him, Jerry said, that he wasn't going to any coffee shop and risk stumbling into a trap. See, they could both set conditions.

Michael was stuck on a two-man chessboard in which Jerry wouldn't depart and Howard wouldn't come. Michael asked how he could even improvise when Howard had forbid him from touching a company phone that Howard assumed was bugged. "Not my problem," Jerry responded. A minute elapsed, and Michael shopped the only compromise he could hatch. What if the two of them went to the payphone down the street, where he could contact Howard without fear of eavesdropping to tell him that Jerry wanted to rendezvous someplace else? Jerry thought it sounded like a reasonable counter and said he would go along. He just happened to forget something in his calculation. Whatever he did, detectives had chastised him earlier, don't leave the company grounds.

Michael strode down Wilshire where the traffic heaved and stopped and a jackhammer somewhere munched concrete. Jerry followed about ten feet behind, watching Michael's construction boots clomp on the gum-stained sidewalk and lamenting that this was his existence now. The two of them had barely traveled a block before Jerry sensed he was tempting danger. There was something waggling in the back pocket of Michael's corduroys that stood his neck hairs on end. Jerry stopped moving to study the object, which had the rough dimensions of a hairbrush or tool that a benign messenger might carry. What was it? Finally, Jerry made his identification. The L-shaped item was steel in the form of a small caliber pistol. Michael was armed. Jerry's second cold sweat in the last hour broke.

He was inert on the sidewalk when Michael swiveled his neck to see if Jerry was following. "You all right, man?" Michael asked. "You look terrible." He doubled back towards Jerry, wrapping his arm around Jerry's shoulder as Benjamin had before their graveyard stroll. No, Jerry answered, he wasn't okay. The stomach bug that laid him out last night was making a return appearance. "I can't go with you," he said. "Have Howard call me." With that declaration, Michael's previous concern for Jerry's well-being hardened to irritation. He yanked his arm off of Jerry and curtly said he would deliver the message. He then marched away with the gun silhouetted in his corduroys to inform his boss about the stalemate on Wilshire.

Jerry had ducked Howard's first curveball without knowing what would be hurling at him next. He walked back to the mansion, sat down at his desk and sighed long enough to fill a balloon. He would wait for the LAPD to appear for further instructions. Approximately five minutes after he gave Michael the heave-ho on the sidewalk, Jerry got his wish with a commotion rivaling an animal stampede. The next thing anyone knew, a clique of officers in dark clothing, protective vests and helmets, each of them brandishing automatic weapons and ammo belts trampled through the front door. They dispersed around the office, shouting orders at each other and flying around corners. Some used walkie-talkies to communicate, every footstep exact. Space Matters had been invaded.

Jerry hadn't known that the LAPD's very own Special Weapons and Tactics (SWAT) team, a new, elite force more paramilitary than traditional law enforcement, had been concealed outside along Freemont Place with the plainclothes detectives. (Daryl Gates, the department's recently sworn-in chief, had formed the squad the previous year; police forces across the country were already imitating it.) Jerry merely assumed the LAPD had extra patrolmen on standby. The SWAT guys galloped from one room to the next, sealing off entryways when their commander redirected the focus. "EVERYBODY DOWN! EVERYBODY DOWN NOW!" he yelled at Jerry's staff. "GET YOUR FACE ON THE FLOOR, PEOPLE!" Space Matters' entire workforce was soon prostate, cheeks pressed into places where their quality shoes had just been. As they did, many of the dozen plus SWAT officers, pinned their bodies along the sides of the windows, peering out from the whites of their eyes.

After five minutes, the SWAT leader shouted "ALL CLEAR" and his officers lifted Jerry's people up off the floor. Except for the hissing walkie-talkies, a silence hugged the building. Clothes were dusted off, underwear unbunched. Slowly, the sounds returned with a few sobs and side comments followed by a scattered grumbling. A couple of the draftsmen muttered in Jerry's direction. Others tugged at the elbows of the SWAT members to inquire what this was about, and if something else surprising was going to happen. Michael, the flaming decorator, was a mess. He was in the arms of Lillian, the French decorator, crying and forgetting about the wallpaper he would been agonizing over before.

They were all a steampot of questions. Why were they made to get down? Was this connected to Richard? Were the police planning on leaving? But Jerry was the most common denominator. Why in God's name, they wanted to know, were they learning about this situation after the LAPD stormtroopers had raided the office and not in a conference room where their leader should have forthrightly explained it? Jerry stood to the side near his ground floor office, absorbing the looks and feeling the heel. He remembered the strict faces of detectives at the Venice Station who had ordered him to dummy up about what was happening.

Now, though, the moral heft was too much. Jerry knew he would turn to stone from the *how-could-you* scowls if he didn't level with his people.

After a few minutes he pulled the SWAT commander aside, arguing in a loud whisper that his crew deserved to "know the basics." The commander agreed. The barn doors were open after what just happened, so he spoke. Howard Garrett, the leading suspect in the murder of their former co-boss, had approached Space Matters in his car after his gofer Michael had left Jerry. The SWAT team had to rush in to get everyone down in case Howard tried squeezing off a wild shot. A ringing silence fell over the mansion again.

None of it made sense. Why would a man bent on collecting seventy-five thousand dollars murder the man he required for that money? The commander, now joined by some detectives, said there was no predicting how a sick fuck like Howard behaved. It was the reason that a police helicopter, as unbeknown to Jerry as the SWAT team garrisoned around his office, had been tailing Howard for hours when the El Camino cruised by. They couldn't chance a bullet taking out an innocent, no matter the panic the commandos inflicted. If anyone spotted Howard or Michael again, detectives said to alert them immediately.

Howard on his end probably would've whinnied uproariously about the alarm he had bred without trying if he had known about it. After Michael had picked him up at the café and described Jerry's refusal to go with him, Howard had Michael him drive him by Space Matters to assess what he could. An hour later, when he had returned to his Pasadena apartment with Michael, Howard discovered a message on his answering machine from Jerry.

Pasadena, one of Southern California's envied suburbs, spread out from the base of the San Gabriel Mountains like a pearl broach. The town of about one hundred thousand was a mélange of middle class comforts, New Year's Day extravaganzas, blue blood lineage and shady slums hidden by a modern freeway. Howard, who had moved here from Arcadia, could not have been more out of place and yet less disturbed by it. He had Michael call Jerry back while he fixed himself a cocktail, snatching the receiver when Jerry's voice came on. The dialogue was beyond cold. Jerry, having received fresh instructions from the detectives, asked Howard to meet him on the bench in front of the Los Angeles County Museum of Art adjacent to the La Brea Tar Pits. Howard croaked he would be there.

As Jerry understood it, the LAPD's revised plan involved new, moving parts and old hazards. Facing Howard out in the open was more complicated than dealing with him inside an enclosed office. Outside, the variables were endless. Wardrobe-wise, it was the same as before: Jerry would still be donning the recording device with no bulletproof vest. Detectives tried comforting him that they would be watching and taping every sound from the undercover van they would park on the curb in front of the museum. They said that Jerry was to remain composed if during his time with Howard he looked south, across Wilshire, to the roof of the Mutual Benefit Life skyscraper. SWAT team sharpshooters would be stationed there, high in the air, ready to fire. LAPD marksmen would also be on the roofs of the Art Museum's three buildings. See, they had it covered.

Here, the detectives told Jerry, was what he needed to remember. Should Howard flash a gun or a knife, Jerry was to slowly back away to avoid being hit by police gunfire in the event sharpshooters took preemptive action. Alternatively, if Howard were to grab him and try shoving him down the museum steps and into the El Camino, Jerry was to either duck down below the car roofline or dive into the vehicle to avoid whizzing bullets. Same as before, the police wanted Jerry to prod and coax Howard into being a criminal braggart. Try, they said, to get him talking about Richard's murder, the treachery he planned for him if he failed to deliver the money and Howard's other lunatic agenda. Jerry left for his meeting about 1:20 P.M. with a brain soaked in instructions.

He headed west on Wilshire, allowing his eyes to trace the sweeping architecture—the regal Gothic churches, the black steel towers—that had intoxicated him once. The faster he drove, the more the boulevard skyline cleaved the sunlight into repeating sequences of light and dark, a photographic negative effect on a day of icky surrealism. Under normal circumstances, Jerry could have chatted for hours about many of Wilshire's signature structures, because he had worked in so many and was intrigued by their history. *What did a marble column matter now*, he asked himself? It was all inanimate.

He swung up off Wilshire onto Curson Avenue east of the museum and parked the Seville. His legs were putty sticks as he walked toward the largest of the fenced tar pits. The viscous, black pools, filled with naturally occurring, forty thousand year old asphaltum, had been a popular tourism site delighting school kids and natural history buffs since World War II. On Jerry's day there, the pungent, sulfur smell dancing off the tar made his eyes watery. Of all the places to meet Howard in a city-state like L.A., it had to be next to gooey ponds that trapped once indigenous creatures—bison, ground sloths, saber-toothed cats, mammoths—in writhing, quicksandish deaths.

Jerry edged closer to the designated meeting spot. As he did, he was unable to resist gazing up at the roof of the Mutual Benefit Life building, where the heads of SWAT sharpshooters formed a parapet of unmoving, black dots. Arriving at the bench, with Wilshire over his right shoulder, he sensed more of them on the museum buildings. Somewhere behind the high rises he could hear the thumping blades of a helicopter eager to remain unseen.

Despite the LAPD armada, Jerry's insides were a puddle waiting for the man who had stuck Richard into that mausoleum. That this could be the same person who nearly welled up seeing Jerry at his bedside after his booze-fueled diabetic coma illuminated the viciousness within. "How about a hug, man?" Howard had asked. So, Jerry stared at the tar pit with its replica mammoth stuck in black sludge, snout pointed skyward, braying at its lethal error wandering here. Jerry wanted to laugh ruefully, because he and that beast weren't all that different. Both of their lives had reverted to survival basics.

At 2:03 P.M., Michael dropped Howard off at the plaza and pulled away in the El Camino. Howard marched up the steps in his blue ghost getup, a wink to Jerry that the murder contract on him was pending, and got to the rendezvous bench. There was no shaking of hands. Howard leaned himself up against the rail, his fingers pinching a Kool, looking as relaxed as any museum-goer. His counterpart could practically gargle saliva.

"You alone?" Howard asked.

"Yes."

"Oh hell, I bet you're wired," Howard said dryly.

"Then you bet wrong," Jerry lied.

"Yeah, well, whatever. Say, how's the wife and kid?"

"Fine. They're fine."

"So, do you have anything for me?"

"Like what?"

"Let's not play games again, Jerry."

"This isn't a game. Not to me."

"Then do you have my money? It's been a week."

"No. No I don't. Nothing's changed from the last time we spoke in my office. Richard's mom still has the [life insurance] claim tied up. She thinks her family deserves all of it. I can't do anything about that."

"Yeah, but you could have hit Tammy's parents up. Remember what we covered before?"

"Yes, I do. I remember you threatening me and my family. But I've thought about it since then and I can't bring myself to ask Tammy's dad to clear out his bank account. Seventy-five thousand dollars might break him. He's not that liquid. He's a businessman. Like all of us."

"I see."

"If you'd just give me a little more time; I can't close my eyes and make that money appear. I can't be responsible for what an insurance company will do. Maybe you'd consider taking less than you asked for before. I just went through this thing with Richard. I had to pay lawyers. I don't have money right now."

"There you go again with your *poor me* routine. I can't, I can't, I can't."

"I don't know why you don't believe me."

"You don't, huh? I once believed Richard, and see where that got me? All I'm hearing now is what I heard before. You're useless, Jerry. You really are."

"But I'm not Richard! He screwed me just like you. The whole company might go under because of him."

"That's not my concern anymore."

"Obviously."

"Don't get flip."

"I'm not. I'm trying to make you understand."

The dialogue circled around this same point until Howard had heard enough to adjourn the meeting.

"Jerry, all I have to say is this. You've made your choice and I've made mine. See ya around."

Howard heeled out the second cigarette he had smoked and threw Jerry a smirk. Leisurely, he walked diagonally down the museum steps, towards the west where his silihouette dissolved into battleship-colored air of Los Angeles. The show was over.

After a few minutes lapsed, Jerry stomped his toes on the concrete steps to get blood pumping through his numb legs. By then, the heads of the sharpshooters on top of the Mutual Life building had vanished as had the police van. The evidence had been collected. On the drive to meet detectives back at the Venice Boulevard station for the debriefing, Jerry wore a big smile, expecting Howard would be arrested within a day or two, having now strung himself up by his own words. Tammy and Jude could come home. There could be delirium and a party. Architecture might even become germane again.

The briefing that Jerry believed would lead to them took place in the same drab room where he had been this morning. Jerry felt electric and hyper. The detectives' eyes were lightless. They said that they would need more time to assemble their case against Howard. He had committed some grisly acts during the last few years, acts that went beyond Richard and an earlier victim that they still needed to sift through. They envisioned a multi-count, omnibus indictment that'd guarantee life in prison for him, if not the death penalty. Jerry's smile began flattening as the detectives' explanations continued. Deep down he knew they were about to unload crushing news.

They were. The LAPD was no closer to arresting Howard than they were twenty-four hours ago, detectives acknowledged. The setup had been for naught. The bulky recording device that Jerry had worn underneath his clothes had, in fact, too sharp a hearing. The constant, low frequency street bustle, particularly from RTD public buses grinding up and down Wilshire Boulevard, had rendered his entire conversation with Howard static-laden background talk. Where officers said they expected to hear Howard's voice admitting that he had ordered Richard's execution and his pressure tactics on Jerry was hissing white noise—engine revs and car horns, gear-shifting buses, and a distant ambulance. The drone and static had overwhelmed the recorder's capabilities, or more specifically, the LAPD's.

The tape was inaudible.

Jerry was stupefied. Stupefied and gut-punched. He wasn't electric about a family reunion anymore. He wanted to bolt from the briefing room and scream at the sky. Quietly, detectives asked him to remove his jacket, vest and shirt. They needed to rip the tape up and get the flunky contraption off his reddened skin. Don't despair, they said. Howard was not going to be loose much longer. They would find another way. Jerry grinned thinly. He still had faith in the detectives, just a bushel less than he had at sunrise.

As the debriefing progressed, one of the detectives offered an aside that cut right through Jerry again. He remarked that if the SWAT men reading Jerry's lips through their binoculars had seen his mouth say "Don't shoot" in response to something Howard did, the sharpshooters could have opened up. Under rules of engagement, they would've had the legal authority to fire at Howard. It was ridiculous. Just those two words, barely a clause—*Don't shoot!*—and this whole saga would have ended within a few seconds on the museum plaza. *Don't shoot!* Why hadn't the LAPD told him that earlier?

Jerry wracked his mind, rewinding it to the morning session when he was being prepped, and was positive they had skipped the instruction. Or had they? After the drama of the vest, detectives had schooled him about what to do if Howard attacked and maybe being in his midst crimped his recall for contingencies. Whatever the truth then, knowing those two words would've silenced Howard with a sortie of SWAT bullets created its own half-life of better outcomes inside him. He couldn't stop dwelling over it, fantasying about what could have been the marvelous headline: DE-SIGNER TRICKS POLICE INTO KILLING MURDEROUS CONTRAC-TOR. Why did authorities always term mechanical catastrophes "glitches"?

Detectives volunteered another tidbit about the meeting that gave him unease. They said that after Michael had dropped Howard off, he had parked the El Camino and hid in some nearby bushes. As Howard and Jerry spoke, Michael had surveyed the meeting armed with his own set of binoculars and, likely, that pistol in his back pocket. At least, Jerry reckoned, that was the last heaping of bad news he would be hearing. Officers would be getting to the round-the-clock police protection for him next. Sly Howard was on to them. His "I'll bet you're wired" was their exclamation point confirmation. He knew Jerry was cooperating with authorities and that meant Jerry needed to be shielded. The LAPD was going to need more time to stitch its case against him than was safe for Jerry to be exposed in the wide spaces of Los Angeles. No other way to interpret it.

Actually, there was. The department would not be sending officers to Jerry's side, the detectives informed him. Armed men in blue would not be at his house, sitting with him at the mansion or in his car. What detectives did say in the strongest possible terms, terms that verged on a direct order, was that it was best Jerry relocate after everything that had played out. His new address would be the seventh floor of the Wilshire Hyatt on the east-ern edge of the boulevard between Miracle Mile and downtown. He would be far safer at the hotel, where other threatened witnesses and informants stayed under LAPD watch, than remaining at his unwalled, foothill home whose address, incidentally, Howard knew. Jerry's heart drooped hearing the news that he was about to be warehoused because the LAPD's secret microphone had malfunctioned. But it practically sank into his gray, knit socks when detectives laid out another mandate: Jerry could only go into

Space Matters on a limited basis, once a week at most.

He alerted his private eyes about the dispiriting chain of events from the Venice Boulevard station, and they had their first significant task in the aftermath. They needed to drive him to his Northridge house so he could collect enough clothes and effects to ride out Howard's reign. Jerry discovered his anxiety was nearly as elevated as it was on the museum steps as they chauffeured him to the edge of the Valley, where the good life with Tammy and Jude once bloomed. Being out there now under these circumstances flushed him with a dread he never could have conceived of a month ago. Dread that Howard had staked out his block and had already snuck into the house; dread he would stick a knife into his liver or a bullet into his ear while the *Dragnet* duo stood in the hallway tapping their toes. A little time in the house before mothballing it would have been calming, but Jerry had never packed quicker.

His new living arrangement at the Hyatt amounted to a high security box hundreds of feet above Wilshire. It featured a hard bed, a small closet, a toilet sanitized for his protection, blackout shades and a sunset obstructed view. Jerry was not here as an official, protected witness whose tab taxpayers were picking up as if he were testifying in a blockbuster, federal mob trial. He was merely a citizen guarded by police and paying his own way in an era of gutted public budgets. Even so, LAPD officers rimmed the floor and controlled everyone's movements. Informants were barred from fraternizing with each other and cloistered in rooms arranged by the type of criminal activity that they had gone to authorities to report. Protocol bested liberties for all guests, including Jerry. Authorities warned him, for instance, that he could not venture outside the Hyatt for a millisecond without his private eyes or someone else like Ari on his hip. When he was outdoors, he was hardly free, either. He had to keep his eyes peeled for Howard and detectives apprised of his schedule.

That evening, Jerry phoned Tammy in Ann Arbor from the Hyatt with a rundown on the day Howard's noose tightened a full length. She asked where he was and he told her the police would not allow him to specify it. The gloom in his voice was as obvious as the crackle of the police-bugged phone. Tammy tried cheering him up by describing the new words that Jude had learned and how he attacked Lego blocks with Jerry's same peculiar creativity. Where he normally would have laughed, a tired snigger was all Jerry could manufacture. Tammy reminded him that it would only be another week before he was slated to fly back for a visit. They would enjoy some alone time then. "Can't it be tomorrow?" Jerry exhaled. "Really."

After she hung up, Tammy had trouble forgetting Jerry's portrayal of his terrible day. Howard's wicked gleam, the inaudible tape: would her husband live to see twenty eight? She went to her father, a pragmatic businessman, and told him that the L.A. situation had turned darker. He saw the fear contorting her face, and wanted to do something for his daughter and so he did. He phoned case detectives that very night and announced that he was prepared to wire Jerry seventy-five thousand dollars from his personal bank account. Forget it, the cops chided him; rotten idea. Once Howard had his money, he would have no motivation to keep Jerry and his memories around as witnesses. The game plan, detectives said, was to keep Howard deluded into believing that seventy-five thousand dollars remained his to collect until there was enough sound evidence to pop him. Tammy's father set the phone down.

Knowing nothing about Tammy's intercession, Jerry spent his first night at the Hyatt trying not to fixate on how long his predicament would last. The LAPD should've had Howard doomed with a few of his careless slipups yet all that was lost in white noise. *Technical difficulties, glitches*—Jerry never wanted to hear those expressions again. Still, he promised himself to stay upbeat and keep his nerves hidden better than he had before. He already knew not to linger in front of exposed windows. In his room, he ate what passed for a cheeseburger, took a shower, and tried losing himself in a tedious sitcom. It didn't succeed. Neither did the late night news, where Jerry vaguely heard about how Billy Carter, the president's redneck, beer-swilling brother, had promised never to drink again. There was also something about chaos in Iran, but Islamic nationalism had nothing on Howard's clench.

Howard had spent the rest of his day more productively than Jerry. That afternoon after the SWAT team tracked him, he and Michael went to inspect a building whose owner wanted remodeling bids. That night, Howard sampled the mood around Jerry's city. He phoned Bert, whom he hadn't seen since the Langer's lunch, acting the harried contractor. Bert, a hardworking, chubby Filipino with a kind smile, was chilled. He tried veering the conversation away from anything involving murder to a problematic remodel near downtown, and Howard said he had disengaged from that crap job. Since he *was* bitching about work, Howard complained that a project he and Jerry were technically collaborating on was lagging; CM-2, he said, hadn't "rigged the blinds" or restretched the carpets.

Howard wanted Bert to know it was just business, saying of Jerry, "I still like him." Bert replied he did, too, and if he could wish reality, this would be the last creepy-sweet call from Howard he ever logged. It wouldn't be. Howard explained that his existence would be a lot easier, and thus everybody else's, if Jerry handled his responsibilities. Bert said he would do what he could to hasten a settlement. Before he hung up, Howard reiterated the shop talk was blurring the goodwill behind his call. "I just called to see how you are. We're not enemies. I hope we remain friends for the rest of our lives."

***

Though he had vowed to maintain his composure, Jerry was pacing in his room with cabin fever barely forty-eight hours into his stay at the Hyatt. His private eyes, the one's he paid by the hour and thought of as his *Dragnet* duo, observed it in their second visit there and realized it would only deepen. They spoke out of his presence and returned saying they had good news. Jerry could move around the city feeling relatively secure about it provided he was willing to ditch his old skin. What he needed, they said, was to fashion a disguise that Howard would neither recognize nor expect. Jerry to achieve this needn't undergo a facelift, cross dress, act crippled, or pierce his nose punk rocker-style. He only needed to leave behind the persona of the traditional, young executive for a remade identity. Jerry took their suggestion to heart and knew where he could fabricate a new appearance. He phoned Ari, who sent a box over to the hotel.

When he stepped outside the Hyatt that first time, Jerry no longer was a space designer in nice threads intended to make him look ten years older. He was an unapologetic hick. Instead of a Givenchy suit, Italian silk tie and razor shaved face, Jerry was outfitted in a bumblebee yellow Caterpillar Construction T-shirt, matching baseball cap and a five o'clock shadow. The long hair he had begun growing into a ponytail would take its time coming in. Strangest of all, Jerry forsook trousers for something he had never worn, Levi Strauss blue jeans. The new Jerry, thanks to Ari, could have fallen off a Midwestern tractor.

He dressed in his usual business suit the few times he visited Space

Matters with his private eyes. Jerry couldn't explain away his farm boy attire to his staff if he was still forbidden from telling them everything. In general, his private eyes kept him out of his hick getup anytime they thought Jerry might bump into acquaintances. They worried that otherwise harmless gossip about Jerry's camouflage might trickle to Howard, who seemed to have an ear for such things.

There simply wasn't that much Jerry could do in those first weeks except to force himself to plug along within the restricted geometry of his new Hyatt lifestyle. A little daylight amnesia would have helped. His sketches lacked punch. Each time he picked up the phone, the background hiss on the line reminded him that the LAPD was eavesdropping. When he looked down at his watch and flexed for his commute home, he remembered his wife and boy were closer to Lake Michigan than the Pacific Ocean. Cash flow was no friend, either, shakier than it had been during the trough with Richard. Jerry had to hustle to gin up new clients at the same time he tried restarting jobsites frozen by Howard's liens. "Things going wrongly or haphazard" he wrote himself in a note. "No direction." If it weren't for Fegen's business, Jerry would probably have to consider lopping off some of his staff.

"Don't shoot!" That's all he had had to say to earn his old life back.

CHAPTER THIRTEEN

WHERE JERRY LEARNED FEAR

As a boy growing up in North Hollywood, Jerry was never quite sure whether the outlandish things he was told were true or imagined so he invented a little game he called "the opposite test" to figure it out. If he was having difficulty, for example, accepting his mother's insistence that nuclear weapon testing was suffocating mankind with cancerous radiation, he asked himself if the reverse was likelier—that lethal rays couldn't possibly be present, because no one was dropping dead on his block—and felt better. Failing that logic, he could always stomp his legs to see if authentic pain ricocheted back.

Regrettably, none of those strategies prepared him years later for Howard because Howard's existence was as palpable as Richard's removal from the earth. Jerry's ignorance about folks like him was homemade. In his childhood, apocalyptic dangers and infectious germs were more commonly discussed than people able to trick the world they were harmless until the blood ran. It was the invisible threats that killed you in the Schneiderman domicile.

Jerry's father was an elementary school principal, pro bono lawyer, and likable guy who had a blast acting as a child. Innocence tinged with mischief burbled through Art Schneiderman, not macho ambition. At toy stores, he was on the floor playing with the latest models while Jerry stood guard for humorless sales clerks. The other dads on their block northeast of downtown were different. Many of them spent their work weeks as factory grunts employed at defense contractor Lockheed Corp. in adjacent

149

Burbank. Weekends for them circled around beer drinking and car tinker-ing. Not Art, a short, athletic guy with brown hair and intelligent eyes. He played the accordion and rode his Harley Davidson.

Peter Pan-like to be sure, Jerry's father nonetheless provided him with a more grounded upbringing than his mother. Vera was the dominant figure in Jerry's youth, ruling the family with a neurotic gyroscope that she prob-ably wished she didn't possess. She was bright and inquisitive as Jerry would turn out, but also paranoid, manipulative and challenging to understand. Bouts of depression could immobilize the dainty woman sometimes so cru-elly that she required young Jerry's assistance picking out her clothes, fixing her coffee and other chores not required of most boys. And her unortho-doxy was just getting going.

Vera was a germaphobe who made her family schlep its own silverware to restaurants and banned Jerry from sharing in friends' birthday cakes. When Jerry's paternal grandmother contracted leukemia, she refused to let her kids eat at her house, suspecting that cancer was contagious. Mysterious chemicals scared her, as well. Once after she once noticed a yellow truck with a hazard symbol triangle tooling around, she forced Jerry and his sister to strip off their clothes to take a decontaminating, backyard shower. The television itself was hardly guiltless, either, with her conviction that modern electronics burped unsafe radiation. Best her kids not watch much of it. The air was already infected with enough isotopes. In fact, on the day of a big Soviet nuclear test, Vera picked her kids up early from school, drove them home and made them wait in hallway while she paced anticipating a cloud of Dr. Strangelove fallout about to encircle the globe. There would be no meatloaf that night.

Hardest about all this was that Vera would not regularly take the anti-anxiety medicine that would've tempered her affliction and made the fami-lies' life easier. Jerry, in some ways, was a casualty of her disorder, confused by his mother's fear-mongering and arguing with her about the causes of disasters. After the explosion of December 14, 1962, when he was eleven, Jerry started appreciating how the unpredictable the world that his mother mistrusted was.

It was on that evening that a silvery cargo plane came pitching out of a wet fog and toward the earth with its propellers spinning full bore. The Flying Tiger "Super H" Constellation loaded with 40,000 pounds of freight and still sloshing with jet fuel was not going to make it to the runway at

Burbank airport a mile and change away. Rather, it was destined to become an inadvertent ICBM aimed directly at the gritty, little block where the Schneidermans resided. The aircraft with a wingspan half the length of a football field slammed into Jerry's neighborhood just after 10:00 P.M., creating a sidewalk-shaking wallop that people felt miles away. The impact killed all five people aboard instantly and three more on the ground, while obliterating six homes, two small businesses and locals' sense of tranquility. The plane hit the ground with such violence that it sheared the nose cone from the fuselage and stoked a one hundred foot high fireball visible for miles.

For Jerry, that night of fire trucks and chaos, gas fumes and death, was evidence that separating terrifying reality from the deceptively untrue would be his lifelong riddle. He need only walk around the next day to sop that up. A nearby billboard had survived the accident, but you wouldn't know what it was advertising anymore because one of the plane's propellers had gouged a hole through it. Also unrecognizable was the wispy rubble of the house across from Jerry's, which entombed the body of Jerry's friend's sister. Cathleen had been a cute, sixteen year old girl getting ready for a late date when the plane that should've been thousands of feet above her canceled her future. The Schneiderman neighborhood had detonated because the thirty-eight year old Flying Tiger pilot had suffered a fatal heart attack and slumped over on the controls next to a co-pilot unable to reverse the nosedive. Jerry didn't know those particulars, or consider it miraculous that his family and nearby apartments were untouched by flying debris. He only remembered hearing his fraught mother, who must've had a special instinct that night, holler at her husband as the aircraft plunged out of the mist and towards their rooftop. "Arty, Arty," she said. "It's going to crash!"

Thanks to the role reversals with his parents, Jerry half reared himself and his sister, Carol, who was two years younger than him and trapped in the same, odd household. Some days their mother's melancholy was so all-consuming that she was unable to pry herself from bed. This further estranged the Schneiderman kids from those whose mothers drove them to the beach and ice cream parlors, even if there were pesticide trucks around or a nuclear test scheduled for a Russian steppe. At public school, the normalcy was only marginally better. Jerry was classified as a pudgy, smart kid who the teachers wrote off as "unmotivated and bored." He earned Bs on half effort, preferring to daydream over memorizing formulas and battle dates, and was skipped a year ahead on aptitude. The bullies had a ball thrashing the kid from Bellingham Avenue, anyway. Their fists bruised Jerry's body, busted his nose and sometimes stole his lunch. They taunted him as a whale, a loser and a Jew. They dared him to punch back and he usually refused. Drawing and artwork is where Jerry's talents shimmered, and his tormentors were powerless there. Shapes and dimensions ballooned off his pencil. Engineer, architect—Jerry's talented left hand could draw his future.

Nobody would have expected that an underachieving, tubby kid like him would've been endowed with a special athleticism. But he was. During summer, Jerry's father and a partner ran a kiddy day camp near Laurel Canyon. Swimming constituted a major pastime there and who didn't love pool races? Answer: any child pitted against Jerry. His butterball body plowed through the water, defying fluid mechanics, ahead of the disbelieving competition. Sometimes he didn't bother using a single stroke and melded windmilling arms with hectic leg chops. He beat almost everyone to the finish line. The water was his natural habitat. At ten, he jumped into a chilly pool at a friend's birthday party to save a drowning little girl that no one had noticed had been underwater for forty seconds. At eleven, he had earned his junior lifeguard certificate.

Jerry's block was populated with lower, middle class Angelenos in standard ranch houses and post-moderns. It had been a whitebread neighborhood, close to the Hollywood Freeway and yet a million miles from the real Hollywood. By the early 1960s, more Jewish families like Jerry's moved in and redneck types packed up for outlying towns. The Schneiderman house was no ode to modernity, though, even for its small, nondescript street. At 1,100 squarefeet, it contained only a few small rooms and its original appliances. Jerry and his sister shared a bedroom there until Jerry turned eleven. Nearing puberty, he relocated into the den, but the typical teenage decorations—posters of all-star shortstops or NASA rockets—were absent. Jerry had no ardent notions of what he would be in life. He merely wanted an exciting future without irrational worries rammed down his gullet.

At thirteen, he began saving for a car. Soon he had a part time job drafting for a real estate appraiser. When he wasn't there or at school, Jerry socialized with the local rabbis, who saw something unique about him. They slipped him advice about making it and sometimes a little whiskey that they fibbed was schnapps. They recounted war stories to him, and why not? Jerry's childhood for the most part was pre-adulthood. Ski trips with his father to Squaw Valley in Central California's High Sierras constituted his treasured moments. The rest of the time he pined for independence.

Jerry dressed like the little grownup he was. For as long as he could remember, he wore plaid shirts and dark colored "dress slacks" to school. Blue jeans that his blubbery thighs made swish when he walked were off limits. Capping off the peculiarity, he toted a briefcase to school instead of a book bag. Alex P. Keaton, the precocious teen in the 1980s television sitcom *Family Ties*, had nothing on 1960s Jerry. At thirteen, he decided to do something about his weight. Being porky in L.A.'s culture of vanity was going to impede whatever he decided to do and it was no way to attract girls, either. Jerry, for these reasons and the challenge of it, put himself on a strict diet, eating once a day and then only meat and lettuce. There would be no ice cream, no slipups. Five months later his protein diet had knocked 50 pounds off his once flabby frame.

He enrolled at the renowned Art Center of Design downtown, where his talent for geometric sketching was honed and praised in technical school fashion. It was in graduating a year and a half early and one day shy of his twentieth birthday in 1971 when Jerry winced at the lesson of post-college existence. His diploma was worth about twenty-four dollars a day in salary in the impersonal world of corporate space planning. His bosses billed clients tens of thousands of dollars for his schematics and then rewarded him with janitor's wages. Whether a firm hired him to design offices at city halls or libraries or to develop plans for cloud-poking high rises, it was always the same formula: his creativity cheaply bought.

When Jerry was poached by a competitor and relocated back to his hometown from Chicago, he believed he had gotten his break. He would march up that corporate ladder now, show what he could do. Instead it was his naiveté that was showing, because the job was another step ladder to invisibility. Management was so paranoid about its eager beaver, young designers poaching clients that they were forbidden from interacting with them until they had hoarded five years of experience. Jerry lasted three subjugated months at the company before skipping to another. Now he was only slightly less dejected with his career choice.

Even so, it was at his last job where he first shook hands with Richard, a gifted planner and even better salesman that management mysteriously underutilized. When Jerry could take the corporate turnbuckles no longer, he suggested that they should be their own bosses and Richard agreed. In alphabetical order, Jerry had passed through industry bigwigs Carnelly

Seleine; ERD, Heitschmidt Mounce Associates; Richmond, Manhoff &. March; and SLS Environetics. Since he had never made much money from them, he intended to capitalize on the experience that he received and the exploitation that he had withstood to build something better. Something his. Now he had a likeminded partner to accomplish it.

And still he was flying blind. Jerry knew little then about Richard's tempests and roguish behavior from his first marriage, or the whirlwind trysts and irate ex-lovers that ensued. He was ignorant about his partner's dabbles with pop psychology to slay what ailed him, including several treks to Esalen, a famous retreat on California's central coast that combined Eastern mysticism with sex, "gestalt therapy," yoga and other New Age self-enlightenment. Jerry, similarly, was unaware that Richard's escape to places like that shredded his future with another promising space planning startup. In many ways, Jerry preferred not delving much into others' pasts, because his own background was too painful to revisit.

Tammy's entrance into his life promised the stability that'd always ducked him. The two crossed paths around 1973 at the ABC Entertainment Center in Century City when Jerry was space planning there and Tammy worked as a corporate secretary. One look at him and the whip smart Michigan girl was smitten. Jerry, however, had another reaction to the crush. He was indifferent, having little experience with women interested in awkward him. Besides, Tammy was so youthful looking herself he wondered if she were jailbait, and he was too swamped with work for flirtatious questioning. One of Jerry's jobs was salvaging bonehead space planning leases negotiated by Nixon Administration campaign operatives—men paid to discredit the president's opponents (think "Communists for McGovern")—that ABC hired in off-election time. Jerry assumed that the network had retained them as political thanks to Nixon or for future patronage. Either way, the sordidness of it burrowed into him.

Tammy continued cajoling friends to get Jerry to ask her out even after she left ABC in the post-Watergate era. Nothing happened. Eventually, she jettisoned the intermediaries and forthrightly asked him to accompany her to a new sports bar. Tammy might've been a daddy's girl barely out of the University of Wisconsin, but she knew that Jerry was her knight. Their natural chemistry was so obvious that on their first date she brought him to meet her parents, who were out in L.A. on vacation. Later that night, she phoned them to declare that Jerry *was* the man she would marry. He never went home after his second date with her. He moved straight into Tammy's apartment and into the first significant romance of his undersexed life.

Eighteen months later, they wed at an elaborate Jewish temple ceremony in Michigan near Tammy's hometown. (Horndog Richard tagged along, bedding one of Tammy's promiscuous bridesmaids, then imitating Jerry later by settling down with his own young wife.) Tammy's prophecy that she and Jerry were meant to be had been prescient. In their first years they scrimped and lived modestly. Tammy earned her teaching credential and accepted a job with Cedar Sinai Hospital near Beverly Hills. On the weekends, the doe-eyed administrator who resembled one of Marcia Brady's girlfriends was responsible for signing papers for terminal patients.

They moved to Northridge, a master-planned suburb with blocks formed like clamshells and backyard barbecues standard. This was frontier Los Angeles, the last of the countrified suburbs. There was a just-built freeway, the 118, to get commuters where they were going, and markets and pharmacies down the street for seedling families. South of the Schneidermans' house was Chatsworth, fast becoming the pornography capital of the U.S. North of them swelled bedroom communities like Santa Clarita, where many LAPD officers resided for the cheaper housing, and Palmdale, where the new Space Shuttle sometimes landed and secret military aircraft pierced the sky.

Even as Jerry later struggled with Richard's mood swings, his life with Tammy beat to a homey, circadian predictability. Once every week was *Bunco Night*, an evening of competitive dice throwing lubricated with friends, finger foods, and glib commentary. A few days later it was *Gourmet Night*, a dinner party potluck with culinary themes. These were not excuses to imbibe too much wine or gorge on carbohydrates during the work week. Tammy organized the fun and sought family order in service to the picket fence lifestyle that she had been dreaming about since her Midwest youth.

After their first son, Jude, was born, Tammy showed herself to be a devoted stay-at-home mom. She just wished Jerry spent more time in Northridge and less at the Space Matters mansion. Many weekends he was so fried he could barely peal himself off the couch. Tammy, by early 1979, lobbied him to pare back his maniacal hours so they could get to a movie or a play. The offerings were tremendous: *Deer Hunter, Grease, Superman, The Wiz*—just something not involving square footage. Someday, Jerry would say. Despite the workload, he knew he had it good with Tammy, loving her right onto a pedestal. "She's everything I ever wanted," Jerry told friends.

***

All those years removed from North Hollywood, and weeks after Richard was shot dead where he should have been the safest, Jerry tried acclimating to life in his hotel room—all 350 square feet of it. He phoned in work instructions to Bert, called Tammy long distance and made late night visits to Fegen with his private eyes. It was a black and white existence of joyless routines. The *Dragnet* duo reminded him what the detectives had, saying that he would not live forever under Howard's thumb. Because they had worked at the LAPD and the Sheriff's Department and still had peers there, they were able to extract fragments of firsthand information about the investigation. The evidence collection was progressing, they said. What they did not reveal to their client—just yet, anyway—was the shit-kicker Howard seemed to metastasize into after he punched the clock for the day.

At first, the omissions were anesthesia for Jerry, who had a hard enough time complying with the LAPD's instruction that he be non-specific about his living conditions to the friends and family that he contacted. His standard line was that he was residing under police protection at an "area hotel," next question. For most of his kin that he phoned from the Hyatt, this was bothersome but tolerable. Jerry's Chicago grandmother wanted him to know during their conversations that he wasn't going through his crisis alone. She was confident that she had secured him a cosmic guarantee of victory. Upon first learning about what'd befallen her California grandson, she had gone immediately to her favorite rabbi and made a donation to his temple. Her rabbi was not like the other Windy City rabbis. Jerry's grandmother believed hers had a direct connection to God. And God had assured him who then assured Jerry's grandmother that Jerry would outlast Howard. As insurance in case her rabbi was mistaken, she told Jerry that she prayed for him all the time.

True to form, Jerry's mother was a tornado of ideas and conspiracy theories in their exchanges. Vera Schneiderman was not content to sit back and let the authorities do all the extrapolating. She frothed with suggestions and hunches about his predicament that he would hear nowhere else. What exactly, Jerry finally snorted, did she want him to do? She was thankful he asked. She wanted him to do the wise thing, and to her that required Jerry flip through his Rolodex and place a few calls. Somebody, she said, would have to know how he could reach the West Coast branch of the Israeli Mafia, because nobody was as competent as them. Vera was sure that they would cheerfully rub Howard out if Jerry paid them well. Jerry slapped his head. *The Israeli Mafia? Really?* She was the second person, after his business lawyer, to advocate preemptive murder of Howard as a way out of the Hyatt.

His mother harped on another theme while she had Jerry listening. She would not stop questioning him about what *he* had done to ensnare himself in a killing that had driven him and his family into hiding. "What did you do, Jerry?" she kept asking. "It must've been something." He had answered, louder with every response that nothing happened, but she had clamped onto his triangular dealings with Richard and Howard. She even hypothesized that they must have been in cahoots against him before turning on each other. "What did you do, Jerry?" she continued asking. Nobody ever called his mother dim.

Before this madness, Vera had enjoyed Howard. When she had phoned or visited Space Matters while he was CM-2's construction boss, Howard had poured on the charm. He angled for information about Jerry and acted dismayed that Jerry wasn't more appreciative of his mother's attentions. "Your son isn't treating you right, Mrs. Schneiderman," he would say. "I'm going to tell him he better, because you deserve it. He should be buying you flowers every week." Now that she knew that Howard had puppeteered Richard's murder and was hunting her son, Vera revealed her long-simmering hunch about him to Jerry. To her, Howard was more than a psychotic. Far more. She believed, in fact, that he was a Los Angeles foot soldier in a far-reaching international conspiracy trafficking in bloodshed, narcotics, and other contraband that she loathed saying over the phone. So, she badgered Jerry to confess about the tentacles that had suctioned around his ankles, and any sordid global drug deals they involved, even if she knew almost nothing about drugs or any theoretical deals for them.

After hearing as much of it as he could, Jerry told her to stop her ranting about loony shadow networks. "Enough, mother! Enough." Vera bit her lip on the subject, then turned her mind to tangential ones. She implored Jerry to let her come into Space Matters to tidy up his messy office while he was out. Jerry told her no, and next bickered with her to stop phoning his staff to see how they were faring during the crisis. Three words came to Jerry about his mother's mania: Howard strikes again.

***

This was no pleasure flight. It was a blast off from California. Jerry boarded the jetliner that would deliver him to Tammy and Jude in Michigan with his company adrift and an intuitive killer waiting for his return. He took any good he could find, and hearing those plane doors hermetically sealed was comforting, even if it did nothing for inner peace. Bringing Ari along in the event Howard or his men showed up was no breezy move itself. Traveling with Ari involved tolerating his oversized personality and Jerry wasn't sure his nervous system could at the moment. *Just enjoy the clouds*, he thought.

The first plane trip to Michigan was more relaxing. Back then, Jerry still believed in a sequence that would locate Richard's killer and reunite his family in Southern California with their emotional register intact. Back then, when the jet out of Los Angeles International Airport crossed above Hillside Memorial where Richard was interred, he felt differently about his ex-partner. Jerry had wanted to shed a tear for him then. Today, he could have denounced Richard for uncaging Howard into his world.

Halfway into the trip, probably somewhere over the Nebraska cornfields, Ari, who never could sit still, unbuckled his seat belt. The stewardesses had begun serving cocktails to the first class passengers from the drink cart and Ari was gearing up to join them. As the flight attendants fussed over people a few rows ahead of he and Jerry, Ari lifted out of his chair, snuck up to the cart and began wheeling it comically down the aisle. "Cocktails, cocktails. Sir, would you like a drink?" The former mercenary pranced through the first class section with a towel draped over one of his arms and his stocky derriere swishing side to side. "What about you, madam?" he asked with a saccharine tone. "I mix you something strong. You forget trip." Within two minutes of his hambone bartending, Ari had the front rows of the aircraft in stitches. The stewardesses thought he was a riot, too, a real original, and allowed him to entertain their passengers. When the plane de-boarded at Detroit International, they filled up Ari's duffel bag with close to one hundred mini booze bottles. They said he was welcome anytime as entertainment. On rethinking things, Jerry was glad he had invited him.

Meeting them at the gate was Tammy, Jude and some of Tammy's family. Jerry looked dead at them as he entered the terminal and they didn't recognize him or Ari. For fun, Jerry walked around and came up behind them, tapping Tammy on the shoulder. "Jerry!" She jumped into his arms while little Jude clutched his pant leg. After a long kiss, Tammy stepped back for a view of her husband and saw that he was Jerry, devolved. He wore a jean jacket, yellow Caterpillar shirt, yellow Caterpillar hat, and black and yellow Caterpillar construction boots. Adding to the new him was long hair he straightened every morning with a blow dryer and roped into a ponytail. Tammy's folks looked on probably thinking she was flirting with a farmer.

At home in Ann Arbor, Jerry and Tammy took a walk to update each other on the occurrences in their respective cities. Tammy was distressed about how gaunt Jerry appeared. He didn't feel any better as Tammy recounted to him how her kin, the Wilsons, were handling the stress. As a whole, they were sympathetic to Jerry's life in hiding. They just couldn't understand how he had entwined himself with an embezzler and a killer. How someone as gentle as him could ever have been in the same business with despicable sorts like that? It was his mother's doubts all over again. "Jerry, what did you do?"

Tammy acknowledged there had been a family dustup before he had landed. It had erupted after one of her two brothers, a collections attorney, predicted that Jerry's endangerment might become their danger. If killers were pursuing Jerry in California, he said, it was reasonable to assume they might stalk him in Michigan and take out the lot of them. Howard knew about the family, right? Tammy resented her brother's insinuation, and the barbs zinged inside their childhood house. "Where do you want us to go?" she snapped. "Iowa?" Tammy's father told his grown kids to restrain themselves. Whatever they made of Jerry, they supported Tammy.

She had gotten noticeably thinner since the murder, even with the baby bulge, but was determined that her marriage outlast the spring of 1979. Jerry's five days in Michigan confirmed that to her family. On the day he left for L.A., it was as if he were returning to the battlefield for a second tour of duty. Tammy, just as before, cried in his arms at Detroit International. Before long, they told each other, there'd be a reunion in Northridge and a continuation of Bunco nights.

CHAPTER FOURTEEN

WHEN ACQUITAL BURNS

On some mornings when his private eyes visited his hotel room bearing coffee and donuts, Jerry wished he could just write them a check to omit reciting to him the wicked things they had learned about Howard's past. With each revelation they gradually presented to him, a portrait emerged of a blue collar burnout done with the pretense of trying to be a respectable contractor anymore. Whatever the tripwire—money woes, the escalating drugs he was ingesting, an ancient malice in him—Howard was not as cautious as he had once been behind his professional handshake and first-rate business cards. He had a new persona spreading havoc-for-profit rather than a mangy opportunist retaliating when he could. Jerry could only hear so much about him in one sitting.

Howard's previous boss learned from experience that confronting him could be hazardous to one's future. Before he had been hired on at Space Matters, Howard had been a freelance contractor generating many of his paystubs from Smythe & Hargill. Sometime in the late 1970s, his boss there, Vic Platte, had purchased a West L.A. home and envisioned Howard giving it a facelift. Howard, conscious that Platte controlled what future corporate work was thrown his way, installed new windows, hinged doors, did some carpentry and added supplemental painting. He billed the work "at cost," which brought no windfall to him. Essentially, Howard's sweat was a gift.

Afterwards, according to what the LAPD uncovered, Howard and Platte wrangled over the job. Apparently, Howard got in the last word by torching his boss' garage in retaliation and possibly threatening him. So what had Platte replied when Richard phoned him for a reference some time later? He described Howard as solid. Jerry marveled whether it could be true. A killer had been handed off to Space Matters by someone who had personally witnessed Howard's dark core, and now people in West L.A. avoided standing in front of large windows.

At first blush, one never would have gleaned that Howard was an animal behind his tool belt. Outwardly, he was the gruff embodiment of red blooded, American self-reliance. He had started with nothing and by 1977 raked in twenty-five thousand annually, doing double that in his best year. Before his debt problems, Howard had a house, several cars in his driveway, lawyers on retainer and an impressive collection of equipment. An outsider taking all this in would see his arc. Howard was a bootstraps success.

He had been born in Mount Vernon, Missouri near the Missouri-Arkansas border in September 1932, a Midwestern kid with a decent upside. His parents divorced when he was four, and it was mainly his Baptist mother, Mabel, who reared him. She remarried, and the family relocated to Southern California's San Gabriel Valley when Howard was seven. After graduating from Alhambra's Mark Keppel High School in 1949, he relocated north to the Bay Area, where his biological father—Howard, Sr.—lived. There, junior was admitted to the carpenters' local, taking jobs parceled out at the union hall.

Howard's law-breaking nature debuted up north, too. In December 1949, he was accused of shoplifting from a drugstore on the Fort Ord Army base near Monterrey, making him the first member of his family to be arrested. In subsequent weeks he would be charged with stealing a car, and in ensuing years his mug shot continued to be snapped. He was cited for reckless driving in L.A., and petty theft in Culver City. In 1954, after the Korean War ended, he was apprehended for failure to register for the draft and possession of a phony draft card. The following year he was busted for burglary. But his misbehaving abruptly stopped after that incident—why, nobody knew. For the next eighteen years, Howard behaved like a reformed man. No more handcuffs, no more sirens in the rear view mirror. Carpentry seemed to have rendered him legitimate.

Every hardhat needs a woman, and Howard was no exception. In 1959, he married Alpha Hart. They stayed together for six years before divorcing over irreconcilable differences. Single, he continued his path to respectability with a contractor's license already in-hand and added an AA business degree from Pasadena Junior College in 1961. Before long, the Missourian had his real estate license and, broadly speaking, proof of redemption. He even contemplated attending law school.

Howard made another commitment instead, marrying Carol in 1969. She had a fleshpot gloss about her with a heavily make-upped face, poufy hair and hour glass figure that reminded some of an aging Vegas cocktail waitress. They had been in Arcadia for seven years and in Monrovia before then. They were divorcing now, or leaning that way. Officially, they were still a couple, living together in their Pasadena apartment with Carol knowing things about him that nobody else alive did. Her husband's return to old habits in the 1970s was one of them.

He was arrested in Los Angeles for driving under the influence in January 1973 and then again on the same charge in June 1977. Police in Mojave County, Arizona detained Howard fourteen months later for second degree grand theft burglary. Trouble was, Arizona authorities were unaware that their man in custody had malice fly-papered to him, or that he personified what the crazed anchor in the movie *Network* had fulminated on camera: *I'm mad as hell and I'm not going to take it anymore!* They saw him just as a common burglar.

***

Unfortunately, Jerry's private eyes told him, they hadn't yet covered Howard's seminal aggression. By the time they had finished, their client laid on the bed with the sheets knotted between his fingers.

Across America, August 1977 was a month of endings. Elvis Presley died of drugs and an irregular heartbeat. The wisecracking Groucho Marx perished from pneumonia at seventy-seven. Even Volkswagen went slightly extinct, announcing it was phasing out its iconic Bug. Howard for his part wasn't so much extinguishing as welcoming when August started, but that was temporary. It was during that month Howard invited a skinny, twenty-six year old heroin addict named Tim Dwight to move into his two-bedroom traditional in Arcadia. A mutual friend thought pairing them would be a beneficial match. Tim was being released from the California Rehabilitation Center in Riverside County east of L.A. with a newly shaved head and a rickety commitment to sobriety. By living with Howard, he would be removed from the temptations of his old haunts in Pomona and around a man who valued a full day's labor. What was in it for Howard wasn't declared.

Wheeling up to his old place on Coronado Drive southwest of the race-track and Arcadia's mall, a newcomer never would've guessed the house was a killing field. The gold-painted residence had a red porch, double front doors and three large, inviting windows carved out of its stucco face. Crown-ing the home was a decorative, gabled sub-structure that gave the illusion of hovering mid-air on misty nights. Howard at the time had room for Tim because he and Carol were no longer living together. Howard divulged to friends that she had wanted to patch things up, and that he was playing along and helping her with chores so he could get her company insurance with Thrifty Drug to pay for his spinal surgery.

If Tim hoped to make a good first impression with Howard, scoring heroin just hours after state rehab released him showed that he knew noth-ing about etiquette. A few days later, Tim underscored his reckless love affair with the needle when he drove away in Howard's El Camino without permission on a search for more powder. His pursuit led him to Oxnard, a farming town north of Los Angeles known for its strawberries and oil production, where he scored an ounce and took it to a friend's place to party. Police were waiting, too, busting down the door and tossing Tim and his friends in jail. The only intelligent move Tim made was giving the cops an alias so they were unapprised that the state had just freed him.

But Tim was the uninformed one. Being a stranger, he could not have realized that by gallivanting off in the Chevy, he had infuriated Howard on such a venomous level that it awakened the misanthrope in him for the rest of his life. Any morsel of goodwill that Howard had retained through his unsatisfying existence was squished in the tracks of the car that Tim took. The newly constituted Howard, as Richard, Jerry, Luis Buonsanti and so many others were about to learn firsthand, harbored a necrotic hate for anyone he believed had wronged him. No longer would he restrain him-self; the victimized must act. Moreover, Howard's beloved El Camino kept secrets that its owner was desperate to maintain. He would have preferred it reduced to scrap metal than have it implicated, investigated or otherwise scrutinized by police. That car with the sightline of a prowling hammerhead shark was an extension of him.

When a week passed with no sign of the El Camino, Howard's vileness ruptured. He pressured Glenn Colley, the man who had recommended his houseguest, and another acquaintance nicknamed "Caveman" to accompany him to the Pomona home of one of Tim's friends. Inside, Howard told the family that if they didn't disclose Tim's whereabouts, they would be sorry. Neither Robert nor Emma Robertson furnished him with what he sought, so Howard and Caveman tied up the couple and their two children. Howard reverted to old tricks for the next stage. He shoved the barrel of his pistol into Emma's mouth. Her husband got it next, Howard firing his gun next to his ear and smacking him for good measure. On the way out, Howard gave the family twenty-four hours to locate Tim or he might return, presumably to get Medieval with them.

Tim blithely phoned Howard a few days later to say he was out of jail, no harm, no foul. Not to Howard; to him it was all foul. Immediately, he got a lift to Oxnard to bring his car and houseguest back to Arcadia. From thereon in, Howard deemed Tim an intolerable threat. Around dusk on Monday, September 13, 1977, he invited Glenn to the house to discuss the predicament. Howard and Tim were sitting in the study when Glenn arrived. Howard gripped a drink, legs casually crossed, with painkillers out for his back. Tim nursed a Greyhound, bobbing his head and behaving high. Glenn said he would join them after he used the bathroom. He was just zipping up his pants when he heard a "thunk" that he would never forget. It sounded like someone thrashing a watermelon with a cane. Another thunk then registered followed by a heavier, crashing noise.

When he jogged to the study, Glenn noticed that positions had shifted. No longer was Tim lounging in a chair near Howard's desk slurping a vodka cocktail. He was face up on the floor with a couple of bloody gashes on the side of his head from where Howard had clocked him with the butt of a rifle. Howard now loomed over his houseguest clutching the weapon while Tim pleaded to hear the reason that he had been clubbed. "Why, Howard?" he begged. "What did I do?" Howard, in a trance-like state with bulging eyes and veins, said nothing. He whacked Tim again with the wooden stock, this time so ferociously that it split it down the middle. Tim wasn't talking anymore after that. The only movement was blood coursing out of his skull and onto Howard's yellow shag carpeting.

Before Glenn could do anything, Howard aimed the rifle at *him* and said stonily, "You're involved in this, too, so help me." At that instant, Glenn realized that he had been duped into being an accomplice to a felony. Then Howard was yelling he that couldn't have blood all over his house, and demanded Glenn grab towels from the master bedroom to sop up the mess. After he bashed Tim once more, Howard kneeled next to him, putting his ear to his chest and said in a voice returning to usual. "I don't hear anything." He rose from the body, and noticing Glenn's dismay, tried justifying the bludgeoning as self-defense. "I'm tired," Howard sighed, "of having to sleep with a gun under my pillow."

They rolled Tim's body into a tan, fuzzy blanket and another covering. It was dark outside as they carried the freight out of the house with the hovering window and laid it in the El Camino's open cargo hold. They added a white painter's drop cloth next and busily addressed the mundane. Howard made Glenn drive to the corner market to rent a rug cleaner to remove the blood stains from his carpeting. After it was steam cleaned, it was time for a burial.

They drove east, away from the downtown skyscrapers that Howard once serviced, and toward the sagebrush spaces. They stopped briefly at Glenn's parent's home in Covina in the central San Gabriel Valley so Glenn could snag an empty gasoline container. Afterwards, they were on the San Bernardino Freeway again with a skull-cracked junkie wrapped in the back. At the interchange with the freeway that led to Las Vegas to the north and Disneyland to the south, Howard swerved to the right. Glenn, on Howard's word, tossed the brown paper bag containing the bloody towels out the window and the bag holding the dismantled rifle next. Some of it landed in a flood control wash.

They continued east and steered off the freeway when they reached Redlands around 10:30 P.M. Howard stopped near a Union 76 service station and had Glenn fill up the five gallon metal gas container. Howard jumped back on the San Bernardino Freeway and drove until they arrived at Live Oak Road in Yucaipa. They were in the boonies now, closer to Palm Springs than L.A., in rattlesnake hills that nobody sane would stumble around at night.

Howard went to the most lightless area he could find and slapped the brakes. They hefted Tim's shrouded body out of the cargo hold and set it down. Quietly, they got out the red-and-gold gas can and soaked their freight. So as not to burn with it, they poured a trail of fuel from the body to a safe area away. Howard, wearing a blue parka and tennis shoes, lit a match and flicked it without reservation. Tim's body was engulfed in seconds. Time to go, Howard gestured. He later told Glenn that by dumping

Tim here instead of the Angeles National Forest behind his Arcadia home police might try pinning the murder on Tim's Pomona heroin connection. Apparently slipping Howard's mind was the possibility that Tim still might have been alive, screaming silently as his flesh burned to a crisp under the desert stars.

San Bernardino County Sheriffs discovered the body the next day. It was still smoking, as if it had a story to share. The corpse was so severely charred that police had to send dental records to Loma Linda University nearby to identify it as Tim Dwight. Police interviewed Glenn thirty-two days later. Petrified as he was about what Howard would do to him if he knew he was squealing, he offered police a skillful account of everything. He told them about the takeover at the Richardson house, Tim's rifle whipping on the shag and his funeral pyre in Yucaipa.

Detectives pressured and wheedled Glenn to give them Caveman's real name, which he ultimately did. They believed Caveman was aware of Howard's involvement in a bloody—and apparently unsolved—crime that had occurred in September 1976. Howard, went this theory, had brutalized somebody else and gotten away with it. Asked what Howard had been doing since that night in the desert, Glenn said he was preparing to bolt Southern California ahead of any murder rap. He suspected that Mexico could be Howard's destination, because Howard had monkeyed with the idea of leaving California and buying into a small hotel there. Whether he left the country or not, Howard intended to make hell for prosecutors, Tim said. In the days after the killing, Howard replaced all four tires on the El Camino and had the car washed.

Police arrested Howard a few days after hearing Glenn's story. San Bernardino prosecutors adamant that Howard was a risk to flee the area if released on his own recognizance motioned the judge not to set bail. The judge did anyway, pegging the amount at a then-astronomical one hundred fifty thousand dollars. Howard surprised them all by posting it through a local bail bondsman with his mother's financial assistance on December 30, 1977. When he faced the judge, he pled not guilty despite the D.A.'s eyewitness.

Proceedings in the People of the state of California versus Howard Landis Garrett, Jr. commenced in late March, 1978, at the San Bernardino Courthouse in an area now called the Inland Empire. (Some might say after the 2008 housing crash, ghost towns of foreclosed-upon subdivisions left it more inland than empire today). The timing was sinister. The gavel banged weeks *after* Richard had informed Jerry that Howard was the perfect man to run their new construction building arm and hired him. Richard had been so impressed by Howard that he approved his leave for the trial. Then again, Richard had been under the impression that Howard was a key witness in some case, not the star defendant in a ruthless killing.

Marc Frenkel, one of the two attorneys that Howard would later sic on Jerry, represented Howard on the murder charge. He posted technical objections about admissible evidence and Howard's locale at crucial times. He squawked that it was unfair for the jury to hear about Howard's previous legal brushes and his drug use. Soon, Howard testified on his own behalf, and so did Carol, his estranged wife. Prosecutors countered skillfully. They won the right to tell the jury about the one-way airline tickets to Mazatlan on Mexico's Pacific Coast that Howard and a friend had purchased approximately a month after Tim was bashed and burned. Would somebody innocent behave like that?

Lawyers presented their closing arguments in early May. Howard was granted permission not to be present during jury instructions without any public explanation given. The jury members–average citizens named Norma, Julie, Benny, and William—got the case. They deliberated, if you could call it that, for all of sixty-five minutes. They found Howard not guilty on every count. With that, the judge thanked the jurors for their service and had Howard's bond exonerated. The lawyers packed up their stuff and their client was free to do as he pleased.

The verdict out of San Bernardino rippled with morbid consequences elsewhere. Within days, Howard was loose in Los Angeles hiding behind his veneer of real estate respectability, cocksure that he could commit just about any viciousness with impunity. Gigantic Southern California had suddenly shrunk. Tim Dwight's charred remains anticipated the scattered shards from Richard Kasparov's patio. Evil had beaten the system, because the system had laid off an animal on the next group of suckers a freeway to the west.

Prosecutors had Glenn's depiction of Howard's carnage. They had Howard's plane ticket to Mexico. They had other evidence, too, and yet the jurors could not swear he was the killer.

This, Jerry's private eyes told him, was the *real* Howard.

PART III

THE MAKING OF AN L.A. MUCKRAKER

CHAPTER FIFTEEN

UNFORTUNATE RECALL

Dragging into his third week at the Hyatt, Jerry could have sworn he was in a cell fitted with invisible bars. The stay he had guessed would last five days had stretched into fifteen, and who knew how much longer he would be cooped up here. Each hour the room grew tinier, its features—the small desk, the view overlooking another hotel—more spirit gobbling. Jerry, knowing something about layouts, was trapped in a box of Howard's design. Big whoop—he had daily maid service. As well-bunkered as he felt with armed cops outside his door, he had never wanted anything as much as checking out.

Six weeks had passed since those men crouched on Richard's landing.

Jerry's private eyes continued urging him with backpats and sunny clichés to bide his time while LAPD homicide collected evidence and interviewed witnesses. "Take a deep breath," they said. Forget it's May. Detectives were steaming towards a knee-capping indictment against Howard, and there were multiple layers to him to tear back first. Rushing his arrest with his skill for wiggling out of charges would be tempting blowback revenge. More shoe leather needed to be burned. "Don't get me wrong," Jerry told them. He was grateful for the detectives' hard work and the SWAT guys' nimbleness the day of the museum meeting. He respected what L.A.'s finest was doing to shield him at a time when dead bodies were bobbing up all over town. "But, for crying out loud, how much proof did they need?" he asked. "When is this going to end?"

Jerry's men could hear the testiness creeping into his voice and less of the nervous confidence he had met his days with before. Now, they saw, Jerry rubbed his hands sometimes so unremittingly it was as if he expected to conjure a personal genie to save the day. For all his anguish, a formidable enemy motivated by spite and seventy-five thousand dollars was after him and the *Dragnet* duo had no way to sugarcoat it anymore.

According to their LAPD contacts, Tim Dwight and Richard Kasparov were just two of Howard's pelts. Evidently, he had fallen under suspicion two weeks before Richard's murder in an unusual, takeover-robbery in Monrovia that had nearly culminated in the execution of six people. Delving further in his background, officers saw his name flagged in several unsolved crimes, among them a suspicious break-in at the Roosevelt Building years earlier and that bloodshed in Pomona in 1976. Another lead to chase down emanated from Howard's supposedly cheating heart. Word was that he had a mistress, and that he had intimidated her to keep quiet about something with his patented persuasion technique. He slipped a gun into her mouth.

After digesting this latest bit, Jerry had to re-accept that bringing Howard down required exceptional effort. He had not yet heard the names of the thugs in Howard's criminal employ—Johnny Williams, Robert Freeman, Hector "Chaser" Villa, James Jones, "Crazy Eddy" Reyes—or the identities of those they were supposed to eliminate besides him. Like everyone else, Jerry was in the dark about the star-crossed campaign it took to polish Richard off, or Johnny's aborted murder of his old friend Robert in Haight-Ashbury. He had no forewarning that Howard was plotting to target at least one Space Matters client, Dr. Marmet perhaps. Faith that authorities would get their man before his own shaky fortitude gave out was his creed.

Thus, it was life by telephone jack on the hotel's seventh floor, and Jerry developed cauliflower ear with the phone receiver up to his head for hours a day. Mainly, he was alone in his room, keeping the television on for company. He listened absent-mindedly to *M*A*S*H* and *That's Incredible*. He heard segments blaring about the ebbing panic at Three Mile Island and the surging interest in the mysterious drowning of Carroll Rosenbloom, the silver-haired owner of the NFL's Los Angeles Rams. Much as he wanted to get hooked on a story, the news hound in him was fading. Neither was he built for confinement. He didn't puff marijuana or down Scotch to decompress, and he wasn't a bookworm or a spiritual seeker. Sitcoms and wall-staring were all he had.

Practically the only relaxation that he enjoyed was being able to phone a tight circle of family and friends if he kept the conversations short. Even that was controlled. Detectives limited incoming calls to the Dragnet duo, because the LAPD hadn't ruled out that Howard would try to tap into the Hyatt's phone system with his technical chops. Still, Jerry spoke to Tammy and Jude for a few minutes every couple of days. He even gritted his teeth and occasionally phoned his mother.

She had, as he had demanded, stopped urging him to hire the Israeli Mafia to eradicate Howard, which was not to say she had stopped pestering him. The longer her son remained stashed at the hotel whose name he could not divulge, the greater Vera's compulsion to plumb Howard's depths. Jerry would've preferred they talked about what an amazing grandson Vera had in Jude. His ears, all the same, couldn't help but unclog when his mother asked if ever listened to the Toni Grant radio show on KABC-AM. Grant was an engaging female psychologist with a predominantly female audience, a forerunner for the Dr. Phil's and other celebrity shrinks of today's touchy-feely world who concentrate on fraying relationships. Occasionally, the help-me carousel of the late 1970s stopped for the more nefarious, and that's why Vera asked her son if he tuned in the doctor.

"Can't say I'm much of a listener," Jerry said. "I'm not exactly her market."

"Well, I wish you did listen to her, because there's something I have to tell you. There was a woman who called in to the program saying she was scared, because her husband was about to be released from jail and she wanted advice about how to handle him. She thought he had already killed two people."

"My heart goes out to her, mother, it really does. But so what? This better not have to do with any more conspiracies."

"I'll tell you why I brought it up since you're skeptical. The woman who called was Carol. Carol Garrett. You know, Howard's wife."

"You can't be right," Jerry shot back, twisting the phone cord around his fingers. "You've got to be mistaken."

"I'm not. I know what I heard."

"But why would you wait so long to tell me? That's not like you."

"Because, I put it out of my head until now...I'm sure it was Carol who called. Maybe I assumed it was another Carol until Howard did all these awful things and it rang a bell...Jerry, you're being so quiet."

"What's there to say, mother?"

If Carol knew the score, Jerry knew that meant Howard had murdered someone other than Tim Dwight, and maybe Carol wasn't counting him. At any rate, his mother thought Jerry should know about Carol's trepidation, and Jerry was conflicted about how much to accept. "Watch yourself," she said in summation. "Howard must've rationalized that the people he hurt had it coming. He's sick, Jerry. Mentally ill. Who knows how his brain works nowadays?"

Jerry slumped on his bed grinding over what his mother said. "*Rationalized?*" Masqueraded was the better term. He had sat across the negotiating table from Howard mere months ago as his lawyers had brayed about how the earnest contractor's credit had been trashed by his lowlife bosses. When the meeting that Howard barely spoke at concluded, he must have gone home to scheme murder as his alternative justice. L.A. was a city of masks. The deceptions that Jerry now realized had engulfed him were sharp proof.

They had probably started when Richard offered to renovate Neddy Hertel's Valley home using construction materials that he deceitfully billed to CM-2. This method guaranteed pure profit for Richard's secretly chartered company and a loyal, tight-lipped client in Neddy—the same Neddy that had known Jerry since they were teenagers around North Hollywood; the same Neddy who had once done legal work for Jerry as an adult. Sometime during the remodeling, Howard must have uncovered the scam and beckoned Richard over for a talk with a one-finger—*get over here*—curl. He probably growled that he wanted some of that ill-gotten money and if he didn't get any he would blab about it. Howard just never dreamed that Richard would've had the nerve to charge supplies he didn't fraudulently charge CM-2 on his credit lines. Most people familiar with Howard's glower would nary flirt with such a scheme. But Richard wasn't like most people. For him, rule-playing was as optional as a sunroof when buying a new car.

Lying there on his bed with crumbs on the sheets, Jerry drew an unflattering portrait of himself in the character assessment department. By accepting Richard's let's-build-what-we-design spiel, he had become either a complicit dupe to his partner's quest for easy money or an idolizing enabler of it, and they had jeopardized everything as a result. Jerry's ardor that Space Matters would flourish if he worked his tail off and trusted his older cohorts to do the same had been self-serving fantasy, the greed bucket kind. He should have lit into Richard for even considering hiring a man who needed to testify in a criminal trial. A little digging around into both of their pasts would have uncurtained the truth about them. His mother's question shook him all over. "Jerry, what did you do?" Not enough, he saw.

Club himself as he did, Jerry also comprehended that Richard the "user" had instigated this drama. His whole life he had gotten away with escalating behavior—malingering to shoplifting, infidelity to embezzling—facing little more than immolated relationships or delinquent bills. It had all finally caught up with him when he hoodwinked a man unwilling to let his shenanigans slide with a wagging finger. Who was around besides Jerry to "rationalize" that?

***

The call patched through to Jerry sometime in May 1979 was a death threat of brevity and exoticism. "Pay up or you're going to die!" a Hispanic voice said. "The contract's written." Behind the words was a fuzzy, crashing sound reminiscent of breaking waves, as if one of Howard's henchmen was calling from a beach phone booth to mock him. The LAPD technicians who had bugged Jerry's office phones said they would try to zero in on where the call was placed. Jerry already knew the voice's inner intent. Howard was in charge.

"How much longer?" Jerry badgered his private eyes. "Can't the police arrest him now and investigate the rest after he's in custody?" *No can do,* they countered. More and more, the *Dragnet* duo was inquiring if he knew this person or remembered that incident, repeating anything important he recalled to their LAPD contacts. Jerry, in return, was hearing further about Howard's layers. He had ties to a prison gang and associates with connections in the white supremacist Aryan Brotherhood. He had his mitts in this and his nose in that.

Jerry phoned Ari to mope about the situation, spurring Ari to pepper Jerry about whether now, after all the delay and debacle, he could take Howard on. "You don't worry, Jerry. Me kill that mothafocker," Ari said in refrain. "The police afraid. Me not." Again, Ari might have been the only civilian thinking like that.

Howard had a gift, a grievous talent. Some of the people he strongarmed and terrorized during the spring of 1979 incessantly adjusted their car mirrors for him, lest he pounce on them from behind. Among the superstitious were whispers that he might have been half-devil with his capacity to know precisely what you dreaded. Whatever the particular fears, everybody understood that Howard was not someone you vanquished with an indignant response or a motion detector. In his eyes—eyes described as bee-bees for pupils and cracked plates for irises—no pity could flow.

Icy stare, necrotic soul: Janice Freeman, the sister of Howard's first hit-man, could not shake Howard's fix on her any more than Jerry could. Three days after Richard's murder, Howard and Johnny had tried breaking into her house while she was at work, smashing a door handle and removing screens probing for unlatched windows. Who knows what they wanted besides Robert's whereabouts? It might have been to engrave the message that the surest way to invite them back for thuggery was to tell the police what they knew about the dead man in Van Nuys.

Janice's eleven year old daughter had been homesick from school the day Howard and Johnny attempted clawing their way in. Freaked, the girl phoned her mom, and Janice rushed home to protect her child. When Johnny phoned her that night to explain their skulking, Janice told him not to bother and hung up. A few days later, the phone rang again and an unfamiliar voice told her, "You are going to die tonight." Janice and her family were done with surprises after that. Within a couple of years they moved off the street to another block, still in Ontario but no longer within the predators' memories.

Luis Buonsanti never felt the same affection for his foothill home in Monrovia after Howard's men held his family at gunpoint in pursuit of money that wasn't there. How could it be? The fifty-five thousand dollars represented Luis's equity stake in the house, not stacks of cash wadded under a mattress or a wall safe. Howard, in his coarse lust for moola and resentment of Luis' success, had misunderstood what he had heard when Luis told him in his Argentinean brogue that he had "money in his house."

Since then, the torment from not knowing who had hatched the take-over was lashing Luis' psyche. He reached out to Manuel, Howard's step dad, with whom he had developed a warm friendship, for consoling and to snoop. Manuel willingly offered his sympathy. Then he complained that Howard had leaned on his mother, Mabel, for ten thousand dollars to get him through another rash of bad months. Wading into his own situation, Luis asked Manuel if he thought Howard was capable of ordering men to invade his house. To Luis' shock, Manuel answered yes.

Here was something else: Manuel had long nurtured a hunch that Howard had something to do with the death of his ex-wife, Alpha, in the early

1970s. A mystery persisted, he said, into whether she had expired from a drug overdose, as most believed, or an intricately planned, unprosecuted homicide. Manuel speculated that materialism could have been Howard's motive. He wanted her San Gabriel Valley house and other possessions that he could not otherwise acquire through divorce laws and such. "I bet my life he killed her," Manuel remarked. If true, Luis was closer to this killing than he realized. When Howard and his mother donated clothes to the Buonsantis after they had emigrated from South America, Howard threw in some of his dead, ex-spouses' wardrobe. Anything else he should know about Howard, Luis quizzed Manuel. Yeah, his friend said: "He thinks that murder for hire is sweet."

Flashbacks from March 13 belted Luis more than ever after Manuel's revelation. For relief, he did what Jerry had, hiring his own ex-LAPD-turned-private-eye. The memories weighed on Luis enough to take his security one step further, sweet-talking the man to lend him his .350 Magnum when he was not there. The J.C. Penney rifle that Luis bought the day after Howard's men visited gave him the confidence of owning a "pea-shooter." When Luis went out, he often toted that .350 with him.

On a Friday three weeks after the assault, Luis drove home in a gleaming, used Cadillac that he had just purchased. He was northbound on Santa Anita Avenue in Arcadia not far from Howard's place when he punched through a yellow light. A Sheriff's patrol car saw the transgression, switched on its red light and Luis pulled over. Luis had that cannon of a handgun on the seat next to him, and when the officers approached, he panicked, shoving it to the floor. No one, he figured, would believe his explanation for carrying it. He was right. The Sheriffs resorted to standard operating procedure for an armed motorist. They drew their guns and gave Luis the business.

Afterwards, they hauled him to the station, denied him his phone call and strip-searched him. The car's belongings were confiscated next and Luis was held overnight. When he was released the following day, he left charged with possession of a concealed weapon. The car repair shop owner and part-time real estate flipper had to lawyer up. It took six months of hassle and cost to resolve the arrest. At first, Luis blamed his incarceration on bad luck and carelessness. As his read on Howard improved, though, he remembered something. He had confided to Howard shortly after the home invasion that he had purchased a gun to defend his loved ones. For the price of a dime, Howard could have later placed an anonymous call to the Sheriff's Department to alert them about an "immigrant" traveling with a weapon. Was that why the police had stopped him, Luis asked himself, and not someone else? It could be.

The way he analyzed it, his house on Hillcrest was either cursed or marked. His wife, Norma, never could relocate her serenity there. So Luis did what Janice Freeman would do, except faster. He put his home on the market and resettled in an adjacent community that Howard was not known to frequent.

Glenn Turner, the man who had testified against Howard in Tim Dwight's murder trial, would've probably liked to have rented a room from Luis in his new residence if he was assured it was bulletproof. Just as sure as the tides, Glenn was positive that Howard had a murder contract on *him* for not keeping secret the wretched things he did to his houseguest.

Yes, Howard had a gift. He haunted by getting between your ears.

***

Jerry in early May 1979 flew to Michigan to visit Tammy and Jude on his third trip to the heartland since Richard's death. Ari was with him once more, still nagging about letting him handle Howard. This time, something noteworthy occurred before Jerry departed for LAX. His detectives asked him in passing if he remembered the kidnapping of an heir to the J. Paul Getty fortune in the early 1970s. Jerry said he did, and inquired why they had raised it. His detectives said the issue could wait for his return.

The flight back was uneventful, Ari deciding against performing an encore of his comedy-stewardess routine. Jerry assumed that he was done with surprises after the detectives had asked him about the Getty abduction. Nope. If he thought the Midwest was frosty when he stepped outside, it was balmy compared to what Jerry walked into at his father-in-law's house in Ann Arbor. As before, the Wilsons remarked it was good to see him and offered him a post-flight snack and drink. Unlike the last trip, Jerry felt aloofness in their hugs and mistrust in their eyes.

Together in her room, Tammy admitted that her family had become increasingly fearful that the pandemonium in L.A. *would* migrate toward them. Sooner or later, they expected to peer out the window at the snowy, white landscape and see California killers skulking toward their house.

Eerie movements in the shadows had already prompted her family to call the local police once. It turned out to be nothing—this time. Tammy then confessed something else. She said that when her father had offered putting up the seventy-five thousand dollars to pay Howard off, LAPD detectives had lectured him that he would have a corpse for a son-in-law if he did. *Weightless*—that's how she felt about that news. You couldn't fault her kin, she said, for secondhand fear.

Jerry wore his crown of suspicion uncomfortably just the same. Didn't his in-laws understand that he had been confined in a claustrophobic hotel room, forced to dress like a country bumpkin if he wanted to eyeball the sun? They had to know he was not like Howard or Richard, that he was still the same sweet, hardworking lad from North Hollywood who had married Tammy. Somehow, the events since March had mangled what they thought of his character, and Jerry wallowed in it; condemnation by association. *How could they think I'm involved? Where's the benefit of the doubt?* He would so admired the family now reevaluating him, particularly Tammy's father. He was the embodiment of the wholesome patriarch up at 5:00 A.M. for his auto scrapping business without ever neglecting his kids at home. He was Tammy's broad-shoulder, a man disinclined to risk. Jerry lately just made her weep.

Near the end of this trip, Jerry found himself uneasy with Tammy's eggshell emotions. Not only was she sobbing continually, her pregnant belly protruded even more over her reedy frame, which had gotten thinner since his last visit. Weighing less than ninety pounds entering her second trimester, a stiff breeze could have carried her off. "What's wrong?" Jerry asked, "You've been crying almost the entire time I've been here." The pressure, she answered, the corrosive unknowing. Tammy had no choice but to expound on it.

While Jerry had been in L.A., her lawyer-brother had recommended that she seriously weigh terminating the pregnancy. "He what?" Jerry stammered. "An abortion? He has no right to do that. That's between us!" Tammy, however, said her brother foresaw a grim progression on the march. He expected that Howard might well get to Jerry, just as he had Richard, leaving her pancaked as a single mother of two. "Nobody," her brother had said, "has problems like these" unless they were partly deserved. Tammy explained her brother was just being over-protective. Don't take it personally.

"But you're not really considering ending the pregnancy, are you?" Jerry inquired. "We might not survive it."

"Of course not," she said. "I love you and Jude and what's inside me more than anything. That hasn't changed. I just don't understand why Howard is still free or, to be honest, why this all had to happen to us."

"Me neither."

Jerry sat in a stupor on the flight home with Ari, who had stayed in the house basement most of the trip.

CHAPTER SIXTEEN

CRACKING FOR GOOD

The goon who spoke again over the sound of crashing surf had Jerry's managed schedule down pat, as if he had been leaked a copy. Jerry and the detectives sworn to protect him were whipsawed over its timing. During the past weeks, Jerry had only been into Space Matters a few times. When he was at the mansion, the LAPD and his private eyes had kept his unannounced visits short and controlled. Somehow, the Hispanic voice from Howard's team was privy to his itinerary knowing just when to dial in. "Jerry?" the voice asked with a breathy intonation. "Yes," he replied. "Pay up or you're going to die. The contract's written."

It was the second time that Jerry had heard that same language from the same throat. The first time it had spoken was the same day that LAPD techs had wired the Space Matters telephone system so department techs could eavesdrop. Following this latest call, they isolated the background noise and determined that the voice was phoning not from a beach but from a bowling alley. Crashing pins were responsible for the frothy hiss, clinking beer bottles for the tinny notes following it. LAPD intelligence gathering had penetrated part of Howard's murder corporation. It might've even greased his arrest if the police had been able to winnow the bowling alley address down. Yet the caller had been too disciplined, trained to speak and hang up in less time than it took the LAPD to trace his coordinates.

Had Richard's widow recovered her bearings enough to share her experiences with Howard's stalking patterns, Jerry might've been tempted to wing back to Ann Arbor on the first jet out of LAX. Paige could have relayed to him how Howard had obsessively called and spied on their house prior to Richard's assassination. While she was at it, she also could have detailed her and Richard's revealing dinner with Howard in Palm Springs a year ago. He had snorted coke down there in the sandy heat, but it was the shiner that his wife, Carol, wore sunglasses over that made them two hours late to the restaurant for what was supposed to be a pleasant meal among colleagues and their better halves.

Carol had lamely tried explaining her black eye away by saying she had stumbled into a door when any fool knew that door was Howard's balled fist. Once the dinner was over, Paige had elbowed Richard if he had considered having a background check conducted on Howard. Even before that night, Paige said there was just something about him, a sort of malevolent energy field that trickled out of him that gave her goosebumps about what lied inside of him. Brie, Richard's ex-girlfriend that he later hired as Space Matters' office manager, had felt the same creepy sensation the first time she had seen Howard—from a good twenty feet across the mansion. They just knew. In each instance, though, when Richard was warned that Howard tripped female intuition for danger, he shrugged it off as false positives. It might have taken Howard's threatening phone calls to Paige months later for Richard to appreciate that his wife's willies were on to something.

Enlightening as all that would have been for Jerry to digest, Paige was in no shape to retell much during her gothic spring. Since the shooting, guilt had slashed her, especially her use of Richard's secret payment ledger in their dispute over child support payments. Equally raking were memories of the warning call about the murder contract from that anonymous woman two days before Richard's fatal disregard of it. Between virulent regrets over that and teary what-ifs, all the while caring for a daughter that a kidnapper tried snatching, Paige was too brittle to communicate much to her dead husband's old partner. As it was, she refused to leave her rental after sundown, feeling as though she was being watched. Sometimes, a plainclothes officer stood guard outside Paige's door.

Jerry, to be sure, wasn't a fountain of disclosure, either. The LAPD remained adamant that he keep his employees from knowing too much, including about those bowling alley calls. Detectives said the information blackout was as much for the employees' welfare as it was Jerry's. He had to go along. Any staffer asking him personal questions—*How's Tammy? When you coming back full time?*—invited a vague non-answer. Jerry yearned to tell them how he had risked his life in a circulation-stopping encounter with Howard at the museum, among other scares. All he could do instead was writhe about the jeopardy in which he had placed them.

Some scorching space planning shop he had going. His employees had already weathered Richard's embezzlement and banishment from the company, only to live through his murder by hitmen. They had had the SWAT team trample into the office and yell at them to hug the floor. Unnerving enough, they now watched their remaining boss traipse into work pallid and semi-mute. Office disheartenment was natural. Many of the designers and draftsmen fretted that Space Matters would go belly up before Howard was arrested. Some buffed their resumes and sniffed for openings at other firms. A few just wanted out of the danger perimeter.

Inside the office, there had been a well-circulated ghost story that the mansions' previous occupants had all died—some inexplicably—before old age. Jerry used to laugh at the silliness of the tale but he wasn't sure he should be smirking about it anymore. What could Bert, his lieutenant, say to motivate the crew? In 1980, they would rebound like Magic Johnson had in the NCAA title game? That the chaos that they had witnessed before would never smash through the front door again?

Jerry had little appetite with these pressures festering in his digestive tract. Sauce-smothered hotel chicken and salty patty melts were unappetizing when assassins searched for where you were sleeping. A slab of chocolate cake and milk might as well have been Spam when so many people you loved swung in limbo. Jerry was starting to think that his paranoid mother was right all along in saying to watch your head—you never knew what might fall into your lap. One day a Flyer Tiger's cargo plane, the next someone like Howard.

Halfway across the country, Tammy grappled with the predicament that required her husband to create a bubble wrap of protection around him. She wasn't trying to be high maintenance or pound nails into her hands as a martyr. She was slowly adopting some of her family's faraway perspectives. After hours upon hours in her old room sequencing what had occurred, she found herself in the philosophical swampland of *why*. Howard had not snapped without cause. Executions aren't accidents. Maybe just maybe her brother's suggestion about her aborting the baby before it got too late wasn't as deplorable an idea as it first sounded. Tammy understood that none of this would have transpired if she had wed someone else. To contain her dismay, she slept loads and prayed. The personal eschatology of *why me?* was less productive.

Jerry's sleep was more interrupted. Howard, he knew, had been embold-ened by the police wire that he guessed that he was wearing. From what his private eyes were picking up from their LAPD sources, Howard or an associate was rolling by Jerry's Northridge home every couple of days on surveillance trips. Other times, as the pay-up calls confirmed, they must have been watching the Space Matters building from a well-concealed spot. Howard also continued to dial Bert at home, usually around midnight, to check if he had let anything slip. Remind Jerry, Howard laced into his good-byes, that "I really need to talk to him."

Paul Fegen had less difficulty reaching Jerry, because Fegen's national leasing empire was helping to keep Space Matters solvent. The police had forbidden Jerry from meeting with him or anyone outside the Hyatt during normal business hours, and the only way he could attend a late night meet-ing was with his hick disguise on and his private eyes alongside. Fegen, the eccentric, had accepted those conditions. So the *Dragnet* duo drove Jerry to Beverly Hills, usually in one of their used Chevys, and Jerry tried giving Fegen the creative gusts still flapping in him.

Tooling along Wilshire Boulevard one foggy evening in mid-May, the private eyes noticed in the mirrors a suspicious car hanging back in traffic. When they turned, it did, too. When they sped up, it gunned it, as well. In the black and the mist, they could not discern faces. Traffic thinned out as they neared Fegen's tower and the car seemed to be still tailing them. The *Dragnet* duo started talking fast, exchanging possible escape routes and ordering Jerry to slide down into the rear seat. By the time they arrived at the building, the tail, if that's what it was, had veered off Wilshire

***

When Jerry returned to the Hyatt after his meeting with Fegen, he didn't just flip on late night television and try to doze off. Rather, he emptied his briefcase searching for a document that wound back the clock. It was Howard's take action letter, the one that Howard had mailed to him and Tammy before he commissioned Richard's murder. Re-studying it, Jerry had a different interpretation of its inner meaning. The letter wasn't just some vulgarly written business correspondence. It was Howard's mechanism for announcing that he was unleashing himself on Space Matters, just as he had unleashed himself on Tim Dwight, Luis Buonsanti and probably a couple dozen more.

Everybody should have recognized the pre-homicidal manifesto for what it was.

Dear Jerry:

...Somewhere along the way I think that you have the opinion that I just fell off the pumpkin truck. Well let me inform you Jerry that I have more time in the pay line than you have in the chow line. And I will be damned and go to hell before I will stand like a tall dog and let you or other members of your firm screw us. That, my old friend, you can bet on ...

I also don't give a damn if your attorney reads this letter or not. But you can bet your ass that mine is going to. At the present time my wife is suffering very much, and is under the care of a doctor, because of the nervous condition she is under. We are still receiving threatening calls and letters resulting from... failure to pay the material bills. I would appreciate you starting to work and getting some correspondence to those people involved. I would suggest that you do this very quickly...at least making an attempt to cooperate and resolve this fucking mess you have gotten me into.

I will tell you one more time now Jerry to get off your ass and get something done. I will not tolerate this shit much longer.

Since my wife is now involved in this I do not like it all.

Very truly yours

Howard L. Garrett

One line Jerry had flown over before shanghaied his attention now. It was the part where Howard declared that he would be screwed no more. "That, my old friend, you can bet on." Jerry's brain thumped with Howard's resentful phraseology as he lay on his pillow. The surreal was the real in a town awash in sunshine and treachery. Anybody discounting the possibility that the boring rhythms of daily life couldn't become a razor to the throat if they incensed the wrong person was deceiving themselves to color humanity kinder than it was. If Jerry thought he was being histrionic, or that mental exhaustion had rendered him punch-drunk, he knew that he wasn't when his private eyes came to his room without thin smiles the next day. They brought up the Getty kidnapping again. Whatever he may have remembered about the case, they said he needed to bone up on the specifics. And he better sit down to hear them.

In July 1973, while the Watergate scandal rippled and Vietnam still raged, the seventeen year old grandson of American oil tycoon John Paul Getty was kidnapped in Europe. His captors whisked him to southern Italy, where they chained him in a cave and demanded a multi-million dollar ransom. The Gettys initially doubted the abduction was genuine, speculating it was either a hoax or maybe even a scheme by the grandson himself to trick his moneybags grandfather into shelling out some of his fortune. When no money arrived, the kidnappers wrote a second pay-up letter that was delayed by an Italian postal strike. John Paul, Sr., once named America's richest man by *Forbes* magazine, dug his heels in further with a strident promise. No negotiations with criminals!

The men who held his grandson, bandits from Italy's mountainous Calabria region, had a response for the old codger. In November 1973, a newspaper in Rome received an envelope from them. Inside of it was a lock of hair and one of the teenager's decomposing ears. The game had changed to escalation by mutilation. "This is Paul's ear," the kidnappers wrote in their third ransom note. "If we don't get some money within ten days, then the other ear will arrive. In other words, he will arrive in little bits." The boy's severed appendage motivated his punctilious grandfather. The elder Getty bargained directly with the kidnappers, whittling the demand down to two million nine hundred thousand dollars. After the ransom was delivered, the abducted, deformed heir was found alive after six months of confinement.

Jerry was mystified why his private eyes expended so much time retelling a sickening incident about someone he never knew. "What does this have to do me?" he asked, just as he had questioned his mother about the Toni Grant show caller. Too much, they said. From what they were hearing now from the LAPD case detectives, Howard was an enthusiast of the Getty kidnappers. Indeed, he was scheming to apply the same technique to little Jude once he unlodged his whereabouts. Howard and his men were still searching to find and bully Jerry into producing the seventy-five thousand dollars and would exuberantly kill him if he refused. But Jude had become their top priority. They wanted to sever one of his ears, or another body part like a finger. They planned to send it to his father to throttle him to do what he so far had refused, and that's pay up.

The next morning, Jerry awoke dizzy and sweaty. He chugged a glass of water, and then another. He had never experienced such a ravenous thirst. Was it that salty, room service burger or an SOS from his subconscious? The night before, Tammy had confessed. She admitted that she *was* wavering about whether to keep the child in her belly, and wasn't sure she wanted to return to California even if Howard was apprehended. Jerry sprawled back onto his bed, letting his legs flog down hard on the ungiving mattress to test that he was awake. *Jude's ear. Tammy's baby.* He thought about his weakness distinguishing reality from illusion, and back again to how his mother had screamed as that cargo plane was about to half detonate their block. "*Arty, Arty, it's going to crash!*"

In that nanosecond, that shudder of a second hand, a tidal wave of sulfurous anger pounded through Jerry's capillaries, up his carotid arteries, dumping directly into his own brain's reptilian ganglia. In twenty-seven years, it was the first time undiluted rage had commandeered him. Since Richard's murder, Jerry had cycled through spurts of depression, apathy, self-pity, semi-denial and quasi-rationalization. And now Howard wanted to imitate the Getty kidnapers on his boy. Hoped to kidnap him and monetize him. Maybe He would snatch and torture Tammy afterwards. Hell, maybe Howard would pursue Jerry's parents or burn down his house in Northridge.

The bleak lines from his past nipped him. This was no hallucination. This was the world that Richard had bequeathed.

""*You fucking Jews—you're all alike,* "Howard said.

"*I recommend you kill him,*" Benjamin said.

"*EVERYBODY DOWN NOW. GET YOUR FACE ON THE FLOOR!*" the SWAT leader said.

"*Pay up or you're going to die,*" the voice from the bowling alley said.

"*This doesn't happen to normal people,*" Tammy said.

When his private eyes showed up for their next briefing two days later, Jerry met them at the door looking flush-faced and, well, a little unhinged.

"You okay, Jerry?" the older, red-haired one asked stepping into the room. "Howard didn't call you here last night, because if he did we would have problems."

"There wasn't any call, but we have problems. Make that, *I* have a problem."

"And that is?"

"I can't take this anymore."

"Well, you have no choice. We keep telling you that."

"Don't I have a choice? Look, I've done everything the LAPD has asked of me. I was their bait on the museum plaza, and they screwed up their chance to get Howard because all that damn recording device picked up was street noise. Then I later find out that the police would have gunned him down if they just saw me say to him, 'Don't Shoot!' That was three weeks ago. And Richard was killed weeks before that. This feels like forever."

"We know it's excruciating, Jerry, but the department has a full plate of leads to follow through on. Howard, as you know, was involved in a lot of bad things besides what he did to your partner and you. They can't ignore that because you're impatient and miss your family. I know that's not what you want to hear. We're sorry."

Jerry paced in front of the bed and stopped. He made sure he was out of the window line.

"Impatient? You realize, don't you, that if they string this out another month my company may go bankrupt, and a dozen people will be out of jobs. My marriage may not last, either. Nobody's could with this guy after them. My wife's family is freaked out about gunmen coming after them in the middle of the night—and they're in Michigan. It's too intense for everybody."

Here's another thing that's too intense. After the molars of a crisis masticate you long enough, fear transfers its potency to an indifferent form of bravery. One way or another, the strain must end. That explained why little bubbles foamed in the corners of Jerry's mouth. That answered why sweat dewed his hairline.

"Jerry, what did you do?" his mother asked.

"Calm down, Jerry," the detective told him. His partner nodded robotically, using it to show he agreed with his associate."You may only be a week or two away from getting out of here. Let the detectives finish their job. The cold ones will be on us."

"A week away. Oh, I don't think so."

"I'll have to call my [LAPD] sources to see if they can move double time, but I don't think its a matter of days. I wish we could tell you otherwise."

"That won't be an issue and I'll tell you why. You're going to be the ones giving instructions. Mine. I want you to pick up that phone and call the case detectives and tell them they either arrest Howard tomorrow or I'm driving out to Pasadena to finish the job. If they refuse, then call (LAPD police chief) Daryl Gates or (new mayor) Tom Bradley."

"I understand this is torture for you and your family but it would be stupid as all get out for you to go there. You'll probably ruin the investigation, if you didn't get shot first."

"I don't care. If Howard shoots me, he does. If they arrest and convict me for killing him, that's fine. I just want a chance to get my life back by getting the hell out of here."

"Look, you're not thinking straight. You've hit a wall. We get that. It's to be expected. You're not the first witness to go stir crazy."

"My thinking is fine. Again, you tell the detectives either they arrest him or I'm going out there and ringing his buzzer. Maybe I'll have a gun and the LAPD will have to decide who to shoot."

"Relax Jerry."

"NO! How many more people is Howard going to hurt while they're taking their sweet time? I want him arrested tomorrow. He's squashing me."

"Give us a sec," the private eye said.

"Know anything about the Getty kidnapping," his detectives quizzed him.

The Dragnet duo left Jerry's room to speak privately in the hallway. He watched them confer, feeling liberation and a damp back. His men understood his reasoning and disagreed with it. When you had a repeat killer to haul down, it could take months to weld a steel case against him. Jerry's detectives looked down at their shoes. He thought he heard the dark haired one who had been nodding the remark, "You can't blame him."

They shuffled back into his room with solemn mouths. It was the first time that Jerry had seen them looking anything but unflustered pros. As former cops, they understood that if Jerry did travel out to Pasadena and challenge Howard, one of the two might not survive it, and it would probably be Jerry with a toe tag sliding into the coroner's truck. The press would crucify the LAPD once they discovered what he had gone through.

Since Jerry was undissuadable, the Dragnet duo had a wrenching choice to make: humor him until he shook out of his folly about a confrontation with Howard, let him go to Pasadena or quit. In the end, the duo worked for Jerry and that's what sealed it.

"We can't promise anything, but we'll deliver your message. You've done everything asked of you so far and maybe that will help."

"Good," Jerry answered, arms akimbo. "Somebody finally heard me."

"There are things about Howard you don't want to know," Richard said.

The police did not loaf on Jerry's ultimatum, or whatever his cracking point signified. The next morning, May 11, 1979, the LAPD gathered outside Howard's Pasadena apartment on Del Mar Boulevard. They went to the second floor unit and pounded on the door, guns ready. It was 7:20 A.M.; in a few hours, Bullocks' white glove tea room down the block would be serving scones. Carol answered the door. From the reek of marijuana, emptied booze bottles and other paraphernalia scattered about, it was obvious that she and her estranged husband had partied to dawn. Where is *he*, the officers asked her? Carol pointed. The officers brushed by her and threw open the bathroom door.

There sat Howard Garrett on the toilet, naked, high and flabbergasted that somebody had the nerve to topple his reign. "Oh shit," he said loudly, as the handcuffs clamped on.

CHAPTER SEVENTEEN

OUTING THE ANIMAL

The trial united them all: the gunmen and their instigator, the innocents and the marginally involved, the detectives and the defense lawyers, Richard's widow and the besieged Buonsantis. Over the next year and a half, the case would draw the dozens connected to Howard, Richard and their fetid dealings to a small, wood-paneled courtroom in Van Nuys with ground zero, the Chandler Boulevard house, a nothing distance away. Many noticed that Howard looked different in court than he did on the outside. Sure, that frosty glare still dominated his face, but he was out of the blue jeans Hawaiian shirt combo that he favored and garbed in a standard prisoner's jumpsuit that somehow reduced him. Call it a defanging by zipper.

The wardrobe change was infused with a grim justice thanks to Vera and Art's boy. By not caving in during the roughly two months after Richard's murder and then going half berserk in his hotel room, Jerry hastened a killer's arrest before he fled to Mexico or "got away with it again." It was existential stamina fortified with underdog brawn. The self-conscious, ex-Art Center graduate had, in his own fashion, guaranteed that Howard would stand trial on murder charges that Howard himself had crowed would never happen during his "Hitler" speech. And Jerry hadn't required a secret LAPD microphone to beat him.

He phoned Tammy in Michigan jubilant with the news the day that Howard was sent into lockup. You can come home soon now, he told her. Book the flight. Tammy answered she would, and what a tremendous relief it was with Howard incarcerated. After he hung up with her, Jerry flopped

191

back on his hotel bed in victory, having flopped there before to test if the chilling things he had just heard about Howard were true or not. (In nearly every case they were real.) *Bye, bye Hyatt*, he thought. *So long, salt burger*. He tossed his clothes into his suitcase and checked out of the hotel after twenty-plus days of confinement. His private eyes cheered on his departure.

Since Howard's minions had not been identified, detectives suggested that Jerry stay with Ari for a spell. It couldn't hurt. Ari said he would love the company and Jerry knew deep down that all was not peachy again despite his lightheartedness. Howard could be released on a technicality, and no one would put it past him to barrel towards the man who had flouted him. Ari's lament, meantime, was his earlier one. He had never been granted five minutes alone with Howard, just clenched fists and will. Ari's magnificent moment would've been watching Howard suck his final breath while standing over him.

Soon, Jerry became Ari's houseguest at Ari's duplex off of Melrose Boulevard in West Hollywood. It was an unconventional place for his recovery to begin because in retreating here, Jerry had left the sterile cube at the Hyatt for a post-marital demilitarized zone. Ari and his wife had split up and in *War of the Roses* fashion bifurcated their home so they could keep living there rather than sell it for a steep loss. As Jerry scanned the interior—half-demolished walls, posted rules about room use—it wistfully reminded him of one of Richard's old remodels-in-progress.

Besides offering him a bed, Ari believed he had other means to cushion Jerry's pain. He wanted his pale friend to hit the L.A. nightlife with him for cavorting and laughs. When Ari was off his bulldozer, he savored his partying, and savored it in expensive European suits with open-collared shirts and thick, gold chains. He tried persuading Jerry to grab drinks with him at a couple of hangouts to celebrate the fact that the "mothafocker" was in custody. Jerry shook his head no. Considerate as the offer was, the liquor sounded unhelpful. "Go have your fun without me," Jerry said. "I'm crashing." He did, too, sleeping better in Ari's divided house than he had since Richard's slaying.

After some days there, Jerry thanked Ari for the hospitality and, just as vitally, his undying friendship. It was worth more than brute protection and his jetliner slapstick. Jerry then climbed into the Seville and steered towards Northridge.

Driving up to his street as the loamy foothills filled his windshield made him mistier than he had expected. Everything considered, the house that his family had evacuated for fear of hitmen outside was due for a raucous homecoming party. A stiff cleaning was in order first. The property looked to be a slipping toward permanent desertion and into a squatters delight. Flyers were piled up in the entryway. Cobwebs embroidered the sidings. The grass was shin-high. Jerry had scarcely seen anything so picturesque.

***

As the years passed, Jerry wished that he could have bottled that stirring feeling and occasionally drank from it. Howard's trial produced more than communal relief. It laid bare the unsuccessful, untold effort to disrupt his plot to assassinate Richard and the others. Robert Freeman, Howard's first assassin, actually had much in common with Jerry. In their own ways they would each tried taking Howard's legs out from underneath him by exposing their jugulars.

After Howard had screamed at Robert's sobbing wife in early March 1979 that he was a "dead sonofabitch" for not killing Richard as promised and swiping the El Camino, Robert knew he had to take a noble stand, maybe for the first time ever. One week before Richard's shooting and perhaps just a day after the assassination attempt on him in San Francisco, Robert had flown back to L.A. to deal with an old burglary charge. He would gladly have skipped the hearing at the Van Nuys courthouse if not for the excuse it gave him to spill his guts to the closest lawyer. Holding it in was pulverizing him. If his heads-up warning earned him immunity for his involvement in Howard's criminal franchise or reduced jail time for unrelated crimes, that was gravy. Robert, the career burglar, wanted the man Howard had depicted as a plastic charlatan to escape the bullet earmarked for him.

Robert's medium to try was Susanne Greene, the same, young lawyer that the court had appointed for him when he was stuck in the San Bernardino jail in winter 1978 without enough money to make bail. At the time, Susanne's law license was still dripping ink. She had only been a member of the California bar for a month. Her well known uncle was the veteran. Harry Weiss was an elegant, monocle-wearing character considered one of the deans of L.A. criminal defense lawyers. Still, he wasn't representing

Howard's maiden hitman.

In Van Nuys, Susanne won a continuance on Robert's case and the two retired to a bench outside the courtroom. Robert there told her that he had to unburden himself. Whatever the secret was, it made the iron-pumping ex-con seem like a timid mouse who swiveled his head and fidgeted despite being in a police-guarded structure. Robert explained everything he could remember through his fugue of fear and heroin—Howard's kill list, his Svengali magic for knowing things and escaping charges, his guns and his lackeys. After hearing his story, Susanne understood Robert's tremors so well that she began nervously watching the court hallway. For a moment, she thought she had scored a break when she saw an assistant district attorney that she recognized nearby. The tenderfoot lawyer approached him for guidance about Robert's warning of contract murders to come, but he couldn't be bothered. He was leaving the D.A.'s office soon for another job.

Of all the clients that Susanne could have represented, Robert was an improvised explosive device. His description of Howard's efforts to kill Richard was more than scary for Susanne to hear: it was chancy for her to know. On one hand, anything Robert said to her was covered under strict attorney-client privilege. Disclosing their private dealings, no matter the reason, could be grounds for disbarment, effectively terminating her career before its first anniversary. Withholding the information wasn't much better. Technically, it might make her a murder conspirator. Or, it might bloodstain her hands if Robert's outlandish yarn came true.

Susanne, struggling with a *Catch-22* dilemma that sounded copycatted from a pulp novel, called around for guidance. She consulted her law school ethics professor, who told her that he had never heard of such a situation. Next, she met in the chambers of Armand Arabian, then a Superior Court judge and himself a former prosecutor. (Eleven years later, then-Governor George Deukmejian appointed the conservative jurist to the California Supreme Court, where he served for six years.) Arabian explained to Susanne that he couldn't assist her much. As an impartial judge, he was "not in the business of giving legal advice," even to skittish colleagues in need of hand-holding, and worried about conflict of interest accusations should Susanne appear in his courtroom on future cases when he was presiding in his official black robe. "So, not to be rude to her and knowing she's inexperienced to some degree, I let her blurt out whatever it was, because she blurted it out anyway," Arabian testified. "I had no control over that. I selectively listened to what it was (and) instantly knew" the conversation had to cease.

But the judge did not completely stiff-arm the seemingly isolated woman, suggesting that she track down a seasoned, criminal defense lawyer. Robert Shapiro, Arabian said, might be able to ferret out whether Susanne's "problem" involved "ethical, legal or moral" dimensions meriting action. (Seventeen years later, Shapiro would be one of O.J. Simpson's "Dream Team" lawyers. Celebrities Daryl Strawberry, Johnny Carson, Linda Lovelace and Lindsay Lohan also received his services. More recently, he was one of the founders of the self-help law site, LegalZoom.com.) In Shapiro's considered opinion and others that Susanne probed, Robert's tale was almost certainly fiction. Veteran defense attorneys, she testified learning, get harebrained stories all the time from clients trying to exonerate themselves.

The newbie attorney adopted some of that professional skepticism. She gave Robert's contract murder account a half-percent chance of authenticity. Still, what if Robert was being honest? What if he had grounds for his tremors? After pondering her options, Susanne decided to manage her risk by palming the phone. So, on the Sunday when Richard was planning to take Rebecca, his baby daughter, out, Susanne called Paige from her home playing the mystery woman with a lifesaving warning. She exhorted Paige to grill Richard about who would want him dead and to do something about it. Just don't sleep on the threat. In Susanne's mind, her urgent words transcended the fact they were anonymous. Logical as that might have been, it didn't succeed. The LAPD officer who Paige contacted that Saturday claimed the department required more specifics to get involved. Richard himself discounted it, accusing Paige of a stunt to win child support. Or so he contended on that fateful day on her stoop.

After Richard's murder, Robert reminded Susanne that Howard wanted him killed, too. Now that she had reason to believe him, she postponed his future court dates. About May 1, while Richard's homicide investigation sputtered along inside the LAPD's teeming caseload of unsolved crimes, she contacted detectives about a client ready to implicate a monster. Beware, she added: the informant, a lifelong crook, was frightened to death. Up on the stand herself, Susanne was hazy about what Arabian counseled her. Shapiro did not appear to have been part of the court's incomplete trial record. Nevertheless, her client's confession yanked the tarp off of Howard's murder corporation and its ham-fisted efforts to execute Richard.

Once Robert laid the entire scheme out, LAPD detectives soon interviewed James Jones, the transvestite thief. Next to crack, in early December 1979, was the sneering triggerman himself, Johnny Williams. He had had his father contact the District Attorney's office with a proposition: his son would agree to testify against Howard in return for prosecutors dropping the murder with "special circumstance" rap that they hoped to hang on him. It would make him eligible for California's death penalty, assuming the courts reinstated it.

***

Howard was arraigned on the September day twenty-two years before Al Qaeda crashed jetliners into the World Trade Center buildings and the Pentagon. His trial commenced a year later in 1980. The lead prosecutor's question to Johnny set the atmosphere for the proceedings. How many people have you killed in your lifetime, Mr. Williams? Johnny's answer was four, and that included his headshot on Richard. Pressed whether taking those lives bothered him, Johnny answered no. Honestly, the fuss confounded him. Murdering to him was no different than ordering a cheeseburger – just something you did.

But Johnny, the epileptic, was more than a sociopath on the stand. He guided the jury into the underbelly of the city of Spago and the Fabulous Forum, explaining that murder-for-hire was a common occurrence in L.A. Most people, he said, just bought the official cock-and-bull that it was a robber, and not a well-trained hitman, that killed a businessman or rich wife during a break-in. Just by himself, Johnny proclaimed knowing of twenty-five contract killings that'd netted no arrests. In a 1984 *Los Angeles* magazine article on the topic, Johnny described a vengeful Los Angeles where sadism was as prevalent as silicone. Assassins looking for employment congregated like day laborers at pimp bars in South Central and at Valley watering holes. Back then, a hired gun would charge you less than a big transmission job. Five hundred dollars was the going rate.

Before Howard's trial began, Johnny pled guilty to first degree murder for shooting Richard. He was sentenced to twenty-five years to life at Soledad State Prison on the Central California coast, and already marked the mid-1990s for a possible early release. Perturbing him wasn't his willingness to testify against his old boss or his own gun-loving DNA. It was Howard's cheapskate ways. Johnny was disgusted that his employer had welched on his compensation package after taking Richard out and everything else he had done. Howard was supposed to have rewarded him with twelve thousand dollars, a fortune for him, and hadn't. What do you know? Howard was as much a deadbeat as he accused Richard of being.

Robert and Johnny were the DA's star criminal witnesses against the man who had forever tarred their friendship. They admitted to practically everything. Whatever they lacked in book smarts, the two seemed to know as much about the California penal code that they had been busting since acne adolescence as their lawyers. The only subject besides criminal statutes that Johnny had collected more lifetime expertise with were the different chemical powders used to dilute pure heroin.

Johnny's rendition of events on the stand contradicted a few details that he gave to LAPD investigators early on. Hair-splitting aside, he recounted a spellbinding story in an impassive voice for the court, painting what he observed through Richard's sliding glass window:

> "Susan is reading...(what) looks like a book and she's sitting with her back up against the bed. (Richard) is laying kind of like (he's) got his hands under his head...He's got lights along the bottom of the wall up to the glass door that are facing the bed and...it is dark out (on the landing)...He looked right at us (but) he couldn't see us...I shoot him...(later. I saw his) head drop forward. I knew I hit him. I have been shooting guns since I was nine years old...He jerked and relaxed. I figured he was dead."

Johnny's other qualm in addition to being stiffed by Howard involved the Buonsantis and whether his foiled home invasion-robbery with Crazy Eddy qualified as attempted mass murder. Johnny said that the prospect of shooting children sickened even *him*. If Howard ordered him to kill Luis in the doorway, he would have gone along; Luis' family just didn't need to witness him crumple to the ground. Johnny said see, he had his limits.

His description of his crimes before and after Richard's shooting sounded more like the mobbed-up East Coast than mellow California except for one element. After they bailed from Chandler Boulevard, self-satisfied with a job finally checked off, they had a gun they needed discarded. No crisis there. Johnny disassembled the M-1 that he had been so proud to fire and chucked the components out the car window near the Magic Mountain theme park northwest of L.A. (They were traveling that direction after the killing to drop Chaser off before returning east to Ontario). "It's part of the freeway," Johnny testified, backpatting himself. Evidence destruction for him was an onramp away.

Robert, facing his own jail time on older charges unassociated with Howard, freed his wife, Elena, before he returned to the slammer. He suggested they divorce, thinking she would be better off without him after exposing her to Howard's venom. James Jones, the cross-dresser who hadn't been at either Richard's murder or the Buonsanti home invasion, was less forthcoming on the stand. Prosecutors knew he had a damn good reason. During Howard's preliminary hearing in May 1980, the Sheriff's Department had transported Howard and James from the men's lockup to the courthouse in the same bus. The D.A. had requested that the men be separated to protect James and somebody in the Sheriff's office evidently forgot. James had already been *uber*-afraid of Howard, so his jitters burned ablaze after Howard threatened him about testifying against him. Following the bus ride, James refused to speak under oath. The hearing had to be cancelled.

This wasn't surprising, for Howard had alibis, fall guys and scare tactics in place well before the proceedings began. He had walked away from the Tim Dwight killing, if not others, and he intended to replicate the feat. His swagger could still strut. Before he had heard Johnny was a prosecution witness, Howard had boasted to him that he "had" someone who would testify that he had observed Robert selling coke to Richard at a West L.A. restaurant. The impression that Howard hoped to manufacture was that Richard was executed over a soured drug deal. It sounded plausible enough in a powder-crazed city.

Howard, at least in his 1981 appeal, scoffed at suggestions that he openly discussed four contract hits. How laughable. The buffoons testifying against him, he theorized, must have misinterpreted his words or failed to recognize that he was being a blue collar loudmouth when he talked *jobs*. Anybody who thought he was lying should consider how Richard had flimflammed him and all the generosity he had showered on the Buonsanti family. Nudged by prosecutors if Richard had cheated him, Howard had an illuminating response: "not anymore" than anybody else. In ear-numbing repetition, Howard denied connections to anything sordid or psychopathic. He had never driven an assassin by Richard's house, never stood lookout for the Buonsanti robbery he supposedly staged, never threatened Jerry for seventy-five thousand dollars or directed menacing calls to him. He just wanted Richard and Jerry to repay him.

Howard did acknowledge that he had worked for Richard's company, Kasparov Design, which Richard used to embezzle materials and mine profits from CM-2. Howard stressed tactics like that were the norm in dog-eat-dog real estate and not immaculate collusion against young Jerry. The cynical notion that he had uncovered Richard's skimming on Neddy Hertel's house or other projects and manipulated it to blackmail Richard before Richard bilked him was nonsense. Same for the prosecution theory that the screed he mailed to Jerry and Tammy was a shot across the bow. Howard said he had only hoped to "get his points across" about his determination to have his debts retired and belongings returned.

The denials stopped briefly with Howard's admission that he was aware of the one hundred fifty thousand dollar life insurance policy that Jerry and Richard bought in case one of them perished. So what, he argued. Knowledge did not equal motive. Howard said there was a crucial nugget about him that he hoped the ladies and gentleman of the jury would accept. When questioned how he felt about Richard and Jerry, he remained magnanimous. "I liked them both."

Incidentally, Mr. Explanation expressed ignorance about an unsettling incident involving Janice Freeman, Robert's sister, several months after he had been arrested. Men representing themselves as police officers working Richard's homicide showed up at her Ontario house in July 1979. They drove her to a restaurant in the southeastern San Gabriel Valley, pressing her for her brother's whereabouts. Janice, sensing something fishy about the men without IDs, told them she didn't know Robert's locale. Nothing else was learned at trial about the imposters and their possible ties to Howard, because his attorneys nixed the line of inquiry.

Throughout the case, Howard's lawyers were always doing that, casting themselves as masters of objection and deflectors of the embarrassing. Indeed, they came off as abettors themselves for returning to Howard the .45 caliber handgun that San Bernardino authorities had confiscated after they arrested him for allegedly brutalizing Tim Dwight. Not that the jury was allowed to hear that. Los Angeles Superior Court Judge Leonard S. Wolf ruled that Howard's role in the Dwight murder was inadmissible evidence. Smarting as they were about the judge's decision, prosecutors noticed something about the defense counselors as the trial wore on. They appeared to grow concerned about what revenge their client might visit upon *them* if they failed to win his acquittal again.

You could fill the cargo hold of Howard's El Camino with the charges filed against him and still think some were forgotten. In regards to Richard, the D.A.'s office accused him of murder with special circumstances because of the premeditation and planning, a death penalty charge, plus conspiracy to commit murder and solicitation for it. As for Jerry, Howard was charged with a single count: attempted extortion. On the Buonsanti incident, they slapped him with attempted robbery and five counts of attempted murder. Investigators could never mold their suspicions about Howard's connections to other killings and bloodshed into additional counts.

Paige testified and the trauma was still not done with her. Under oath, she admitted that while Richard had periodically gotten physical with her, her love for him was undiminished by abuse or time. Paige also bumped into Susanne Greene, the lawyer on the other end of the anonymous warning call. After Susanne introduced herself and her voice struck a chord, Paige fainted in the courthouse hallway. Little or nothing was made about the man on the deck who had tried kidnapping her and Richard's baby daughter. Had Howard commissioned Robert Freeman, during an unknown respite from jail, to do it as a way to force Richard to pay off his debts? Or had it been somebody else on the landing, maybe one of Howard's toadies that he had kept hidden? The identity of the intruder that the Guatemalan housekeeper rebuffed with a broom stick has remained unsolved for more than three decades.

During his court appearances, Howard tried squelching the hate inside him, knowing he had the jury's hearts to win over. He couldn't let them see that gamma ray demeanor that Jerry and others knew plumed within him. Thus, Howard focused his glare away from the jury box and toward many of the prosecution's witnesses—people who once would have called him their friend—when they testified. From the defense table, he glowered and smirked with a telepathic message impossible to miss. Though jailed and charged, he was still deadly; prosecutors described him as a self-styled "lawnmower on a grassy street." Everybody speaking out against him should remember that he knew how to bide his time even if he was doing "time." San Francisco, the Miracle Mile, Ann Arbor, Ontario—distance was immaterial. He would find you.

Jerry strove not to look his way during his hours on the stand, and his stomach thanked him for it. The D.A. advised all witnesses implicating Howard to avert their eyes from him, as if he were a California Medusa. The Buonsantis said they had try as prosecutors made the family members point at him, Johnny, and Crazy Eddy. The D.A. later requested that Maurice, now eleven, answer affirmative questions on the stand with a simple yes, and not the "Uh huh" that he had been. When prosecutors asked the boy if he understood the instruction, Maurice nervously responded, "Uh huh." It produced one of the few courtroom-wide guffaws.

Except for when he testified, Jerry was barred from hearing others describe their experiences with Howard since he was an official prosecution witness. His father, Art, had no such restrictions, and he wanted to assist. He was present for much of the trial, eventually falling in and befriending the little platoon of old men courtwatchers who regularly waited around the Van Nuys courthouse for scintillating cases. When Art wasn't trading commentary with them, he sometimes tailed Howard's lawyers as they broke for lunch and tried coyly sitting nearby. Art even had a tape recorder running to capture their conversations. If they said anything spicy, he told the D.A.

Prosecutors shoved Howard's face in his description to Jerry of the bullet hole in Richard's window; he had incriminated himself with his own hubris there. They interrogated him over dates, inconsistencies, hostile testimony against him and his working class alter ego. If he were innocent, why had he cut out and preserved newspaper stories about Richard's slaying and the Buonsanti robbery? He clumsily tried explaining away the Buonsanti article by saying that he had been saving the story to mail to his mom in Barstow, good son that he was.

To all these shoddy explanations, the jury basically said "yeah, right." On October 30, 1980, they convicted Howard of murdering Richard in the first degree and every related count. The sentence *was* kneecapping: life in prison without the possibility of parole. If prosecutors were disappointed, it was that the jury did not convict Howard on all the special circumstances counts that might have plunked him on Death Row. Likewise, the jury acquitted him for plotting against the Buonsanti family. By then, however, Luis and his clan had no misconceptions about who had dispatched Johnny and Crazy Eddy to their door. Howard was no friend. Anybody who could have terrorized children he had once entertained as Santa was a Neanderthal.

His new home was Folsom State Prison northeast of Sacramento. Like

Johnny, Howard went there convinced it was temporary, that his tenacity would get him out of his cellblock on appeal. He wasn't wrong much, but all that hate can erode one's I.Q. His appeal was denied. Prosecutors, meanwhile, requested that prison officials ensure that Robert did not serve time in the same penitentiaries as Howard or Johnny. They believed that if he did, Robert would exit feet first. No one knows what became of him or lesser members of Howard's disbanded murder corporation.

CHAPTER EIGHTEEN

DEATH OF SWEETNESS

In Northridge, the lawn was cut, the newspaper resumed. Jerry's Mercedes and Tammy's Seville were parked home again, and nobody fretted anymore about a bomb under a carhood. Jerry's farm hand disguise was gone. So, too, were his private eyes. Take away the drawn curtains and an outsider never would have guessed that the household had been knocked off its foundations.

Tammy and Jerry hoped the renaissance of their old routine would bind their scars. By Jerry returning full-time to Space Matters and Tammy to motherhood in California, they expected to banish the spring to the foggy corners of memory. Entomb it in a box. The Schneidermans wanted their humdrum, old bliss back and at first it seemed attainable. Tammy delivered a healthy son whose existence had been debated, and Jude grew into a marvelous little boy with both ears attached. From the exterior, the family was whole again. You had to gaze deeper to behold the fissures. It wasn't just Howard's trial they had to endure or his notorious gawk they had to forget. California's revolving door penal system made it possible that someday he might be sprung. Bills from Jerry's lawyers and detectives had also stacked up, and post-Richard Space Matters was gasping for fresh contracts. The new normalcy was expensive.

Tammy, try as she did to be sunny, was not the same woman by March 1980 as she had been in March 1979. Some days she was phobic, others survival-minded. Predictability mattered more than ever. She had asked an LAPD detective during Howard's trial how long she would have if Howard were released from prison unexpectedly. Long enough, he advised her, to stuff a bag and scramble to the airport. In other words, once the warden gave the order to cut Howard free, she and Jerry would have just a few hours to make their family invisible in a new city. As much as she tried focusing on her little ones and Jerry and not what was crouching in the shadows, Tammy's evacuation scenario spun behind her eyes.

She now disliked things that she could not identify. She scribbled down the license plates of unrecognizable cars near their home. One evening, panic trembled through her when she overheard two men that she hadn't been expecting speaking on her porch. Jerry, it seemed, had extended a last minute dinner invitation to a friend. Tammy was furious over it, her tolerance for surprises depleted. "If you're going to keep this up," she said later, "I'm going to leave you." She voiced and rephrased this line with other post-trauma jumpiness in the months ahead. After hearing as much of it as he could weather, Jerry told her that she had a decision to make. She could live with him happily, coexist with him dolefully or flat leave him. Jerry said he hoped she would pick choice number one, but Tammy refused to make a selection. She did speak authoritatively in one area. She wanted out of L.A. where things were "not normal."

But which Jerry was Tammy talking to? If it was the reserved North Hollywood cuteypie who used to doodle cartoons of adorable rabbits for her, that Jerry was dissolving by the day. The manic relief arcing through him after Howard was incarcerated had slackened. Jerry now assumed every new person he met concealed something poisonous. Just like Tammy, he was less than he had been. Howard had sucked dry his predilection to trust, Richard his willingness to accept facts at face value.

Soon, Jerry emulated Luis Buonsanti to feel safer. Following Howard's arrest, he went out and bought a gun for protection—a Walter PPKS, similar to the pistol James Bond kept. Jerry carried it in his waistband to work, home, the car, everywhere. The piece even accompanied him on a business trip to Denver without setting off the airport screening machine.

What did it matter, though? The gun-toting Jerry was just as torn up inside as the unarmed one. He was a muddle—a muddle of smoldering, contradictory, mostly unlanced emotions. He never could have believed after all those weeks in hiding that he would feel so spacey and tense all at once in the afterglow of Howard's capture. *I just want to be back where I was,* he whispered. Yet, there was little time to know when that would come as he returned to sixty-hour workweeks, fighting off lawsuit claims and re-securing Space Matters' corporate clientele. Some victory lap this was. Out of the Hyatt and back on the hamster wheel.

Jerry's psychic reboot proved more slippery than he had imagined. The therapy sessions that Tammy eventually convinced him to attend brought out more about her anguish than his. She wanted a resumption of the simple life and wanted Jerry to want that. He would like to know how he was supposed to interpret the dreams pecking his head, or the tears streak-ing down his face. They had begun along with a heave or two while he and Tammy had been on the freeway to someplace. "I just got to get it out," Jerry told her. "My system can't take it." So let it out he did, uncontrollably for about three days. Unfortunately, when the tears ceased, the disequilibrium remained.

Gunmen were all over. The Schneiderman's comprehended that just by picking up the newspaper. Johnny Williams had been right about death-for-sale. Accused murderers were hiring contract killers to muffle witnesses. A Japanese importer had commissioned a hitman to kill his wife for insur-ance proceeds. Near Palm Springs, an Indian tribal leader and two others had been executed in a shooting that police linked to mobsters skimming casino profits. A designer had been discovered savaged in the hills. For every airhead caricature of L.A. life there were assassins tiptoeing up some-body's driveway. Nineteen seventy-nine might've seemed a joyride of video Pong, goosedown vests, narrowing ties and smarmy J.R. Ewing, but it was inversion of expectations elsewhere. Snow falling in the Sahara, a rabbit at-tacking Jimmy Carter on a canoe trip, with *C-SPAN* on line as the outwardly détente-adoring Kremlin invaded Afghanistan.

Space Matters was barely afloat in the post-Richard doldrums. Those illicit remodels that Richard had undertaken were not all untangled. Three homeowners with uncompleted renovations demanded their money back, cavalier as could be about Jerry's executed partner as they harped on un-fulfilled contracts. Others filed lawsuits or insisted on project completion. Never mind that a few of the grumblers had been complicit in Richard's cheating. Jerry tore holes in his gut settling the jobs, and sued a few home-owners who knowingly received stolen building materials. Neddy Hertel was one of them.

Afterwards, the ruins were still there. Jerry owed hundreds of thou-sands of dollars in settlements, taxes, lawyers' fees, and other expenses, while generating scant revenue in the bedlam. The stagnation prompted him to suspend paying CM-2's business taxes from the point that Richard's skimming commenced. Sadly, the one hundred fifty thousand dollars in life insurance proceeds wasn't much of a financial tourniquet once it was paid out. After the IRS asked for its slice of CM-2's income, Jerry had to make a harsh decision and did. He directed the taxmen to levy the bank account holding the insurance payout. The agency tapped it and nobody else got a cent. Not Richard's mom. Not Paige. Not Howard. The blood money went to Uncle Sam.

Remarkably, Space Matters and its associated units were profitable by 1981 with work in major highrises and elsewhere and nothing with luxury home remodels; Jerry disbanded CM-2 almost as quickly as Richard had hatched it. Still that was just brush clearance. The next year, 1982, reality scalded Jerry in ways that he could not dream.

Paul Fegen's extraordinary success leasing buildings across the country once had him lording over an empire estimated at seven million square feet in twenty five states. But what was superbly enriching in the 1970s proved to be exceedingly risky in the next decade. In 1982, the U.S. economy sputtered into recession. Office buildings once lushly packed with "Fegen suites" hemorraged tenants. Unoccupied buildings and weakening rents spread. Las Vegas, one of Fegen's hotbeds, was hammered by vacating properties. Texas, where Fegen had done particularly well, was double-whammied by the weak economy and an oil slump. The rise of the personal computer itself was inhospitable. The bulky IBM computers digitizing everything once paper meant endangered species status for the old fashioned secretarial pool. Because of that, lawyer tenants that Fegen had routinely leased 600 square feet offices to could retrench to half of that or less. Banks worried about Fegen's vanishing revenues soon cut off credit to him and tried getting their money back. Jerry had been one of the first to decipher Fegen's funky accounting. His leasing extravaganza was splashed in red ink.

In fall 1982, exactly two years after Howard's murder trial, the landlord of a Las Vegas building that Fegen had leased flew out to L.A. to meet with Fegen's bravura space planner. Jerry was accustomed to Fegen's "Bald Jesus" image causing a stir. He had been in meetings with straitlaced financiers before and asked them if they had ever seen the man with whom they invested millions. Most said they had not. Jerry remembered one Kansas City bank executive who had nearly cartwheeled backwards in his chair when

Jerry had handed him a photograph of Fegen with that oddball haircut and sequins twinkling on his face.

That photographic shock value felt like good times now. The Las Vegas building owner told Jerry point blank that if he couldn't collect his rent, he was going to "have Paul killed" so he could collect on his two million dollar life insurance policy. Just to make sure his ears heard it correctly, Jerry inquired if the property owner was enunciating a pay up or die choice, and the man apologized for his unprofessional language. The financiers who had purchased insurance contracts on Fegen and named themselves as beneficiaries were less talkative. Fegen so appreciated that he might be worth more dead than alive that he turned his office penthouse into a citadel. Jerry could not exactly dissuade him that contract hits only existed in Hollywood screenplays.

In the annals of Jerry, November 1982 stunk. As Fegen's empire took on water, Jerry agreed to lend Fegen two hundred fifty thousand dollars so he could make payroll and avoid immediate liquidation. The man had been a loyal friend. His attorneys, conversely, were just as much money hawks as Howard's yapping lawyers had been. They spun around on their tasseled loafers and filed a two hundred fifty *million* dollar lawsuit against Jerry, accusing him of profiting from Fegen's leasing bonanza. The lawyers had to do it. With Fegen destitute, they couldn't earn fees without having an enemy to litigate. Other than pillow-biting, what could Jerry do?

The only strategy that made sense was allowing his enemies to over-reach. Once more, Jerry had been victimized, this time in what an adviser termed "a legal gangbanging." So, he hired a flashy lawyer with a taste for Expressionist art to handle the complex case, and conceded nothing. He underwent depositions and, thinking ahead, shrewdly bought legal malpractice insurance knowing his attorney would likely commit technical errors. To make a tortuous story short, the insurance company for Jerry's lawyer came to the rescue when errors did arise. It paid the seven hundred fifty thousand dollar settlement against Jerry and gave him two hundred fifty thousand dollars for his nuisance.

Triumphant there, Jerry's home turf was less accommodating. He and Tammy were not sure how much they liked each other's post-ordeal personalities. Where, again, was that downy soft reset? The couple did have another son, their third, and yet Jerry's workaholic binges grew worse in his compulsion to never be defrauded again. Tammy was gloomy that these lessons of self-reliance, not family rejuvenation, were what motivated him. Worry continued pincushioning her. The minute that Jerry was late from work, and he was behind schedule constantly, was the minute she was alarmed. Sometimes, she would phone the California Highway Patrol to see if patrol officers knew where he was. When there was no peep of him after an out-of-town trip, she dialed the tower at Los Angeles International Airport to ask the air traffic controllers if his jet had landed. They recognized Tammy's voice after a string of her calls. Nothing was as it had been.

Tammy believed what her family needed was a do-over in the decent Midwest, where people didn't dart around shooting each other in the skull over business conflicts. You didn't have to be a hardboiled detective to know that L.A. was simmering with irascible people—serial killers, gang enforcers, thin-skinned drivers, surly parolees; a town where the vengeful stuffed rattlesnakes in mail slots of those they disliked. Pound for pound, there were fewer of those types in the heartland than California, and a wealth more civilized human behavior. Tammy at her nub was more Michigan girl than Californian.

Tapping that skittishness, Tammy again broached the sensitive issue of them relocating to Ann Arbor. She had already discussed with her father the possibility of Jerry going to work for him in his auto junking business, and would grant Jerry a year to wind down and sell Space Matters. Tammy's dad was no hack entrepreneur. His company was the largest in four surrounding states, enriched by contracts with the big automakers and insurance companies. One perk for his kids was getting to drive experimental cars before they were demolished. The West Coast had no monopoly on the future.

Jerry delivered his answer about a fresh start in Michigan the same month that Fegen's lawyers whacked him with their quarter billion dollar suit. It was an emphatic no! His heart was here, his survival lesions, too. If Tammy for her own sanity needed to deep-six the household and relocate to the Midwest, Jerry told her to by all means leave. She would just have to do it without him. He would be a lesser man if his post-Howard legacy was abandoning his hometown to haul jalopies through the snow.

Tammy grasped the implication—their marriage was over. It was a love, as the Beatles once sang, that should've lasted years, but the ache of 1979 had swiped their innocence and left nothing worthwhile to replace it. Jerry was jaded at twenty-nine and she obsessed over license plates. Geography was Tammy's balm. She went ahead with her California exit, moving with their three boys to a place near her parents. The supersized Northridge tract home, a virtual McMansion of its era, was leased out.

Divorce loomed. It had been two and a half years since those men came for Richard.

***

With his family resettled in Michigan and his old home rented out, Jerry, the space planner, had no space to live. He leased a condo near Santa Monica that belonged to an associate who had left to run for Congress in Utah and then what do you know? Just when Jerry thought he was in solitary confinement, a secret admirer waiting in the wings made a play for him. Daphne had been his personal assistant and before that, one of Fegen's top secretaries. On their first date, she escorted Jerry to a beach house, where she treated him to a scrumptious meal and then lusty desserts on silk sheets. She was an exotic young woman, half-black, half-Korean, who had been hoping Jerry would come back on the market. *Market?* he asked himself. *What market?* Jerry was overjoyed that anyone would fall for staggered him, let alone someone as gorgeous as Daphne.

Jerry's metabolism had something waiting for him, too. He was parched and had to urinate constantly. He tried slaking his dry throat by downing 7-Eleven Slurpees, and found his chest throbbed with blowtorch indigestion. What was wrong with him? Jerry's doctor examined him and when he smelled Jerry's breath, it was stupendously acidic. After blood tests, the diagnosis was in. Jerry was a Type One diabetic. The physician said with Jerry's off-the-chart blood-sugar levels, he had no business being conscious. He was sent immediately to Cedars Sinai Hospital for treatment and education, where that imprisoned feeling returned. This was a forever disease requiring forever personal care, and that wasn't Jerry, now thirty-two. He wanted to travel, wander, ruminate and eat as he pleased. A glucose meter and syringe had become his tethers. More than that, he felt cursed. Here he was years after 1979, condemned with the exact disease as the man who flattened his household.

Not long after his diagnosis, Jerry was at the Hollywood Bowl for a philharmonic with his sister, who had packed a picnic. She prepared sugary chocolate cake for desert. After it was suggested that Jerry should abstain for the sake of level blood-sugar, he threw an uncharacteristic tantrum. "I'll die if I don't eat this!" he said, giving himself a massive insulin shot to compensate. "I will." Jerry, a couple of years later, interviewed his doctor about what precipitated his condition. The doctor said that since he had the Type One gene, a harrowing shock could have been the last straw for his pancreas. Those four terrible words returned in his mind. *Howard had struck again.*

Newly diagnosed and all, Jerry wed Daphne in 1984, a landmark year if there ever were one. L.A. hosted a successful Olympics devoid of whiskey-brown smog and snarled traffic. More pointedly, Howard died in prison of diabetes-related complications that his brooding, violent nature must've certainly aggravated. When Tammy heard that Howard was gone, her whoop of delirium might've surpassed Susan's murder night scream. Every year since his sentencing, Tammy had called the prison to see if he was still there. Now there'd be no more calls. The reptile was never coming back, at least in physical form.

In the following years, Jerry and Daphne purchased a house in Malibu a long ways from Northridge and welcomed two daughters. Destiny had recalibrated. Jerry would finally put the past behind him and learn to trust again, right? Anyone figuring yes failed to understand that in Jerry's saga, the unexpected was the expected. It was Jerry's new wife dragged backwards into a wormhole of bad history that had to be sorted out.

Daphne's parents had been a South Korean prostitute and a black American serviceman unprepared to raise her. After she was born, they left her at an orphanage, hardly a blessing since Korean families tended to shun mixed race children. Unclaimed, the girl was bundled off to U.S. and right into the homes of cruel, abusive people. Now that she was a grown woman, Daphne's bruising childhood sent her into a crippling depression that sometimes anchored her in bed just like Jerry's mother. She hit the psychotherapy couch to get to the bottom of her breakdown and Jerry attended sessions for spouses, disliking it so much that he tried instigating a mutiny.

His second wife, nevertheless, had reshuffled her values. She converted to vegetarianism, headed her church, explored scream therapy and, inspired by a feminist mentor, enrolled in graduate school to become a therapist herself. The new Sheila was less fiery about resuscitating Jerry and more about comforting the dying. With her degree, she accepted a job at a hospice treating AIDs-infected mothers. When Daphne requested a divorce, as she focused on the new "her," Jerry went along.

He accepted that this was how things would be. That sometimes one gigantic black ordeal produces a low-grade infection that boils up when contentment is within walking range. So many entwined in the slow motion jackknife of Richard's final year were haunted by some part of it. Inside, they knew Howard's trial had been murder dissected and still mystery unsolved. No one had publicly answered why Richard had been so frantic for extra money that he cheated his idolizing partner and misused the credit of his saturnine foreman.

From his own thousand hours of retrospection, Jerry knew Richard shouldn't have required a hitman with a late-blooming conscience or a terrified lawyer to try gumming up Howard's vendetta. Richard was aware of the wicked mouthbreathers after him. There was more than enough time for him to straighten up, settle with Howard or, at the very minimum, flee California. Time hadn't tripped him, though. His shellacked self-esteem had. The Richard whose shimmering success everybody grew tired of waiting for folded into the Richard who simply gave up. How else to explain his plea that Jerry watch out for Paige and Rebecca if something happened to him a short nine hours before something did? Jerry, green no longer, could only deduce the truth.

Richard had leaned into his own demise. He had committed suicide by Howard.

His life ended within hours of Johnny's bullet. Those he left in its wake required years to get blood pumping right again. Howard had endowed a prolific legacy. He had triggered two divorces in the Schneidermans and the Freemans. His home invasions shuffled two families, the Buonsantis and Robert's sister, onto new blocks, leaving them forever wary of shadows. Many others were consigned to therapy, self-medication, self-destructive relationships, seclusion and worse. It wasn't just Tammy, either, vehement about drawing curtains and shades across windows, regardless of sunlight. From Beverly Hills to the Bay Area, dark rooms pervaded.

Paige's life afterwards was a bumper car ride for stability. She purchased a small house in the Valley near the Sherman Oaks Galleria through various legal settlements. Next, she accepted Jerry's job offer to be a decorator. In the years to come, she married three more times, never finding her new spouses as thrilling as Richard. Between those relationships, ravishing Paige dated a medley of famous Angelenos—the owner of a local sports franchise, an actor and a television executive. In the end, none of the men did her right, even after she got sick. She deserved better, and when she finally propped herself up, it was on her own.

Deep into the 1980s, Jerry's dreams remained tied to 1979. Mainly they were about Richard in a recurring scenario in which Jerry would see him at a restaurant immaculately dressed, happy as a clam, and very much living. Jerry's dreaming brain would ask him how he could possibly be there when he had seen his coffin. Richard, though, was not apt to speak of the macabre. He smiled glisteningly, reassuring Jerry that he had faked his own murder on the path to being a "new man."

Jerry himself should've been a revived spirit by the late 1980s and early 1990s. Though twice divorced and living with diabetes, he had five beautiful children, a few trusty friends, a decent nest egg and that supple mind. Nationally, Southern California brushed off its reputation as a seething Valhalla and the sun shone through the hydrocarbons. L.A. *Law* re-glamorized the place, making divorce and patent applications hip. Ronald Reagan's defense buildup rained billions more on local aerospace companies developing stealth bombers and *Star Wars* missile defense. L.A. was suddenly gung-ho about aerobics, crack cocaine, soy diets, the Magic Johnson-led Lakers, and recycling bins. New skyscrapers rose. What a town, back to its old seductions.

Just not for Jerry. Richard's murder had gutted too much of him to be anything but mostly miserable.

CHAPTER NINETEEN

JERRY GETS HIS PAYBACK

"There's a North Hollywood nightclub about to collapse," the stranger whispered over the phone that day in 1995. "Subway tunneling did it." The tip rang at my desk at *The Los Angeles Daily News*, intriguing me enough to call transit officials about the property. The mystery man knew his stuff. The club was about to buckle.

During the next few years, Jerry would become one of my best sources, feeding me leads that led to one exposé after the other. Stories about subway graft and a crony, taxpayer-built museum; stories about a slum housing complex that'd doom a famous Latino politician and, overall, more dirty deal-making than a floor full of FBI agents could investigate, let alone me.

What did I know about my medium besides his reputation for over-the-top antics and high batting average for being right? Honestly, almost nothing. Jerry, at first, never disclosed that he had undergone inside-out evolution in the wake of a cannibalizing murder triangle. Neither he nor anyone else informed me that in outlasting it, he had mutated from an impish, quiet Jewish kid from throwaway North Hollywood into a smirking pot-stirrer happy to kick the civic Establishment in the nuts. All I understood was that Jerry spotted government deception that others missed, and that he fancied himself a weird hero in a town that loved its crusaders flawed.

Jackie Goldberg should've realized that even before Jerry outwitted her on the Gower Street homeless shelter with those phony invitations. The year before in 1994, she had thrown her support behind a controversial, Hollywood needle-exchange program run by a non-profit organization. Giving addicts turning in dirty needles a set of clean, unused ones, as well as distilled water and bleach, had been lauded as a practical way to temper AIDs-infection rates while coaxing junkies into treatment. Every Wednesday evening for six months, volunteers parked their Ford Bronco in front of Selma Elementary School and did their work, and every time it made Jerry's blood boil. He had no high-horse objection with the concept. He was just against running it near a grade-school without neighborhood input.

Goldberg's staff bristled at insinuations that they were endangering kids by importing the hard-drug culture into the midst. Only mean Jerry, they claimed, was dissenting. He knew that was poppycock and decided, this being the movie capital, to publicize the absurdity of the situation with cinematic flair. How? He enlisted old ladies and Scientologists troubled as well about the program, arming them with video recorders and cameras to film what was happening. The non-profit fired back with white sheets, draping them around the rabble-ish needle-users entering and exiting the Bronco to block their faces from the cameras. Jerry's little army got their shots anyway. After he shared the footage with area VIPs, the needle-swap that he had had lambasted in the *Los Angeles Times* as the "height of stupidity" relocated to a new street.

Whether button-down serious or dementedly funny, Jerry's crusading, I'd come to learn, shared one common thread: a brain that remembered the lessons of spring 1979 no matter his heart's yearning to forget them. Jerry's memory disguising himself as a tractor-driving hick to trick Howard and his killers served him especially well sixteen or so years later with another gag. Jerry's new ploy was dressing up as a clownish version of the politician he was scrapping with to see how many official events he could crash. It took ingenuity. To impersonate her, he got a hold of a size 72 tuxedo and a floral vest like her signature one. For girth, he stuffed a sleeping bag into the derriere of his pants and another one around his belly. Two balloons became breasts. Lastly, he tugged a Rush Limbaugh mask over his face, put a pair of half-glasses over the eyes and pulled a Beatles wig over his hair. Meet Jackie Goldberg, the manly sequel.

Some city leaders at a Democrat Party dinner were momentarily perplexed when "she" showed up. In hushed voices with drinks in hand, they debated amongst themselves whether she/he/it was the real McCoy. One cantankerous, white-haired activist believed it, yelling that Jackie should be ashamed of "her" policies as Jerry giggled under his mask.

Disguise removed, that laugh might've been a cry. Anyone with his scrapbook could see that Jerry was a worn version of the baby-faced persona stomped long before anyone had ever heard of Facebook or Osama Bin Laden. In the time since his dealings with Richard and Howard, Jerry had packed a doughy fifty pounds around his midsection and draped a scruffy, beard-moustache beneath his nose. Thick, brown curls of his twenties were now thinning, salt-and-pepper hair that sprang unruly from his large, oval head. Fine, paw-shaped wrinkles rimmed his marble-green eyes with puffy bags the scaffolding. Best to take it all in when you could, too, because in a moment of reflection, an uncanny shadow could wrench half his face into darkness.

Jerry's face other times was getting around in a city still licking its wounds from the 1992 riots, the Northridge earthquake, and O.J Simpson's double murder trial. As a clever joke, he sent a gaggle of City Hall politicians a dartboard ringed with concentric circles, each showing the escalating millions his crusading high-jinx had cost L.A. Overlaying it was Jerry's smug, slightly taunting face. *Aim high, Dick* was his personalized note to Mayor Richard Riordan. Around that same period, he also traveled to his hometown North Hollywood, where he advised residents opposed to a redevelopment plan how to hamstring its future. Politicians, Jerry correctly knew, often used urban-renewal money as "piggy banks" to mow down decrepit communities eligible for rebuilding with subsidies awarded to developer-buddies. It was your basic corporate welfare, so Jerry turned the tables by exhorting property owners to debone it. People who acted on his advice underwent assessments that shaved $311,000 from the redevelopment kitty.

By 1997, after I had left *The Daily News* to write books and freelance, it was obvious that Jerry was addicted to the muckraking and deeply jaundiced toward L.A.'s political apparatus. He prowled Hollywood in a spy-like trench coat listening for the crackle of subway workers' walkie-talkies sending out word that he was snooping. He attended riotous public meetings where foul-mouthed transit activists publicly cursed officials in prefab-meltdowns while he performed intelligence collection. Sometimes while he did, a political aide would mosey up to me and ask what Jerry was up to, because they had no experience with his kind. "Who is this guy?" they would beg to know.

Somebody best not to rile was what I advised them. Recognizing that he would need a battering ram to take on the county's subway-building juggernaut, Jerry formed a company that he called "Hollywood Damage Control and Recovery" and staffed it with motivated people. On board were fired MTA workers, unemployed engineers, claims adjusters and frizzy-haired gadflies with encyclopedic brains. Jerry's guerillas half-resembled G-men as they monitored the subway and other public projects for him in FBI-style windbreakers and canary-yellow construction hardhats. In their hands were seismographs, radar guns, sound meters and gas-testing devices. Jerry was their captain, Hollywood's self-deputized crusader, and where cunning failed to work against the Man, creativity generally succeeded. His people slapped fake red tags from the "Metropolitan Terrorist Authority" on sub-way-compromised buildings. They paid street kids to chitchat with tunnel workers to discover if there were troubles brewing underground. In perhaps their most inspired stroke, they spread rumors of a vapory, superhero-like figure that scaled high walls to snap incriminating pictures of subway-safety violations. "Tunnel Ninja" was its name. Jerry's history had taught him to beat the "animal" you must aggravate it first.

His multi-plaintiff case against the MTA in a sense did that. Though it was settled for far less than the two billion dollars originally sought, the agency held off popping any bubbly. The legal actions and public attacks that Jerry and other activists ignited helped slow the money-eating subway to a crawl, slicing federal support for Metro Rail by ninety-percent. By 2000, momentum for new routes was virtually dead. You didn't need a degree from an Ivy League institution to plumb Jerry's psychology once you'd digested his pre-activist life. He was punching at a city that had dropped murderers in his lap and never apologized for the vast things stolen from him. High jinks were his post-traumatic shunt.

Jerry had more on his mind than bird-dogging Metro Rail and sneaky politicians when we became better acquainted. We'd gab for hours, Jerry and I, about "great" Los Angeles on the sixth floor of the tumbledown office tower where he kept an office. (As I'd find out, he always rented dives when he could have afforded better because it made him less of a bulls-eye for his enemies.) Hollywood—the place, not the industry—then was as seamy as Jerry's digs, and it bothered the crap out of him. Tourists had long clung to whimsical hopes of finding movie stars at soda fountains and shooting stages popping with action on their visits. It was all extinct. Except for Para-mount Pictures, every major studio had deserted Hollywood the place by the 1920s. The boulevard had fallen in abject decay by the 1970s, with a western end that in particular felt like a human landfill drenched in urine and sustained by panhandling. Teenage prostitutes, mohawked runaways, junkies, beggars, the mentally ill and other castoff people made it their living room.

While the boosters overseeing the Hollywood sign and the Walk of Fame screeched all was not lost, Jerry knew there was plenty gone. No longer was he exclusively a gag-playing agitator and legal hellraiser superb at getting under officials' skin. Jerry was a community conscience and a go-to source for newspaper quotes about the need for coherent policies and private investment. Hollywood mesmerized him and disgusted him. He was photographed in a national magazine driving the streets in his Jaguar condemning the rows of tacky souvenir shops and squalor where there should've been real estate fairy dust. "Garbage, garbage, and more garbage," he told a *Los Angeles Times* reporter riding with him one day. "You tell me, is this street ready for a Gap?"

It had happened. Jerry had elevated into a "somebody," a grassroots leader bred from a mysterious past. Underdogs of all kinds contacted him seeking assistance. Yes, history was ready for him to put his fingerprints on it.

East Los Angeles' Wyvernwood Garden Apartments were a series of two-story apartments in a park-like setting of grassy commons and winding trails. With capacity for ten-thousand residents, Wyvernwood (pronounced Y-vernwood) represented one of the largest privately owned housing compounds west of Chicago. For people with modest tastes and the hankering for the urban bucolic, it was an august place to call home. By 1997, though, Wyvernwood had surrendered its quietude to a chemical taint that wouldn't relent. Four children, and perhaps far more had been badly sickened by their exposure to flaking, dangerous lead paint on the buildings. Lead, linked to learning disabilities in children and other maladies, caked older properties across the West.

At Wyvernwood, citations flew and health inquiries began, tipping its slumlord owner, Samuel Mevorach, on his heels. Toxic paint was just one emergency. Working class Latinos who constituted the bulk of his renters had been unable to persuade him to plaster holes, fix their crummy heating, or exterminate cockroaches. He had turned a blind eye; too much graffiti tagging and too many gangbangers. Everybody knew that with L.A.'s paucity of affordable housing, Wyvernwood was too precious to continue neglecting. Still, nobody realized how much backroom-intrigue was swirling until Jerry came on scene with his reputation for tripping up the powerful. He had been sleuthing around East L.A. after he had heard that the MTA planned to use eminent domain to acquire property for a new subway line there. In doing, so he earned the trust of a brave, waifish anti-lead activist named Linda Kite who told him the entire, shameful story. Jerry passed along to me what Kite confided to him and like that I was chasing the slumlord of Wyvernwood.

As I swiftly discovered, Richard Alatorre, the longtime councilman representing the Boyle Heights neighborhood where Wyvernwood was located, had repeatedly intervened with the D.A.'s office in a bid to buy more time for Mevorach before criminal charges were filed. After Alatorre helped then-D.A. Gilbert Garcetti win reelection, Garcetti's office loosened its grip on Mevorach, supposedly so he could have the toxic lead removed from his property and sell it to a more humane owner. The entire thing stunk.

When my exposé linking Alatorre and Mevorach appeared in the L.A. *Weekly* in 1997, I had no idea of the kerosene I had squirted. The *Los Angeles Times* picked up months later where I left off, reporting that Mevorach had secretly—and illegally—given Alatorre tens-of-thousands of dollars and arranged a sham lease on his old condo. Alatorre, a swarthy, knuckle-brawling pol with a gravelly voice, was in quicksand. Once the stories about him and Mevorach subsided, new ones appeared in the *Los Angeles Times* about Alatorre's alleged cocaine habit. By 1998, it was unclear whether Alatorre would survive the onslaught with television news crews camped out on his lawn and authorities butting into every crevice of his life. His once-legendary name was radioactive. The next year, Alatorre saddened his backers when he announced he would not seek reelection.

The scandal that Jerry helped tear open was a political asteroid strike. Alatorre had been the odds-on favorite to take the 2005 mayoral race and when his collusion with a slumlord cost him his career, the decks were cleared for then-Councilman Antonio Villaraigosa to enter and win. Villaraigosa, with his skeletons of philandering and broken promises, has produced a lackluster record at best. Not so for Jerry. He had changed L.A. by outing the graft that the men in power never intended to see daylighted. He had etched his legacy as a giant-killer, a do-gooder who didn't fit the mold of the sign-waving dissident or public interest lawyer in an off-the-rack WalMart suit. And it wasn't about money, not this time, anyway. This puzzled those in the anti-Jerry camp—the ones adamant he wouldn't get involved unless he fattened his own pockets while defending the needy.

For me, calculating his wealth wasn't any simpler than cracking his motives. Sure, Jerry drove a Rolls Royce and a Jaguar, but it was straight into the parking lot of that Hollywood skyscraper with the architectural grace of a dinghy black stake. Grime was more present than humans in the building on the southeast corner of the once-famed Sunset Boulevard and Vine Street. Heels echoed in the lobby and the jerking cage of an elevator teased you with a free-fall before depositing you on your floor. Jerry's office was tucked in the back, and he implored me not to judge him by his rat-hole in the sky. He claimed involvement in two-hundred million dollars in real estate deals. I nodded my head, tamping my doubt. I just wanted to split before nightfall.

Years after meeting Jerry, I didn't really know who he was. On the surface lied a bright, mischief-making personality who enjoyed the media spotlight and the adrenalin of taunting government game. Below that, his identity was murkier. Jerry's gift for making public officials squirm as he defended victimized tenants, land-owners and others flushed endless satisfaction through him. The cape fit him well. But psychic happiness was something else. Jerry's spirit, as measured by his shenanigans, seemed about as tranquil as plutonium.

For the first years I knew him, Jerry revealed nothing about the abyss that Richard and Howard had shoved him in, or the innocence that he abandoned on its canyon floor. If you asked him something too delicate, he would adroitly steer the conversation back to whatever dishonest public entity he was driving batty at that moment. For all that walling off, it was still hard to dislike him and dishonest to suggest he wasn't as original a character as the eminence of exhibitionism himself, Paul Fegen. Jerry could pinpoint deceit in the fine-print of a half-inch document as if it were bolded. He had a cackle that trilled after his stories and a head that cocked sideways to emphasize a point. He couldn't stop bragging about his kids and valued loyalty above all. Categorizing him was puzzling because I had never met anyone with their ying and yang screeching in such opposition. In Jerry were shades of both profiteer and humanitarian, sly opportunist and new breed of agitator. Who was he?

It wasn't until one summer day in 1998, just before the Monica Lewinsky scandal exploded and roughly three years after we met, when my education about the *real* Jerry commenced. I'll never forget it. We were strolling down Hollywood Boulevard on our way to lunch, weaving past a carnival of fast-moving people with no appointments to keep. We had just passed a ruddy-faced vagrant with a banjo when Jerry dropped a bombshell on my mental village of him. "Did you know," he asked matter-of-factly, "that I had a double murderer chasing me and my family?" He said the pursuit speared his first marriage, trashed his health and sent his life skittering. I joked about my good memory to say it was all news to me. Jerry cocked his head. He wasn't laughing. "My ex thinks it killed the old me. Made me untrusting." Braggadocio, I figured. Nothing more than a fabulist at work.

A little later, over crispy duck at a cheap, Thai restaurant, Jerry dribbled out more of his supposed back story. *Interesting*, I conceded. *But so what?* I was here for story leads. He was here to reconcile history. Jerry ate his duck and explained that the best way to neutralize a powerful adversary is to twist their own momentum against them. John DeLorean, Barry Minkow—Jerry enjoyed reading how the weak became strong. My expression must have blinked disinterest. "Why don't you go to the downtown courthouse and pull the trial records," he challenged me. "No thanks," I said. "What do you have to lose checking the facts?" he said. "If I'm wrong, you'll know I'm a liar." Fine, I answered after he pestered me more. "If it'll get you off my back, I'll waste a day in the archives." Nevermind that restaurant's poor lighting. I spotted instigation in Jerry's green eyes. He knew what I would find.

A contest developed between us. I would dare Jerry to tell me something more bizarre and sick about his experience and then I would see whether I could discredit them by chasing down records or peoples' memories. After months of this dare-and-check, my recourse was simple. I had to apologize to him for my skepticism. "That's all right," he would say. "I wouldn't have believed it myself if I hadn't lived through it. Not that I wished it had happened." Had Jerry known his mind games would tempt me to write a book, or did he merely want me to admire him? I still wasn't sure.

Jerry had a chance to prove to me that he would learned from his gashes. Prove it he did.

In December 2001, shortly after the al Qaeda attacks, all twenty floors of that dreary Hollywood highrise where Jerry rented his office pitched into darkness. A blown electrical transformer near the garage had conked out the power, spurring the city Fire Department to evacuate the building and quarantine it. Too risky for human occupancy, officials said. None of the nearly forty tenants were allowed to re-enter the tower to grab their appoint-ment books, computers, files and other belongings. All of them remained precisely as they had been, frozen in time, when the Fire Department red-tagged the property.

Months went by without compromise. People fretted that they would lose their businesses, and with no income, maybe their homes. Stories ap-peared making the city's handling of the situation look klutzy. One of the building's Middle Eastern owners, a scowling man named Roy, tried un-loading his property to another investor. He couldn't. Squatters then broke in and vandalized the suites. Officials deluged by calls finally permitted people to collect some of their stuff if they took the stairs. Nobody was happy. The owners blamed the fried transformer on the city's electrical grid. Tenants railed that an illegally connected rooftop air conditioner had triggered the short circuit.

Jerry was already wise to that, understanding as he did the conse-quences of unheeded warnings. Months before the building went dark, he had written to the city expressing detailed concerns about the property's fire safety. Jerry was especially troubled about what would happen if a fire broke out at the bottom of the elevator shaft and fluted up to the penthouse nightclub. Dozens could burn in a deathtrap above Sunset Boulevard. If officials disregarded the warning that he had provided them and disaster struck, Jerry promised that he would take it public and hold them account-able. As it played out, the Fire Chief ignored Jerry's words, so Jerry adapted.

When the stalemate over the people-less building appeared too conten-tious to ever resolve, Jerry answered the way history had taught him—with step-ahead thinking. He banded renters together into a creditor's associa-tion that effectively tossed the owners into involuntary bankruptcy. They paid settlements to every tenant—except him, of course—and many renters were able to extricate themselves from their leases. Not only that, Jerry's agitating about fire-prone high rises in the post-9-11 era led to inspections and a renewed focus on them citywide.

Young Jerry never would have launched such a counter-strike, not with-out somebody's muscle behind him. The modern version was an improved people-reader who accepted the surreal and stood confidently in front of exposed windows.

EPILOGUE

The kingdom of Jerry rose just off the Harbor Freeway, in a drab industrial zone in the shadows of Dodger Stadium. Trying to make a left turn off the freeway to reach his Lacy Street address with no signal in heavy cross-traffic was Russian Roulette played with a gas pedal stomp. When you did arrive at his headquarters, it was no monument to survival over the bullies of L.A., criminal or elected. The façade of his new company, Creative Environments, was much humbler, if easy to miss altogether, an aesthetic yawn of corrugated metal and bubble glass that led to a deceptively large space with runt curb appeal. You wonder if an architect designed it or a fortress-maker.

A post-modern sparseness greeted visitors inside the reception area snaked with big, black air ducts overhead and smoothed, dark concrete at their soles. The minimalism shouted money being made hand over fist, and Jerry was. His millions, the money he intended on keeping this time, began accumulating in the year 2000 as he focused on property acquisition and management and not contouring square-footage for other people. Space Matters effectively ceased operations and Jerry replaced it by founding Creative Environments with a partner whose background he vetted painstakingly. What timing, too. His company jumped into the lucrative, urban-loft market just as L.A. planners were devising ways to encourage more city living and less corrosive suburban sprawl.

Like ice cream, Jerry's lofts came in all flavors—multi-level, one-floor retail, gallery setups, art studios, etc. They could be decorated in "industrial chic" or "contemporary rustic." They were adaptable to filmmaking, live theater, or design work. It was a splash of vertical New York in horizontal-Southern California. Some of the loft complexes were housed in onetime movie studios in zip codes that most of today's acting superstars wouldn't be caught dead in without security. Jerry accepted this invisibility (quite a bit, actually), attracted to underutilized, overlooked properties seeing gems where others saw quick tear-down. The company was doing something right. Seven awards for architecture, community citizenship, and historic preservation stood in the trophy case. One citation was presented by the institution that Jerry especially bedeviled: L.A. City Hall.

Jerry's own office was ensconced in the middle of the building the way a nucleus is situated in a cell. His desk was solid granite, assuming you could see it under his paper tsunami, his furniture bright red, Italian leather. Wall-to-ceiling glass that covered one set of walls went with three glass doors wrapping around. Know Jerry's story and you'll know that's not by accident. He wasn't terrified of another reptile like Howard bellying up, not outwardly anyway. He just liked seeing what was happening. And a lot was. Jerry, nonetheless, was eternally late, and when he did waddle in, his secretary and underlings followed behind as if he were their shambling monarch. Throughout the day, they barged in regularly to tap into his brain on a development hitch or share a victory anecdote. Jerry hardly ever got mad, unless it was for show.

Despite the changeover and what appeared a rebirth from 1979, Jerry was neither fully healed nor totally rebooted as the 1990s snapped close. Anyone who had really observed him in activist mode knew that behind his mischief, unspoken forces still clenched him. They did, too: cysts of fossilized rage and despair named Howard and Richard that clung stubbornly inside his ribcage, as though longevity had granted them residency. Around the year 2000 juncture, Jerry was introduced to a pint-sized, elderly Chinese woman who would help to evict some of those ghosts. The woman at the time was squabbling with the MTA and an oil company over property it wanted to purchase from her. Jerry volunteered to intervene as the man the MTA loved to hate and extracted a winsome check for her. She asked him afterwards what she owed him and he replied "nothing." But the Chinese woman was determined to repay him, so she gave Jerry some of her money to invest and brought other, wealthy friends to his door. Soon, he had enough capital to acquire a succession of older buildings in or near downtown, Hollywood, East L.A., Eagle Rock, and—naturally—Miracle Mile.

As terrific as the old woman's money was, it was her life story that would inspire Jerry to re-examine his own harshly *Wonderland-ish* journey. In the 1970s, she had transitioned from being a little-known restaurateur into a star businesswoman selling frozen egg rolls to the U.S. food conglomerates. Millions could be hers. Then thuggish mobsters jealous of her success decided they wanted the business that the woman had slaved to build from the deep-fryer's to the packaging. As a sign of their commitment, they locked her in an industrial freezer to intimidate her into selling it to them. The sadistic wise-guys got what they wanted with the funniest of results. The woman refused to let the hypothermic bullying poison the sweet, generous person that she had been before she had been locked up, believing the good-hearted of L.A. still outnumbered its barbarians.

For Jerry, learning the resiliency of the onetime egg roll queen from one of her friends was a light beam to the more compassionate version of himself. He just wasn't certain how to break it loose. He assumed that the only path was to try once more scraping away the remnants of Richard and Howard that'd absorbed into his personality against his will like invisible bio-toxins. Until he did, he would never bust out of the triangle and could never believe he had recovered. Bit by bit in his everyday actions, whether in small kindnesses or helping strays, Jerry strove to zap his associates' lingering presence in him—Richard's ulterior motives, Howard's human-weakness-radar. Simultaneously, he also began studying acquaintances to determine if *they* contained any of his old adversaries and what he could do to purge them. Bizarre as it sounds, "saving people" became Jerry's side-hobby the way murdering Richard once preoccupied Howard.

The best example here may be Jerry's improbable relationship with a former, suit-wearing Los Angeles gang member, the sort of hardened, inner city soldier wise never to upset. This man opened a Hollywood Boulevard confection store after he was released from prison only to discover that he lacked the nitty-gritty management expertise how to succeed. Hearing about Jerry's Metro Rail legend, he sought him out. With Jerry's assistance, the ex-African American gangbanger filed his first-ever tax return, landed a bank loan and invested his money smartly. Jerry said the proprietor turned his life around to become among the "most honorable people" he ever knew. Not so for another man who wanted to partner with him. When Jerry investigated him, he found a "scary guy without a conscience" and severed their dealings. All in all, Jerry's benevolence towards others over time did wonders for him. Anybody comparing the Jerry that impersonated Jackie Goldberg with the later Jerry that mentored strangers had to admit it. At long last, a gentle peace had settled into his face.

Being a modern businessman, Jerry had gone global by early 2000s, striding far beyond the urban lofts and historic building rehabs of L.A. In Japan, he paired with one of that nation's most connected businessmen, the former head-man of Sumitomo Corp's U.S. operations, on a hotel, nightclub and aquarium near Disneyland Tokyo. He wheeled and dealed in Africa, as well, and once more a connection sparked it. Daphne, his second ex-wife, is married to one of the seven kings of Ghana and together he and Jerry worked to acquire a diamond mine in Sierra Leone. Soon, the king wanted to help develop his own dirt poor, war-torn country, where more electrical power is essential. The question was how to pay for it, and three-dimensional thinking could be the solution. A solar farm, financed only as Jerry could have concocted it, may someday hulk over Ghana's flatlands. Affordable, modular housing by Jerry 's friends could be peppered around.

If you added everything up before the Great Recession descended, Jerry was involved in close to two-billion dollars worth of deals and property. Not that his money was easy to isolate. "You won't find my name listed prominently in the records," he once said, "because I've been threatened with financial annihilation by the politicians and developers I have gone after. But if they want to come after me they can. I have had nastier people than them chasing me."

Thus, Jerry's style was educated fearlessness. Deliveries were sent to his office, and associates were not permitted to visit his comfortable Valley house. His staff dealt with construction subcontractors. Jerry had enough with foremen.

As of this writing, Howard has been dead more than a quarter century. His pugnacious lawyers are gone, too. Johnny Williams expired in prison in 2004. At the 1998 parole hearing that denied his freedom, Johnny was classified as depressed, anti-social and a moderate threat to society. Tammy, who eventually relocated back to abnormal L.A. from Michigan, is happily remarried. Ari burned to death in a suspicious fire. The prosecutor who put the sundeck assassins away retired after a prolific career. Richard's daughters themselves are adults. From how Paige described them, they are happy, well-adjusted grown women imbued with common sense that their father tragically lacked.

***

A stroll through Jerry's building was once a tour through his past. Lawrence, the same, easygoing assistant with him when he declared war on Hollywood's rogue subway work, remained. Bert, the space planner that Howard tried using as a steppingstone to locate Jerry while he was in hiding, was still there. The "kid" at the place for a spell was even more recognizable. It was Jerry's oldest son, Jude, the one Howard had wanted to maim during the blight of 1979. Jerry's other grown children have excelled just like him, with jobs on Wall Street, in law firms and in their academic careers. Once in a while, Richard Alatorre-yes, the same ex-councilman that Jerry helped connect to the slumlord of Wyvernwood-dropped by for consulting work. Jerry liked to believe there was some human rehabbing in it.

Until recently, the rarely dull life of sixty year old Jerry Schneiderman pulsated with contentment, workaholic hours and risk management. His health could have been better, his legs stronger, but he had a sweet, fair-haired third wife (his former real estate litigator) and an adorable, young son to lift him up when he fell. Family dinners were amusing and boisterous, reality television caliber. Besides his kids' families, often attending were his two ex-wives and their spouses, folks he had taken under his wing and sometimes even Richard's widow, Paige. If the Creator granted Richard and Ari a furlough, Jerry's dad, Art, too, and Paul Fegen received an invite, you might have marveled that Jerry was living his own adaptation of the film *Big Fish*.

There was but one shred of unfinished business for him to bury. It was about character. It was about blood and consequences. This was my philosophy, anyway. As this book steamed toward completion, I pestered Jerry to hop in his car and drive to the West L.A. mansion of the real estate executive who had employed Howard before he had been hired at Space Matters. I told Jerry that he needed to pound on Vic Platte's door. Bash it off its hinges, if he must.

Rather than stand up to him, Platte sent Howard and that gamma ray personality into Richard and Jerry's doings. A crime of omission, craven and seminal—that's what he had committed. When Richard had phoned Platte as Howard's chief reference, Platte never mentioned that Howard had torched his garage in a quarrel over work at his house. Had the executive come clean, even reckless Richard would've blocked Howard's employment and he wouldn't have had killers crouching on his landing a year later. Just a quick disclosure would've done the trick, yet Platte only saved one person: himself.

In 1980, between the time of Howard's arrest and his trial, Platte gingerly walked up to Jerry at a social event. Please, he implored, "don't mention my name on the stand. Howard could hear you and he never forgets." Jerry was disgusted, disgusted and furious at the symmetry of the request. Platte basically wanted insulation from the insidious events that he set in motion from one of the victims, an instigator sweating through a hairshirt of his own making. To show how he felt, Jerry turned his back on the jerk, letting him sniff his own rancid karma, and then nobly said nothing about him up on the stand. The court docket does not appear to have any record of the executive speaking at trial.

Over and over, I tried whipping Jerry into a mad-doggish lather. This book, I preached, was his excuse to confront the person who passed wickedness down the line as if it were a child's hot potato game. The rules were absolute: the last to hold Howard was the first one he would likely behead. After everything, I told Jerry that he deserved ten minutes to roar about the havoc his silence wrought. I was hoping to see un-athletic Jerry tongue lash the old man into bone and gelatin. The bullet that silenced Richard did not need to go airborne. Who's really worse: an emotionally tortured embezzler or a perfectly functioning coward?

Sitting in his glassed-strewn office one day, Jerry delivered his answer. He wasn't interested in hollering indignantly at anybody. "That's not me," he said. No vendettas, no eternal hate. He had a point. The wounds rotting in him as the trauma-bit muckraker that I had met in the mid-1990s *were* much fainter now. As this sank in, I realized my idea of Jerry confronting Platte would have likely backfired. "Yeah, probably," Jerry chuckled. "We'd both go to jail. Wouldn't that be ironic?" He and I both agreed that the executive will creep towards his demise with a spotty disease.

How could Jerry laugh about something so lethal? Because he knew better than the average person that space matters in L.A.—as in the space to reclaim your goodness after life's inevitable buzzsaw moments. That evil's worst offense is the trust it steals without permission. In this way, Jerry reconciled 1979, his year of rain, assassins, and what-might have been. It was how he ascended from endangered space planner to thankful survivor.

***

Jerry was less animated about his prospects for 2011, sensing perhaps that his teeth only had only so more chomps at the apple. The credit-thrashed economy had bruised any number of his business ventures, whether in real estate, foreign properties or commodities. "Bad times," he would sigh, eyebrows collapsing. "Lots of complications." Whenever I was around, Jerry moved swiftly over these undulating deals (for sugar, diamonds, land, you never knew) and dialed in on provocative, public subjects that we both enjoyed arguing about. Recently, Chinese interests had approached him about partnering on a solar-power conquest of California. Jerry applauded the foreigners' hustle, yet it also galled him that the Asians could make a killing in green-energy manufacturing that U.S. companies should. Smirking, we drew up plans for a delicately crafted article.

What fools we were. By winter, any talk about photovoltaic cells was eclipsed by worrying over Jerry's crumbling health. Some months earlier he had suffered a minor stroke while driving and decided to give up his keys. His secretary now drove him to work, and a cane he cracked wry about over his embarrassment often steadied his gait. At least, there was no group denial anymore that Jerry was failing. He knew it. The relatives and pals who had for years implored him and scolded him and sobbed for him to take better care of himself knew it. The words never took. Jerry, for some byzantine inner reason, seemed to have capitulated to a fatalistic itinerary that after everything there would be no docile, old age for him, that he would walk voluntarily into the misty beyond whatever the bulk sadness heaped on others by his fadeout. Morbid exhaustion—that's what it smacked of from my years of *Jerryology*; a morbid, self-reconciled exhaustion pebbled with light boredom. I joined the nagging brigade, too, with clumsy reminders about all he had to live for—that great wife, the six wonderful kids, each containing some facet of him. Hearing this line, Jerry would throw up his hands claiming it was too late for course corrections. Let him protest, I thought. Someone as tested as him would eventually smarten up.

An imbecilic assumption on my part. In the fall, Jerry underwent emergency surgery at a Glendale hospital to drain fluid from his swollen brain. He must have known he still had some tread on his tires because when he awoke from the operation, he pretended being paralyzed for the momentarily horrified relatives ringing his bed. He was flat on it and un-comedic when I visited him there a day later. After ten minutes, he pulled himself up with a grunt and a heave, a feat in itself, and stretched his weak legs out like origami. This was not the same urban legend who spun the MTA dizzy, or the young, family man who flummoxed diabolical Howard. This was Jerry on the knife-edge of twilight. With my usual Boy Scout enthusiasm, I tried selling him that he would be back in the office in no time. Jerry grinned flatly to humor me or maybe just to shut me up. Then he waddled like an old geezer that he wasn't toward the bathroom.

The next time I saw Jerry, on December 4, 2011, he was too frail to remove the small palm tree that had toppled across his front door after a record windstorm. We sat in his house, me and this enigma I've known for sixteen years, Jerry telling me how much he hoped I'd prosper from *his* story. I told him I felt likewise about him, and only later driving home did I start piecing together how much he had nurtured me over the years, through professional struggles and my own family health issues, with advice and fierce allegiance. Jerry's affection was sneaky: it frequently saw the originality in people before they saw it themselves. Anyway, though his complexion was milky that afternoon, his mind was lucid and a picaresque light still jitterbugged through his eyes. We finished our shoptalk after an hour and softly shook hands in his driveway. "Thanks for coming out," Jerry said, waving. Yeah, he would recover. He had had practice at it.

Three days later, I learned the inevitable on Facebook from Jude without any wall to slump against in gulping disbelief. My friend had suddenly died at his Valley home on December 7—Pearl Harbor day. It felt like a tire iron to the back of my neck. I could still hear his laugh. His service was held at Mt. Sinai Memorial Park, near Forest Lawn, the next Sunday. If the true measure of a man is the size of his funeral, Jerry measured up beautifully because hundreds attended. The crowd was so big, in fact, that dozens spilled out into the auxiliary chamber and towards the doors to say goodbye. Jerry's widow and two ex-wives gave pithy tributes that they leavened with asides about his quirky habits; one of them held up his infamous dartboard to ripples of audience giggles. His sons and nephew spoke glowingly about his principled shenanigans. Creative, maddening, rascally, unpredictable. Through swollen tears and grim mouths, many were "pissed" that Jerry had blasted off before his time. The world had suddenly gotten less interesting.

At the grave site, I tried picking out faces under the chilly, asphalt-colored skies. I wondered if any old Hollywood Boulevard crazies or Space Matters' alumni snuck in. Maybe a politico—someone from Riordan's old office or Goldberg's or the MTA—there to bid a grudging farewell to a worthy adversary? I wasn't worried about any graying killer there with a handkerchief, for Jerry had outlived them. One person I did identify from his stocky frame was the former-gang-chief-turned-businessman. He stood near Jerry's coffin speaking in heavy, sullen tones about his mentor's demise as if his own magnetic north was inside that box. Another longtime associate, he of the ripped-suit-pants-dyed-hair cadre, fidgeted as the rabbi recited a final prayer. This man murmured sweet, inside memories to me about Jerry, but when he turned away I noticed his bravely-girded face dissolved into a collection of disorganized features, eyes and nose roughly lined up. It wasn't just him. Glazed shellshock was a common expression among Jerry's colleagues. Not only did they lose him, they lost the mind that frequently made him the sharpest dealmaker in the room.

After the dirt had been shoveled on his casket and other Jewish rituals observed, mourners dispersed with heads tucked down, car keys jangling in the cold, dead air. Jerry's widow kindly invited me to the Shiva, but I couldn't steel myself to attend; I remembered Jerry's account of the wake he had attended after Richard's murder. The sequence here felt equally obliterating. Just three months more and Jerry and his clan would've celebrated the publication of his life-story, a hero's story. But that was my timeline. Numb, I plopped into my car and wound out of the cemetery. At the Ventura Freeway on-ramp, I debated driving out to Richard's old house not far away. Give it one last glimpse to curse the ever-lasting carnage from Johnny's bullet. Damn thing might as well been a WMD. I couldn't make the trip to Chandler Boulevard. No way. Instead, I drove home, shucked my dark suit and wept in private.